SATAN AND MĀRA

CHRISTIAN AND BUDDHIST SYMBOLS OF EVIL

STUDIES
IN THE HISTORY OF RELIGIONS

(SUPPLEMENTS TO *NUMEN*)

XXVII

SATAN AND MĀRA

CHRISTIAN AND BUDDHIST SYMBOLS
OF EVIL

LEIDEN
E. J. BRILL
1975

SATAN AND MĀRA

CHRISTIAN AND BUDDHIST SYMBOLS OF EVIL

BY

JAMES W. BOYD

LEIDEN
E. J. BRILL
1975

ISBN 90 04 04173 7

PRINTED IN THE NETHERLANDS

TO MY WIFE
MYVANWY

TABLE OF CONTENTS

Part Two

ANALYSIS OF THE MĀRA FIGURE IN THE EARLY INDIAN BUDDHIST TRADITION

Part Three

A COMPARISON OF THE EARLY CHRISTIAN AND BUDDHIST MYTHOLOGIES OF EVIL

PREFACE

This work is the result of both the study of historical materials and conversations with contemporaries who have intimate knowledge of their respective areas. I am indebted to Professors Philip S. Watson of Garrett Theological Seminary and Edmund Perry of Northwestern University for their guidance and encouragement during the formative stages of this study and for their critiques of the section of this book dealing with early Christian materials. Professor Edward Conze introduced me to the Buddhist mythology of evil and sparked my curiosity on the matter of a plurality of Māras. Fulbright and Rockefeller grants enabled me to journey to Sri Lanka and attend the University of Sri Lanka, Vidyodaya Campus. I am grateful to Professors Walpola Rahula and Shanta Ratnayaka, both of whom devoted much time to the second part of the study which deals with early Buddhist materials. The comparative section of the book has enjoyed the criticisms of colleagues from several universities, both East and West. To them I also extend my gratitude, and especially to Professors Bernard E. Rollin, Donald A. Crosby, Holmes Rolston III, and James R. Jordan of Colorado State University. Finally I wish to thank Ms. Sharon Shackleton for devoting several months of her time to checking the accuracy of the footnote references, and Mrs. Myrle H. Phelan for typing the manuscript with such patience and care. I acknowledge with gratitude permission given by the editor of *The Journal of Asian Studies* to use part of the work which has appeared in that journal.

The inadequacies in this study are due to my limitations. I expect to benefit from corrections and suggestions offered by students of the two traditions, and hope that they in turn will benefit from the present work.

INTRODUCTION

This study is an historical analysis of the Satan and Māra mythologies of evil as they appear in selected Greek and Pali-Sanskrit texts. Its purpose is to contribute to a better understanding of the Christian and Buddhist traditions and the relation between them. The literature examined falls within the formative period of the early Christian and Buddhist traditions (*ca.* 100 B.C.-*ca.* 350 A.D.). The analysis of these texts (Parts I and II) seeks to derive a general portrait of the activities, nature and power of Satan and Māra. Part III sketches an interpretive comparison of the experiential meaning of these mythologies in so far as that is possible within the confines of the historical materials. A broader philosophical treatment of the meaning of these mythologies of evil is not within the scope of the present work.

The nature and meaning of what the early Christians and Buddhists experienced and defined as "evil" constitute an important aspect of their religious experience. As counter to what they experienced as ultimately good and true, the experience of evil offers an alternate perspective from which to view and better to understand the meaning of the Christian "salvation in Christ" or the Buddhist "realization of the Dharma" as taught by the Buddha. Recent studies in the symbolism of evil,[1] and more specifically, an analysis of the symbols Satan and Māra undertaken by T. O. Ling,[2] have not only demonstrated the intrinsic merit of such an undertaking but have also revealed the need for further scholarship in this area.

The *early* portions of both the Buddhist and Christian religious traditions have been chosen principally because of the importance for contemporary Christians and Buddhists of the materials that fall within this general period, (*ca.* 100 B. C.-*ca.* 350 A. D.) for it is then that the canonical literature of Christians and Theravādin Buddhists was written as well as important sutras of Mahāyāna Buddhists. It was a formative period containing not only the

[1] E.g., Paul Ricœur, *The Symbolism of Evil,* trans. by E. Buchanan (New York: Harper and Row, 1967).

[2] T. O. Ling, *The Significance of Satan* (London: SPCK, 1961); and *Buddhism and the Mythology of Evil* (London: George Allen and Unwin, Ltd., 1962).

building materials of subsequent doctrine, but also a rich variety of attempts to spell out the distinguishing characteristics of new religious orientations, including attempts to understand the experience of evil.

We speak of the early *tradition* of each religion because we view the selected texts as belonging in each case to a single religious and cultural continuum.[3] It is not assumed that a tradition is an "intrinsically coherent or self-subsisting" entity or that the portraits of the figures Satan and Māra derived from the selected materials represent unified conceptions of evil adhered to by all writers belonging to the tradition in question. Our analysis respects the dynamics and diversity of history, but it is this writer's position that as components of a single linguistic-religious-cultural continuum (Pali-Sanskrit-Indian-Buddhist and Greek-Christian),[4] the various aspects of the early Christian and Buddhist mythologies of evil may legitimately be unified in conception. By abstracting and synthesizing one can arrive at a general portrait which incorporates basic motifs that underlie the whole tradition and structure its expression.[5]

Because our purpose is to clarify basic structures of meaning that govern the use of the symbols Satan and Māra, a broad selection of literature from the early Christian and Buddhist traditions has been made. The Christian texts range from the New Testament and the Apostolic Fathers to several of the early Greek Fathers. The Buddhist texts selected include portions of the Pali Canon, and

[3] W. C. Smith, in his book *The Meaning and End of Religion* (New York: Mentor, 1965), argues that the basis for a proper understanding of man's religiousness is not by approaching religions as though they were entities but rather by studying expressions of the faith of men as they have been nurtured and passed on through "cumulative traditions." Such "expressions of faith" are intelligible and empirically knowable by the historian of religions. This articulates well the methodological basis of this study. The following paragraph is indebted to Smith for its basic argument.

[4] J. J. Jones, in his translation of the *Mahāvastu* (MvJ, II, p. x), states that "one must proceed from the assumption that both Pali and Sanskrit texts preserved as a fixed core a very primitive tradition." As the following study will demonstrate, what is most striking in the relationship between Pali Theravādin texts and other Buddhist Sanskrit texts is the common tradition of a mythology of evil they both express. Pali and Sanskrit texts of Theravādin and Mahāyāna Indian Buddhism are constituent parts of one religious cumulative tradition.

[5] Cf. W. C. Smith, *Religion*, 151ff.; also cf., Anders Nygren, *Agape and Eros*, trans. by P. S. Watson (Philadelphia: Westminster Press, 1953) for a discussion of "motif-research," and below, pp. 65ff.

Sarvāstivādin, Mādhyamika, and Yogācārin Sanskrit literature. Such a broad sampling involves problems of selection but also furnishes a wide perspective from which to analyze and define basic characteristics which remain constant throughout the range of materials.

An undertaking of this scope is possible only because of the contributions of previous scholarship. T. O. Ling's work on the Buddhist and Christian mythologies of evil has already been referred to. In addition, special mention should be made of Francis X. Gokey's careful study of *The Terminology for the Devil and Evil Spirits in the Apostolic Fathers*,[6] and of Edward Langton's books dealing with Satan and demonology.[7] In the area of the Buddhist symbolism of evil, a number of essays have dealt with Māra,[8] but the single most important work is Ernst Windisch's book, *Māra und Buddha*, written in 1895.[9] The present study is indebted to Windisch's findings, but differs in purpose. Windisch's concern was principally philological, and he sought to elucidate the historical development of the mythology of evil in early Buddhist literature. He gave a good deal of attention to the dating of texts and the chronological relationship between them. Our effort is not to establish or conjecture about the position of the Māra myth in the history of early Buddhist literature. Consequently, we do not always treat the selected texts in chronological order. Our present task is to study the religious symbolism of evil as seen within the historical context of each tradition, not to study the history of religious ideas. A comparison of these symbols of evil will not only help define the relationship between the two, but hopefully will contribute perspectives by which each tradition can better understand and evaluate its own religious symbolism.

---

[6] (Washington, D. C.: The Catholic University of America Press, 1961).

[7] Edward Langton, *Satan, A Portrait* (London: Skeffington and Sons, Ltd., 1945) and *Essentials of Demonology* (London: Epworth Press, 1948).

[8] Besides references in general works on Buddhism, a number of essays on the subject of Māra have been written. Among the most important are: B. M. Barua, "Māra," *The Buddhist Review*, VII (1915), pp. 194-211; B. C. Law, "The Buddhist Conception of Māra," *Buddhistic Studies*, ed. B. C. Law (Calcutta: Thacker, Spink and Co., Ltd., 1931), pp. 257-283; J. Masson's chapter on "Māra" in *Religion populaire dans le canon bouddhique Pāli* (Louvain: Bureaux du Muséon, 1942), pp. 99-113; L. de la Vallée Poussin, "Māra," *Encyclopaedia of Religion and Ethics*, VIII (1955), pp. 406-407; Alex Wayman, "Studies in Yama and Māra," *Indo-Iranian Journal*, III (1959), pp. 44ff., 112ff.

[9] (Leipzig: S. Hirzel, 1895).

The criteria for selecting the texts of each early tradition are as follows. First, the text must have material relevant to the topic. References to Māra abound in the *Suttapiṭaka* but are infrequent in the *Vinaya* and the *Abhidhamma*; therefore the *Suttas* constitute the selected text from the Pali Canon. Among the Apostolic Fathers in the Christian tradition, *St. Clement of Rome* has been omitted as he makes only a single reference to the "Opponent"; hence the work contributes little to the topic being investigated.[10]

As a second criterion, the works selected should be representative of each early tradition both in terms of the time of writing and the content and purpose of each writing. Justin, Irenaeus, and Origen, among the Greek Fathers, were selected not only because they were writers who chronologically come after the Apostolic Fathers and the early canonical writings of the New Testament, but also because they represent different theological orientations and differences in purpose of writing. Justin is an apologist who is optimistic about the harmony of Christianity with Greek philosophy, and his writings are intended for the Gentile public.[11] Irenaeus is also interested in interpreting his faith to his contemporaries, but his orientation is far more biblical from the outset than is Justin Martyr's. And Origen, in contrast especially to Irenaeus, does not share the latter's "reverent agnosticism" in matters of high theology and more readily discusses matters of cosmology and metaphysics.[12]

The same criterion applies to the selection of texts in the early Buddhist tradition. In addition to the Sanskrit texts which purport to be basically biographies of the Buddha, such as the *Mahāvastu* of the Mahāsanghikas,[13] and the *Lalita Vistara*, the Sarvastivādin text *Abhidharmakośa* by Vasabandhu has been selected, as well as treatises such as the *Śrāvakabhūmi* by Asaṅga, founder of the Yogācārin school and the latest of the Buddhist writers considered.

---

[10] Cf. *St. Clement of Rome* (51:1) in the Loeb Classical Library Series titled *The Apostolic Fathers* (AF, I, 97). Likewise, the *Epistle to Diognetus* only makes reference to the deceit of the snake (12:3) (AF, II, 379). The *Didache* need not be treated as a separate document as chapters 18-21 of the *Epistle of Barnabas* (EB) contain a version of it which contains the essential references relevant to our topic.

[11] Cf. Henry Chadwick, *Early Christian Thought and the Classical Tradition* (Oxford: Clarendon Press, 1966), pp. 10-11.

[12] Cf. Hans von Campenhausen, *The Fathers of the Greek Church* (London: Adam and Charles Black, 1963), pp. 42ff.

[13] The *Mahāvastu* is attributed to the Lokottaravādins, a subsect of the Mahāsanghikas.

Of the two general types of literature found in the early Buddhist tradition, sutra ("a text which claims to have been spoken by the Buddha himself") and śāstra (treatises which "endeavor to be more systematic and quote the sutras as authentic"),[14] representatives of both types have been selected, including the Mahāyāna sutras the *Aṣṭasāhasrikā Prajñāpāramitā* and the *Saddharma Puṇḍarīka*, and Nāgārjuna's *Mahāprajñāpāramitāśāstra* [15] which is a commentary of the *Pañcaviṃśatisāhasrikā Prajñāpāramitā.*

The third and final criterion for the selection of texts in each early tradition is their suitability for establishing a basis of comparison with the other religious tradition. When it comes to the question of the "nature and power" of Māra and Satan, specifically questions of a metaphysical and cosmological nature, it is necessary to refer to literature of a more philosophical or theological tone, such as the works of Justin or Origen, Nāgārjuna or Asaṅga, so that a basis for comparison of content is established. Furthermore, any discussion of the "activities" of Satan and Māra depends upon material filled with descriptive verbs of action, i.e., a full-fledged mythology which describes experiences and events termed evil as activities of Satan or Māra. Hence besides philosophical or theological treatises, the Sanskrit epic-poetry of Aśvaghoṣa's *Buddha Carita* as well as the Pali *Nikāyas* are profitable selections, as are many of the writings of the Apostolic Fathers (Ignatius, Polycarp, Barnabas) and also the theological letters of Paul whose language is frequently couched in mythological terms.

On the basis of the above stated criteria the following texts of the early Greek Christian tradition have been selected: the canonical literature of the *New Testament* (*ca.* 50 A. D.-*ca.* 150 A. D.) including the Synoptic Gospels, the Pauline and Johannine writings and the Book of Revelation; the earliest post-canonical writings, known as the "Apostolic Fathers" (90 A. D.-140 A. D.): the *Letters of Ignatius* to the *Ephesians*, the *Magnesians*, the *Trallians*, the *Romans*, the *Philadelphians* and the *Smyrnaens*; the *Epistle of Polycarp to the Philippians*; *The Martyrdom of Polycarp*; the *Epistle of Barnabas*; and the *Visions*, *Mandates*, *Similitudes* of the *Shepherd of Hermas*. Texts selected from the early Greek Fathers include Justin Martyr (*ca.* 114-165 A. D.): *The First Apology of Justin, The Second Apology*

[14] E. Conze, *Buddhism: Its Essence and Development* (New York: Harper and Brothers, 1951), pp. 28-29.

[15] Cf. p. 6, n. 18.

of Justin, and *Dialogue of Justin, Philosopher and Martyr, with Trypho, A Jew*; Irenaeus (d. 202 A. D.): *Irenaeus Against Heresies*; Origen (*ca.* 185-254 A. D.): *Origen De Principiis* (*Peri archon*) and *Origen Against Celsus*.[16]

From the early Indian Buddhist literature the following have been chosen: the canonical Theravādin *Nikāyas* of the *Suttapiṭaka* (redacted *ca.* 100 B. C.-100 A. D.): the *Dīgha, Aṅguttara, Saṃyutta, Majjhima* and *Khuddaka Nikāyas*, the last including the *Dhammapada, Udāna, Itivuttaka* and the *Sutta-Nipāta*; the Mahāsanghika texts (1st and 2nd cent. A. D., and later) *Mahāvastu, Lalita Vistara* and Aśvaghoṣa's *Buddha Carita*;[17] the Mahāyāna texts (pre-1st cent. A. D.-2nd cent. A. D.) *Aṣṭasāhasrikā Prajñāpāramitā, Saddharma Puṇḍarīka*, and Nāgārjuna's *Mahāprajñāpāramitāśāstra* (*Le Traité de la grande vertu de sagesse*).[18] The Sarvāstivādin standpoint is represented by Vasubandhu's *Abhidharmakośa* (*ca.* 4th cent. A. D.),[19] the Yogācārin view by Asaṅga's *Śrāvakabhūmi* (section 13 of the *Yogācārabhūmiśāstra*) (*ca.* 350 A. D.).[20]

[16] Concerning quotations from the Greek Fathers, whenever the Greek text is not available in J. P. Migne's *Patrologiae Cursus Completus, Series Graeca* (MPG) the Latin text provided by Migne is cited. New Testament translations are from the Revised Standard Version. The Loeb Classical Library Series on *The Apostolic Fathers* provides on alternate pages the Greek and the English translation by K. Lake.

[17] Cf. M. Winternitz, *A History of Indian Literature*, trans. by S. Ketgar and H. Koen (2 vols.; Calcutta: University of Calcutta, 1933), II, pp. 239ff., 248ff., 256ff.

[18] É. Lamotte's translation in French of Nāgārjuna's *Mahāprajñāpāramitāśāstra* is not from the original Sanskrit which is lost, but comes only through the Chinese translation of it, the *Ta tche tou louen*. Since Lamotte includes reconstructed Sanskrit terms in his translation *Le Traité de la grande vertu de sagesse de Nāgārjuna* it is possible to cite the Sanskrit "original" when necessary in Part II. Due to some indecision about the Chinese character for *śastra* the title of this work might be rendered more accurately *Mahāprajñāpāramitāupadeśa*.

[19] L. de la Vallée Poussin has translated into French the Sanskrit text of Yasomitra's *Abhidharmakośavyākhyā*, using also the Tibetan version of Vasubandhu's own commentary and the Chinese versions by Paramartha and Hsuan-Tsang. Since Poussin includes Sanskrit terms in his translation *L'Abhidharmakośa* it has not been necessary to cite Yasomitra's *Vyākhyā* in Part II.

Concerning the difficult question as to the date of the *Abhidharmakośa*, see E. Frauwallner, *On the Date of the Buddhist Master of the Law Vasubandhu*, (Rome: Serie Orientale Roma, 1951), III, and Alex Wayman's criticism in his *Analysis of the Śrāvakabhūmi Manuscript* (Berkeley: Univ. of California Press, 1961), pp. 19ff.

[20] This particular chapter of the *Yogācārabhūmiśāstra* has been selected for two major reasons: it specifically deals with Māra (more especially the

The procedure of the analysis of these texts is as follows. Passages which describe the activities of the chief figures of evil are grouped according to characteristic verbs and verb phrases of which "Satan" or "Māra" (or established related names) are the grammatical or contextual subjects. Verb forms or phrases which appear in the Greek, Pali or Sanskrit are used to characterize descriptive activities of Satan or Māra. Then passages which describe the nature and power of Satan and Māra are grouped according to characteristic titles and phrases which are applied to them. These titles and phrases, likewise, are derived from Greek, Pali or Sanskrit passages which are directly linked with "Satan" or "Māra" (or related terminology) in the selected literature. A summary discussion concludes each section as well as each Part.

Finally, a note about our use of the terms "mythology" and "symbol." The early Christian and Buddhist descriptions of the activities, nature and power of Satan and Māra are properly called mythologies as they each constitute a tradition of stories about beings conceived as possessing divine or superhuman attributes (*mythos*)[21] who exist in a time and space that the modern mind cannot coordinate with the time and space of history and geography according to the critical method.[22] *Mythological* is to be distinguished from *mythical* (*mythikos*), the latter connoting "arbitrarily invented" and "imaginary" stories. To speak of these stories as mythologies of evil is merely to designate the general nature and content of the narratives; it is not a statement about their truth or falsity. Satan and Māra, as the central figures of these narratives, are both designated "symbols" as they are richly connotative terms which serve as focal concepts for the Christian and Buddhist understanding of evil respectively.

four-Māra formula), and an analysis of the Sanskrit text with a studied translation has been made readily available by Alex Wayman in two publications: *Analysis of the Śrāvakabhūmi Manuscript* (Berkeley: Univ. of California Press, 1961), and a translation and discussion of the *Śrāvakabhūmi* of Asaṅga in an article "Studies in Yama and Māra", *Indo-Iranian Journal*, III, (1959), 44ff., 112ff.

[21] Cf. Webster's *Third New International Dictionary*, 1966.

[22] Cf. Ricœur, *Symbolism of Evil*, p. 18.

PART ONE

ANALYSIS OF THE SATAN FIGURE IN THE EARLY GREEK CHRISTIAN TRADITION

ABBREVIATIONS

Greek Sources

NT	*New Testament* (Revised Standard Version)
AF	*The Apostolic Fathers.* Translated by K. Lake. The Loeb Classical Library, I-II. Edited by E. Capps, T. E. Page, and W. H. D. Rouse. Contains the following writings which are quoted by paragraph and sentence:
IE	*Ignatius to the Ephesians*
IM	*Ignatius to the Magnesians*
IT	*Ignatius to the Trallians*
IR	*Ignatius to the Romans*
IP	*Ignatius to the Philadelphians*
IS	*Ignatius to the Smyrnaeans*
PP	*The Epistle of Polycarp to the Philippians*
MP	*The Martyrdom of St. Polycarp, Bishop of Smyrna*
EB	*Epistle of Barnabas*
HV	*The Shepherd of Hermas, Visions*
HM	*The Shepherd of Hermas, Mandates*
HS	*The Shepherd of Hermas, Similitudes*
ANCL	*Ante-Nicene Christian Library.* Edited by A. Roberts and J. Donaldson, II, V, IX, X, XXIII. Contains the following writings listed by book, chapter, and paragraph where applicable, and cited by volume and page number of author's works in *ANCL* listings:
JAi	*The First Apology of Justin*
JAii	*The Second Apology of Justin*
JD	*Dialogue of Justin, Philosopher and Martyr, with Trypho, A Jew*
IAH	*Irenaeus Against Heresies, I-II*
ODP	*Origen De Principiis*
OAC	*Origen Against Celsus,* I-II
MPG	*Patrologiae Cursus Completus, Series Graeca.* Edited by J. P. Migne, VI, VII, XI (1857-1887).

Other sources frequently cited

BAG	*A Greek-English Lexicon of the New Testament and Other Early Christian Literature* (4th ed., 1952). A translation and adaptation of Bauer's *Wörterbuch* by W. P. Arndt and F. W. Gingrich.
ERE	*Encyclopaedia of Religion and Ethics.* Edited by J. Hastings, IV (1912), VIII (1916).
Gokey, *Terminology*	Francis X. Gokey, *The Terminology for the Devil and Evil Spirits in the Apostolic Fathers.*
Langton, *Essentials*	Edward Langton, *Essentials of Demonology.*
Langton, *Satan*	Edward Langton, *Satan, A Portrait.*
Ling, *Satan*	T. O. Ling, *The Significance of Satan.*
PGL	G. W. H. Lampe, *A Patristic Greek Lexicon,* I-V (1961-1968).
TDNT	*Theological Dictionary of the New Testament,* I-V (1964-1968). Translation and edition of G. Kittel's *Wörterbuch* by G. W. Bromiley.

CHAPTER ONE

TERMINOLOGY CENTERED AROUND SATAN AND THE DEVIL

The terminology designating an evil personage in the early writings of the Christian tradition is widely varied, but there are two dominant terms which pervade all the selected literature. The term "Satan," predominantly used in the New Testament more than in any other early Christian writing, is a Hebrew name derived from the root *sâtan* which means "to oppose" or "to act as an adversary."[1] The term "Devil," which comes from the Greek word *diabolos* used in the Septuagint (LXX) to translate the Hebrew *sâtan*,[2] is a more frequently used term in the writings of the Apostolic and early Greek Fathers. Both terms Satan and Devil, however, are to be found in the New Testament as well as in the later writings. The New Testament writers Mark and Paul show a preference for the term *Satanas*,[3] whereas Matthew more frequently uses the other designation *diabolos*, but all three authors use both terms. And whereas Justin Martyr, Irenaeus and Origen most frequently speak of the Devil (*diabolos*), each writer provides us with his own version of the etymological derivation and meaning of the word Satan (*ho Satanas*).[4] In short, the two terms are treated as synonyms throughout the early tradition.[5]

---

[1] BAG, "σατάν," p. 752; TDNT, "διάβολος," Vol. II, pp. 72ff.

[2] Exceptions to this rendering of "adversary" as (ὁ)διάβολος in favor of ὁ Σατανᾶς and Σατάν occur in *Cod. Alex.* Cf. Gokey, *Terminology*, p. 4. Διάβολος is etymologically connected with the verb διάβαλλειν, "to throw across" (διά = across; βάλλειν = to throw, cast), which in Greek usage came to mean "to set against," "attack," "accuse," "reproach," "slander," and "deceive," cf. Liddell & Scott, *Greek-English Lexicon* (1961), pp. 389-90.

[3] V. Taylor, *The Gospel According to St. Mark* (London: Macmillan, 1952), p. 164.

[4] Justin Martyr's etymology, e.g.: "For 'Sata' in the Jewish and Syrian tongue means apostate; and 'Nas' is the word from which he is called by interpretation the serpent, i.e., according to interpretation of the Hebrew term, from both of which there arises the single word *Satanas*." (JD, CIII [ANCL, 229-230]). Cf. also Irenaeus, IAH, V, XXI, 2 (ANCL, II, 113), and Origen, OAC, VI, XLIV (ANCL, II, 385) who give the term the meaning "apostate" and "adversary."

[5] W. Foerster, TDNT, "διάβολος," Vol. II, p. 79, states: "As concerns the alternation between σατανᾶς and διάβολος in the NT, no material distinction

The relation of these two words to the variety of other terms used to designate evil is a more complex problem. In noting some of the names and titles associated with Satan and the Devil in the literature being investigated, reference must be made to a number of background sources in the context of which the early Christian literature was written. Such background references will clarify the relation of these varied names for evil to the terms Satan and the Devil.

In the New Testament reference is occasionally made to "the evil one", as when Jesus teaches His followers to pray "deliver us from the evil one" (*apo tou ponērou*), literally, "of or from the evil" (Mt. 6:13). It is generally agreed upon that the allusion here is to Satan and to evil in the abstract,[6] and this is also the case in a number of other references throuhgout the early tradition.[7] The term *ponēros* (evil) means in the physical sense "sick," "painful," "spoiled," or "in poor condition," and in the ethical sense "base," "vicious," "degenerate."[8]

II Cor. 6:15 refers to Beliar (Belial) and is reminiscent of apocalyptic literature references, e.g., the *Testaments of the Twelve Patriarchs*, where Beliar is used interchangeably with Satan or the Devil.[9] Mk. 3:22 refers to Beelzeboul, which was a name in the apocalyptic literature given to a chief of evil spirits and in the

may be asserted." Passages in the New Testament which equate the Devil and Satan are the clearest evidence to support this assertion (e.g., Rev. 20:2). The same conclusion, says G. J. Bartelink, *Lexicologisch-Semantische Studie over de Taal van de Apostolische Vaders* (1952), p. 98, is valid for the Apostolic Fathers even though σατανᾶς is seldom found. Interchangeable references to Satan and the Devil, such as the following written by Justin and Origen, are common to the Greek Fathers' usage of these terms. Justin: "The devil came to Him—i.e., that power which is called the serpent and Satan" (JD, CXXV [ANCL, 258]). Origen: "The name, then, of Devil, and Satan, and Wicked One, who is also described as Enemy of God, is mentioned in many passages of scripture" (ODP, I, V, 2 [ANCL, I, 45]).

6 For a discussion of the NT use of ὁ πονηρός, see Gokey, *Terminology*, pp. 113ff., n. 10; cf. also Langton, *Satan*, p. 29, and Part III below.

7 Mt. 5:37; I Jn. 2:13, 3:11, 5:18; II Th. 3:3; Eph. 6:16. Among the *Apostolic Fathers* the use of πονηρός is common: EB, XXI, 3 (AF, I, 409); EB, IV, 13 (AF, I, 353); and also MP, XVII, 1 (AF, II, 335). Cf. Barnabas, EB, II, 10 (AF, I, 347), where the phrase is definitely "the evil one," ὁ πονηρός.

8 BAG, "πονηρός," pp. 697-698.

9 Cf. *The Apocrypha and Pseudipigrapha of the Old Testament* (Oxford: Clarendon Press, 1913), II; BAG, "βελιάρ," p. 138: "worthlessness." Belial also appears in the Qumran texts, cf. e.g., A. R. C. Leaney, *The Rule of Qumran and Its Meaning* (London: SCM Press, Ltd., 1966), p. 126; *The Manual of Discipline*, trans. by P. Wernberg-Møller (Grand Rapids: Eerdmans, 1957), pp. 22ff.

Talmud is regarded as the prince among demons.[10] Various other names and phrases found in the writings of the Apostolic Fathers include: "the Opponent of the race of Saints,"[11] "the Black One,"[12] and "the Lawless One."[13] Irenaeus, besides interchangeable references to Satan and the Devil, notes references to the Devil as "adversary,"[14] and "the wicked one."[15] Origen, besides identifying Satan with Lucifer,[16] summarizes his use of the terminology for evil in the following manner:

> The name, then, of Devil, and Satan, and Wicked One, who is also described as Enemy of God, is mentioned in many passages of scripture.[17]

Apparently, for the early Christian writers, all such terms and phrases refer, however obliquely, to Satan and the Devil.

---

[10] It is not always clear whether Beelzeboul was equated with Satan or regarded as an underling, a demon prince subject to Satan, among early Christians. When Jesus was accused of expelling demons with the help of Beelzeboul, he tacitly substituted the name Satan in his answer, because for Jesus the realm of demons stood under the authority of Satan. Cf. W. Foerster, "βεεζεβούλ," TDNT, Vol. I, pp. 605-606. For a discussion of the relation of gospel demonology to Jewish demonology, see, W. O. E. Oesterly, "Demon, Demoniacs," Hasting's *Dictionary of Christ and the Gospels*, I (1908), 439a. Other oblique references to Satan in the NT include "roaring lion" (I Pet. 5:8), "great dragon" (Rev. 12:7-9) and ὁ εχθρός, "the enemy" (Lk. 10:19; Mt. 13:25, 28, 29). Justin Martyr also refers to the Devil as a "roaring lion" (JD, CIII [ANCL, 229]).

[11] Translation by Francis X. Gokey, *Terminology*, p. 91. K. Lake translates the phrase more literally: "... the jealous and envious evil one who resists the family of the righteous" (MP, XVII, 1 [AF, II, 335]).

[12] EB, XX, 1 (AF, I, 407); cf. also EB, IV, 9 (AF, I, 353). T. H. Gaster's article on "Satan" in *The Interpreter's Dictionary of the Bible*, IV (1922), 227a, notes that "the concept of the devil as a swarthy 'Ethiopian' recurs later in the apocryphal Acts both of Andrew (ch. 22) and of Thomas (ch. 55), as well as in the famous Paris Magical Papyrus (lines 1238-1239) ..."

[13] EB, XV, 5 (AF, I, 395). Concerning the term ἄνομος, see below pp. 24ff.

[14] IAH, I, XXV, 4 (ANCL, I, 95); translation of "adversarium." MPG, VII, 683.

[15] IAH, IV, XLI, 2 (ANCL, II, 51); translation of "maligni," MPG, VII, 1115.

[16] ODP, I, V, 5 (ANCL, I, 51-52). Gustav Davidson, in *A Dictionary of Angels* (New York: The Free Press, 1967), p. 176, says that Satan was identified with Lucifer through a misreading of Is. 14:12: "How art thou fallen from heaven, O Lucifer, son of the morning." Davidson says that the name Lucifer ("light giver") applies to Nebuchadnezzar, king of Babylon, in this passage, but was erroneously equated with the fallen angel (Satan). Cf. below, pp. 38ff.

[17] ODP, I, V, 2 (ANCL, I, 45). Also quoted above, p. 14, n. 5.

The background developments which explain the interchangeable use of these various terms need not be elaborated in full here, but a brief sketch is necessary. In the Old Testament the term Satan used as a reference to a being or personality appears in three passages only, all of which are post-exilic (*ca.* 519-300 B. C.).[18] In Zechariah, "Satan" is used not as a proper name but as an epithet, or descriptive title: "the Satan," "the adversary." In the prologue to the Book of Job, Yahweh accepts the challenge of "Satan" who functions as his angel minister and not as a demonic, malignant being. In Chronicles, "Satan," who continues to function as an angel minister of Yahweh, is said to incite David to number the people, and here, for the first time the term Satan seems to be used as a proper name.[19]

In both apocalyptic and rabbinical literature of the Intertestamental period, Satan undergoes a change in character and function from his Old Testament role as "adversary" angel.[20] Gradually he becomes a malignant evil being, arch foe of God and man as he appears in the New Testament.[21] In this period prior to the New Testa-

[18] I Ch. 21:1; Job 1:6, 9, 12; 2:3, 4, 6, 7; Zech. 3:1, 2. For a more thorough study of this topic, see R. S. Kluger, *Satan in the Old Testament*, trans. by H. Nagel (Evanston: Northwestern University Press, 1967).

[19] All other references to Satan in the Old Testament mean "adversary" with no supernatural being or personality referred to: Numbers 22:22ff., I Sam. 24:4; II Sam. 19:22; Psalm 109:6; I Kings 5:4; 11:14, 23.

[20] George A. Barton, in an article "The Origin of the Names of Angels and Demons in the Extra-Canonical Apocalyptic Literature to 100 A.D.," *Journal of Biblical Literature*, XXXI (1912), 156, states the following: "In the earlier time the various angels and demons in which the Hebrews believed were not sufficiently personal to bear individual names.... A great change is traceable in the literature of the second century B. C. and the centuries which followed. Proper names were then bestowed upon many spirits both good and bad."

[21] It is understood, of course, that a proper understanding of the development of the Satanic character in the direction of evil requires attention as a separate subject of research. A maze of avenues open themselves to this type of investigation, e.g., a study of Assyrian, Babylonian and early Hebrew demonology, the demonology of the Old Testament, and as suggested by G. H. C. Macgregor, "Principalities and Powers" *New Testament Studies*, I (1954), 17-28, the relation of Persian dualistic conceptions to Jewish thought, consideration of the extraordinary proliferation of Hebrew angelology in the intertestamental period, and the whole apparatus of demon-possession in both the Oriental and Hellenistic environments, as well as in the Gospels. G. von Rad's article, "The Old Testament View of Satan," TDNT, "διάβολος," Vol. II, p. 75, mentions another area needful of investigation besides the above mentioned. He says, "Attention should also be paid to the revival of ancient mythologoumena (the fight with the dragon, the serpent of Paradise, marriages with angels). Deriving from very different contexts, these tend to crystallize around the figure of Satan and thus to

ment no conception of one supreme power of evil exists. Rather there are references to many princes of evil, Satan among them. Mastema, Beliar, Sammael, Satanael, Beelzebul, are some of these names. By the end of the first century, Satan or Devil had become the dominant terms. The writings that overlap the New Testament period generally share this emphasis.[22] *The Assumption of Moses* (4 B. C.-7 A. D.), e.g., clearly views Satan as the head of the Kingdom of evil.[23]

This development of the Satanic character in the direction of evil was probably at least partially due to the influence of Persian dualism. Persian influence is also very likely an important factor in the emergence of the conception of one supreme symbol of evil. The predominant tone of the references to Satan in the early tradition definitely points to a single personage, Satan, as the prince of evil. In the New Testament the terms Satan and the Devil are almost always used in the singular with the definite article (*ho satanas*), (*ho diabolos*), the exceptions constituting grammatical or metaphorical usages of the terms.[24] This is also the general usage of the Apostolic and Greek Fathers. In Ignatius, for example, *diabolos* is always used with the article and never in the plural,[25] and when the

---

contribute an essential broadening of content." Basic research in some of these areas has been done by E. Langton and F. Gokey. See also R. S. Kluger (above p. 16, n. 18) and J. Duchesne-Guillemin, *The Western Response to Zoroaster* (Oxford: Clarendon Press, 1958) and *Symbols and Values in Zoroastrianism* (New York: Harper and Row, 1966).

[22] Cf. Langton, *Satan*, pp. 13-25; Gokey, *Terminology*, p. 87, supports this assertion by noting that all Greek mss. of the Testament Asher 6.4 (*Testaments of the Twelve Patriarchs*) translate the Hebrew "Beliar" with "Satan" or "devil."

[23] *The Assumption of Moses*, trans. by W. J. Ferrar (New York: Macmillan Co., 1918), pp. 33ff.

[24] BAG, "σατάν," p. 752, lists the following exceptions: Mk. 3: 23; Lk 22:3; II Cor. 12:7. In all of these σατανᾶς appears without the definite article. There is also the use of the vocative without the definite article: Mt. 4:10; 16:23; Mk. 8:33. When διάβολος is metaphorically applied to men it is never with the article as in John 6:70; I Tim. 3:11; II Tim. 3:3; and Titus 2:3. This treatment of the references Satan and Devil in the singular is not characteristic of the apocryphal and apocalyptic literature written prior to the New Testament. *The Book of Enoch*, trans. by R. H. Charles (Oxford: Clarendon Press, 1893), p. 119, refers to a class of Satans ruled by a chief Satan. Cf. also *The Book of Jubilees*, trans. by G. H. Schodde (Oberlin: E. J. Goodrich, 1888), p. 35, n. 2. The only possible plural reference to Satan in the NT depends on the interpretation of Eph. 6:12, "world-rulers of this present darkness." Cf. later discussion, pp. 42ff.

[25] Gokey, *Terminology*, pp. 75-76, n. 3.

plural reference "devils" is used the term is usually a synonym for "demons." In the case of Justin Martyr it is the translator's consistent use of the English word "devils" to render the Greek *daimones* that obscures the singular importance the Devil had in Justin's thought.[26]

The terminology for evil in the selected writings of the early Christian tradition, as we have noted, is centered around the dominant terms Satan and the Devil. Our primary interest will be, in the following pages, to note and analyze references to Satan and the Devil. Related names and titles will be noted only when they provide an additional perspective which will help in our consideration of the nature of evil as symbolized by Satan and the Devil in the early Christian tradition.

---

[26] The translator himself notes, "There is but one devil, but many demons ...." and "the word διάβολος, devil, is not applied to these demons" (ANCL, II, n. 1).

CHAPTER TWO

THE ACTIVITIES OF SATAN

Theorizing about the nature, origin, and cosmological status of Satan is definitely a secondary concern in the selected writings. It is through his activities that the Devil is best known and a glimpse of his character ascertained.

The activities of Satan or the Devil are many, but for the most part fall into the following categories: temptation, deception, obstruction and torment, possession and instigation, and destruction. This typology is applicable to all the writings being investigated, although varying emphases as well as differences of opinion will be found among the various writers of the early tradition. It is for this reason that discussion of each type of Satanic activity will be developed first as it appears in New Testament writers, then in the Apostolic Fathers, and finally in the early Greek Fathers.

A. Satan as Tempter

Satan has many snares, wiles, and devices.[1] In the Gospels he acts chiefly as the tempter (*ho peirazōn*), principally in the sense of testing one by inducing him to commit sin.[2] The first gospel references to Satan occur in the various accounts of the temptation of Jesus in the wilderness. Mark says Jesus was "tempted by Satan" (*peirazomenos hypo tou satana*), (Mk. 1:13).[3] Matthew gives the following account of the temptation:

[1] II Tim. 2:26; Eph. 6:11; II Cor. 2:11.

[2] BAG, "πειράζω," p. 646, in this connection gives this term the principal meaning of putting to the test (in order to discover the kind of person one is) by enticement to sin. R. Leivestad, *Christ the Conqueror* (London: SPCK, 1954), p. 42, makes an important observation, namely that demons, in contrast to Satan, do not induce persons to commit sin in the New Testament. Such is a demonic activity, however, in such works as *Testaments of the Twelve Patriarchs*.

[3] Matthew and Luke say Jesus was "tempted by the Devil" (Mt. 4:1; Lk. 4:2), although Matthew at the conclusion of the temptation episode quotes Jesus as saying "Begone, Satan!" (Mt. 4:10). Generally when Jesus is quoted he uses the term Satan rather than Devil. B. Noack, *Satanás und Soteria, Untersuchungen zur Neutestamentlichen Dämonologie*(Copenhagen, 1948) pp. 56-57, accounts for this in terms of a predilection of the writers, based on a proper linguistic sense, of using σατανᾶς when quoting Christ. Sometimes Jesus is reported as referring to Satan as "the evil one" (ἐκ τοῦ πονηροῦ; ἀπὸ τοῦ πονηροῦ) (Mt. 5:37, 6:13).

> And the tempter came and said to him, "If you are the Son of God, command these stones to become loaves of bread." But he answered, "It is written, 'Man shall not live by bread alone, but by every word that proceeds from the mouth of God.' "
> Then the devil took him to the holy city, and set him on the pinnacle of the temple, and said to him, "If you are the Son of God, throw yourself down; for it is written, 'He will give his angels charge of you,' and 'On their hands they will bear you up, lest you strike your foot against a stone.' " Jesus said to him, "Again it is written, 'You shall not tempt the Lord your God.' "
> Again, the devil took him to a very high mountain, and showed him all the kingdoms of the world and the glory of them; and he said to him, "All these I will give you if you will fall down and worship me." Then Jesus said to him, "Begone, Satan! for it is written, 'You shall worship the Lord your God, and him only shall you serve.' " (Mt. 4:3-10; cf. also Lk. 4:3-12).

All these temptations are peculiar to Jesus' calling as Messiah.[4] The point of departure for Satan is, "if you are the Son of God" then show yourself to be such in terms of popular messianic expectations. What follows is a testing of the obedience of Jesus to his own messianic consciousness. Satan asks Jesus to work a miracle by turning stones into bread, which in effect is asking him to use messianic powers for his own use. Then Satan asks Jesus to fly from the roof of the temple presumably in view of the people, thus rejecting messianic anonymity and suffering for recognition and popular acclaim. Finally, Satan suggests that by showing him obeisance Jesus will be given the power and title of "prince of the world," the expedient and unsuffering way to the messianic goal. The temptations are always related to the concepts of traditional messianism but not in accord with Jesus' own messianic consciousness, characterized by the elements of obedience and suffering.

Luke concludes his temptation narrative with these words: "And when the devil had ended every temptation (*peirasmon*), he departed from him until an opportune time" (Lk. 4:13). And so it was that later "others, to test (*peirazontes*) him, sought from him a sign from heaven" (Lk. 11-16),[5] just as Satan had done in the wilderness. Peter's rebuke of Jesus after Jesus had begun to teach his disciples that the Son of man must suffer many things is seen by

---

[4] The explanation that follows is indebted to Anders Nygren, *Christ and his Church*, trans. by A. Carlsten, (Philadelphia: Westminster Press, 1956), pp. 75-85, and to R. Leivestad, *Christ the Conqueror*, pp. 53ff.

[5] Mt. 16:1; 19:3; 22:18, 35; Mk. 8:11; 10:2; 12:15; Lk. 11:16; Jn. 8:6.

Jesus as an activity of Satan's, as it bears the same markings as the first temptations. Peter was putting Jesus' messianic understanding to the test and consequently was an enticement away from his own messianic consciousness. Hence Jesus said to Peter: "Get behind me, Satan! For you are not on the side of God, but of men" (Mk. 8:33; Mt. 16:23). The same connotations to the notion of temptation are found in Paul's letters. I Thess. 3:5 refers to "the tempter" (*ho peirazōn*), who entices men from their faith; I Cor. 7:5 refers to the opposing one, Satan, who puts man to the test through lack of self-control. Rev. 2:10 predicts that the devil is about to throw some of the Christians into prison, that they "may be tested" (*hina peirasthēte*).

Among the selected writings of the Apostolic and early Greek Fathers very little use is made of the term *peirazō* to designate Satanic temptation as trial and enticement.[6] The occasions on which the concept is employed are descriptive summaries of gospel accounts of the temptation of Jesus.[7] Origen does have an extended discussion of the question of temptation following his reference to the encounter between Jesus and Satan, but as he develops his ideas it becomes evident that temptation is a general word which connotes instigation, enticement and possession, as well as the idea of putting to the test. These aspects of the activities of Satan will be discussed in the following sections.

In summary, it is Satan's temptation of Jesus that is most frequently referred to in the selected literature. Satan seeks to put Jesus' faith to the test by attempting to induce him into actions not in accord with his messianic consciousness. Satan also seeks to entice the followers of Jesus from their faith and puts them to the test through their lack of self-control.

B. Satan as Deceiver and Liar

1. *Heresies*

In the selected early church writings Satan the liar and deceiver proves very active, especially as these activities underlie heresies.

[6] The *Shepherd of Hermas* refers to man's "being tempted (ἐκπειρασθείς) by the devil" away from faith, even after the "great and holy calling" of believing in the Lord. (HM, IV, III, 6 [AF, II, 85]). Gokey, *Terminology*, pp. 139-140, says of this term ἐκπειρασθείς, that as a compound it has new force, i.e., "to tempt out," "try to the utmost or tempt thoroughly." This is the only reference to this term in the Apostolic Fathers.

[7] Cf. JD, CIII (ANCL, 230); IAH, V, XXI, 2 (ANCL, II, 112); ODP, III, II, 1 (ANCL, I, 224).

The Book of Revelation speaks of "that ancient serpent, who is called the Devil and Satan, the deceiver (*ho planōn*) of the whole world" (12:9).[8] John quotes Jesus as saying of the Devil, "He was a murderer from the beginning, and has nothing to do with the truth, because there is no truth in him. When he lies, he speaks according to his own nature, for he is a liar (*pseustēs*) and the father of lies" (Jn. 8:44).[9] In Acts Peter is quoted as saying to Ananias who had lied and kept back part of the price of the land, "Why has Satan filled your heart to lie (*pseusasthai*) to the Holy Spirit... ?" (Acts 5:3).[10] These two basic concepts, lie (*pseudos*) and deceive (*planaō*), expressed in a variety of ways and with a variety of terms, have meanings that are closely interrelated. To lie is to make an untrue statement with the intent to deceive, i.e., to cause to believe the false. To hold false religious beliefs, in turn, is what the early church termed heresy. The Apostolic and Greek Fathers especially warned against what the New Testament refers to as the spirit of error (*planēs*), (I Jn. 4:6) which seeks to take away the Word that has been sown in men's hearts so that weeds may grow in its place (Mk. 4:15; Mt. 13:19, 25).

St. Ignatius of Antioch admonishes the Ephesians, may "no plant of the devil be found in you"[11] and declares:

> Be not anointed with the evil odour of the doctrine of the Prince of this world, lest he lead you away captive from the life which is set before you.[12]

[8] Caution against being deceived is prevalent in the NT: Mt. 24:4ff., 11:24; Mk. 13:5ff.; Jn. 7:12; I Jn. 2:26; 3:7; Rev. 2:20; 13:14; 19:20; 20:3, 8, 10. Cf. BAG "πλανάω," p. 671. Gokey, *Terminology*, pp. 116-117, n. 12, says: "πλάνη is a word which in one form or another (e.g., πλανάω, πλάνης, πλανήτης) has been used in almost all the figures of speech associated with evil, because evil is (even for the strict dualists) conceived and described as a wandering from the path of good and right. The term is, therefore, so used in Jewish, Christian and pagan writings ... It is most frequently associated with the deviation from truth."

[9] The term ψεύστης explicitly linked to the devil occurs only here in the NT. However, the prevalence of lies and falsehoods, especially with reference to religious matters, is a danger warned about frequently. Cf. BAG, "ψεῦδος," p. 900. The Qumran literature also refers to the "spirit of deceit," the "man of lies" and the "preacher of lies;" cf., e.g., *Manual of Discipline*, trans. by P. Wernberg-Møller, p. 26.

[10] Jesus' prophecy of Peter's threefold denial links Satan to the episode ("Satan demanded to have you ...") and can also be cited as an example of Satan's involvement with lies and deception (Lk. 22:31-34).

[11] IE, X, 3 (AF, I, 185). Gokey, *Terminology*, p. 71, translates this "that no weed of the devil (τοῦ διαβόλου βοτάνη) may be found among you" following the NT parable of the weeds (Mt. 13:24-30).

[12] IE, XVII, 1 (AF, I, 191).

More specifically he criticizes the Docetists who are inspired by the Devil,[13] and he condemns the Judaisers as instruments of the Devil:

> But if anyone interpret Judaism to you do not listen to him.... Flee then from the wicked arts and snares of the prince of this world, lest you be afflicted by his device, and grow weak in love; but come all together with undivided heart.[14]

The unity of the church, its doctrine and discipline, are opposed by Satan, the Prince of this world.[15]

Polycarp, likewise, refers to heretics as the "first born of Satan" or "of the devil":

> For everyone who does not confess that Jesus Christ has come in the flesh is an anti-Christ; and whosoever does not confess the testimony of the Cross is of the devil; and whosoever perverts the oracles of the Lord for his own lusts, and says that there is neither resurrection nor judgment—this man is the first born of Satan.[16]

Barnabas speaks of "an evil angel" misleading those who trusted in circumcision [17] and warns Christian brethren "carefully to enquire concerning our salvation, in order that the evil one may not achieve a deceitful (*planēs*) entry into us and hurl us away from our life".[18]

The *Shepherd of Hermas* tells of the Devil who fills the false prophet "with his spirit, to see if he can break any of the righteous,"[19] and for Justin Martyr that same spirit of deception filled not only false prophets [20] and heretics,[21] but also the fables of the Greek, pagan world. "The devil, since he emulates the truth, has invented fables about Bacchus, Hercules, and Aesculapius."[22] The Devil also imitates and counterfeits truths written in the Scriptures.[23]

[13] Regarding the docetic denial of the humanity of Christ, Ignatius says "the virginity of Mary, and her giving birth were hidden from the prince of this world, as was also the death of the Lord" (IE, XIX, 1 [AF, I, 193]).

[14] IP, VI, I, 2 (AF, I, 245).

[15] IM, I, 2 (AF, I, 197).

[16] PP, VII, 1 (AF, I, 293). Irenaeus says that Polycarp applied the phrase "first born of Satan" to Marcion (IAH, III, III, 4 [ANCL, I, 263]), but the reference is not limited to Marcion.

[17] EB, IX, 4 (AF, I, 371).

[18] EB, II, 10 (AF, I, 345-347).

[19] HM, XI, I, 3 (AF, II, 119).

[20] JD, VII (ANCL, 96): "false prophets, ... are filled with the lying, unclean spirit."

[21] JAi, LVIII (ANCL, 56): "the devils (δαίμονες) put forward Marcion of Pontus."

[22] JD, LXIX, (ANCL, 184).

[23] Cf. "spirits of error," JD, XXXV (ANCL, 130); also JD, LXXVII (ANCL, 196).

Likewise, Origen refers to apostate and refugee powers who invented error and delusion of false doctrine,[24] and Irenaeus states clearly:

> Let those persons ... who blaspheme the Creator, either by openly expressed words, such as the disciple of Marcion, or by the perversion of the sense (of Scripture), as those of Valentinus and all the Gnostics falsely so called, be recognized as agents of Satan.[25]

This recognition of agents of Satan not only pertains to heretics, for Irenaeus, but also to men who practice magical arts and incantations. They too have "been sent forth by Satan to bring dishonour upon the church," turning men away from "the preaching of the truth."[26] In summation, it is Satan who has "obscured the love which God had towards man, and blinded his mind not to perceive what is worthy of God..."[27]

2. *The serpent and the anti-Christ*

It is these characteristics of lying and deceitfulness that lead to the association, made explicit chiefly in the Greek Fathers, between Satan and the Serpent who appeared at the beginning of time[28] and the anti-Christ who will dominate the end-days of time.

Origen says that the serpent in Genesis, "being inspired by the devil, was the cause of Adam and Eve's transgression".[29] Justin Martyr carries the association further, using the term "serpent" as an epithet for "Devil": "the prince of the wicked spirits is called the serpent, and Satan, and the devil,"[30] and it is "the devil... whom

[24] ODP, III, III, 4 (ANCL, I, 241).
[25] IAH, V, XXVI, 2 (ANCL, II, 127). Cf. also IAH, I, XVI (ANCL, I, 72).
[26] IAH, I, XXV, 3 (ANCL, I, 94).
[27] IAH, III, XX, 1 (ANCL, I, 348).
[28] In the NT there are no direct associations between Satan and the Serpent in the garden of Eden. II Cor. 11:3 refers to the serpent who deceived Eve by his cunning, but there is no explicit connection of the serpent with Satan (though reference is made to Satan in vs. 14 of that chapter). As noted previously, Rev. 12:9 (also Rev. 20:2) does see as related, if not synonymous, "that ancient serpent, who is called the Devil and Satan ...." But again this is not a direct reference to the Adam and Eve story for the immediate metaphor being employed is the great dragon (that ancient serpent) whom Michael fought. Cf. also Rom. 16:20. The selected writings of the Apostolic Fathers make no contribution to the association of the serpent with Satan. In terms of the original meaning of the passage in Genesis, the serpent was probably understood as a theriomorphic demon, i.e., a demon assuming the form of an animal.
[29] ODP, III, II, 1 (ANCL, I, 222).
[30] JAi, XXVIII (ANCL, 31).

Moses calls the serpent,"[31] who "beguiled Eve, and was cursed."[32] The "beguiling" characteristic of the serpent's activity leads to its association with Satan. This is also true for Irenaeus. Irenaeus discusses Christ's work of recapitulation as "crushing him who had at the beginning led us away captives in Adam,"[33] and frequently refers to "the serpent a liar."[34]

Satan as the deceiver of the whole world is also closely associated with the anti-Christ of end-time. The New Testament says that before the day of the second coming of Christ, "when the Lord Jesus is revealed from heaven with his mighty angels in flaming fire", (II Thess. 1:7), a rebellion will occur and "the man of lawlessness" (*ho anthrōpos tēs anomias*) [35] will be revealed (II Thess. 2:3). His coming is "by the activity of Satan" (vs. 9) and will be:

> with all power and with pretended (*pseudous*) signs and wonders, and with all wicked deception (*apatē*) for those who are to perish, because they refused to love the truth and so be saved. Therefore God sends upon them a strong delusion (*planēs*) to make them believe what is false (*pseudei*) ... (vss. 9-11).

This lawless one, an anti-Christ, will be excessively powerful as an apostate and deceiver. The Gospels warn of "false Christs" who shall attempt "to lead astray (*planēsai*) ... even the elect" (Mt. 24:24),[36] for the anti-Christ is the opponent of all that is holy and divine. He proclaims himself to be god, and by means of pretended (*pseudos*) signs and wonders makes people believe in him. A principal characteristic of this lawless one, therefore, is his power of deceit.[37]

Among the Apostolic Fathers there is a suggested instance of identification of the figure anti-Christ with Satan.[38] For the Greek Fathers, however, the anti-Christ is seen as an instrument of Satan

---

[31] JD, CIII (ANCL, 229); cf. also JD, CXXV (ANCL, 258).

[32] JD, LXXIX (ANCL, 198).

[33] IAH, V, XXI, 1 (ANCL, II, 110); cf. also IAH, V, XXIII, 1 (ANCL, II, 117).

[34] IAH, V, XXIII, 1 (ANCL, II, 117); cf. also IAH, V, XXIV, 1 (ANCL, II, 119).

[35] For a discussion of the NT use of the word ἄνομος, cf. Gokey, *Terminology*, p. 112.

[36] Cf. also Mk. 3:22.

[37] The constituent elements of the NT anti-Christ are traditional, cf. Dan. 7:25; 8:25; 11:36; Ezek. 28:2; Rev. 13:5 and R. Leivestad's discussion in his book *Christ the Conqueror*, p. 91.

[38] Barnabas appears to identify the anti-Christ with the Devil when he refers to the Son of God's destruction of "the time of the wicked one" (τοῦ ἀνόμου), EB, XV, 5 (AF, I, 395).

who is, as Justin says, "the man of apostasy, who speaks strange things against the Most High...." [39] Irenaeus and Origen use the anti-Christ figure to summarize most of the characteristic activities of Satan which emphasize his role as the satanic counterpart to the Son of God.[40] Irenaeus, however, singles out those characteristics of the anti-Christ which epitomize his deeds. Citing II Thess. 2:9-10, Irenaeus says that the coming of the anti-Christ "is after the working of Satan, in all power, and signs, and portents of lies, and with all deceivableness of wickedness for those who perish."[41]

Thus for the early Greek Fathers especially, Satan the father of lies and the deceiver of the whole world has been active since the beginning of creation and will dominate the end-days of time. Among the earlier writings as well as the Greek Fathers Satan is the spirit of error and falsehood who leads men away from the truth and sows in its place disunity, heresy and counterfeit truths of pagan fables. The embodiment of these characteristics, the near-incarnation of Satan as deceiver and liar, will appear as the future anti-Christ, just as it appeared as the serpent who deceived Eve.

C. Satan as Obstructor and Tormentor

1. *Work of Satan*

In the New Testament several of Paul's letters make mention of the hindrances Satan has placed in Paul's path. Speaking for Silvanus and Timothy as well as for himself, Paul says to the members of the church in Thessalonica: "we wanted to come to you ... but Satan hindered us" (*enekopsen hēmas ho satanas*), (I Thess. 2:18).[42] Referring to himself in a letter to the Corinthians, Paul speaks of "a thorn ... given me in the flesh, a messenger of Satan, to harass me (*hina me kolaphizē*), to keep me from being too elated" (II Cor. 12:7).[43] The nature of these hindrances and of this thorn in the flesh is not made clear. What is clearly stated is that these conditions that thwarted were seen as obstructing and tormenting

[39] JD, CX (ANCL, 236-237).

[40] Cf. OAC, VI, XLV (ANCL, II, 386).

[41] IAH, V, XXV, 2 (ANCL, II, 123); cf. also IAH, V, XXV, 1 (ANCL, II, 121ff.).

[42] BAG, "ἐγκόπτω," p. 215; cf. also: Gal. 5:7; I Pet. 3:7; Rom. 15:22.

[43] Cf. also: I Cor. 4:11; I Pet. 2:20. BAG, "κολαφίζω," pp. 441-442, summarizes various interpretations, e.g., epilepsy, hysteria, periodic depressions, headaches, malaria, leprosy, stammering. If a physical malady is the reference, then disease comes within the scope of Satanic activity for Paul.

activities of Satan,[44] and like the persecuting activities of the future anti-Christ, are efforts to deny and prevent man's full realization of a life in Christ.

Among the Apostolic and Greek Fathers one aspect of Christian life was easily identified as an obstructing and tormenting activity of the Devil: martyrdom. Polycarp considered the "terrible torment(s)" (*deinas kolaseis*) endured by the martyrs as stratagems of the devil, "for the Devil used many wiles against them."[45] Ignatius writes:

> May nothing of things seen or unseen envy me my attaining to Jesus Christ. Let there come on me fire, and cross, and struggles with wild beasts, cutting, and tearing asunder, racking of bones, mangling of limbs, crushing of my whole body, cruel tortures of the devil (*kakai kolaseis tou diabolou*), may I but attain to Jesus Christ.[46]

The *Shepherd of Hermas* speaks of the Devil as hard and oppressive who can cause fear even in the servants of God,[47] but though "the devil can wrestle with them, . . . he cannot throw them down."[48] Justin says that "for our piety, punishments (*kolaseis*) even to death have been inflicted on us by demons, and by the host of the devil, . . . and (Christians) endure all torments rather than deny Christ even by word . . ." [49]

But such severe torments are not the only work of Satan. Mental attitudes and emotional states ranging from slothfulness to anger and irreligious sentiments also characterize the work of Satan. These can be viewed as obstructions to the achievement of a full life in Christ. In discussing Paul's injunction that one should not give place to the devil (Eph. 4:27), Origen says "it is through certain acts, or a kind of mental slothfulness, that room is made for the devil."[50] When, e.g.,

> losses and dangers befall us, or calumnies and false accusations are brought against us, it not being the object of the hostile powers that we should suffer these (trials) only, but that by means of them we

[44] Rom. 16:20 implies that whatever obstructs the peace is the work of Satan: "the God of peace will soon crush Satan under your feet."

[45] MP, II, 4 (AF, II, 317). Obstructions to prevent the martyrdom of Polycarp are also seen as the stratagems of the Devil in MP, III, 1 (AF, II, 317).

[46] IR, V, 3 (AF, I, 233).

[47] HM, 12, IV, 7 (AF, II, 133).

[48] HM, 12, V, I, 2 (AF, II, 135).

[49] JD, CXXXI (ANCL, 265) and MPG, VI, 780.

[50] ODP, III, II, 4 (ANCL, I, 232).

> should be driven either to excess of anger or sorrow, or to the last pitch of despair; or at least, which is a greater sin, should be forced, when fatigued and overcome by any annoyances, to make complaints against God, as one who does not administer human life justly and equitably; the consequence of which is, that our faith may be weakened, or our hopes disappointed, or we may be compelled to give up the truth of our opinions, or be led to entertain irreligious sentiments regarding God. For some such things are written regarding Job, after the devil had requested God that power should be given him over his goods.[51]

In the context of this quote, perhaps Origen's question, stated after referring to Jesus' freeing of the woman bound with an infirmity for eighteen years by Satan, has added relevance: "And how many others are still bowed down and bound by Satan, who hinders them from looking up at all, and would have us to look down also!" [52]

2. *Work of demons*

The above reference to the woman bound by Satan by a physical infirmity (Lk. 13:16) is an exceptional one in both biblical and early Christian literature. Satan is rarely *directly* connected with illness, whether of physical or mental type.[53] Rather the tormenting of people by causing sickness and possessing them tends to be the exclusive function of demons. Demonic activity involves Satan, but in an indirect way.[54]

In the New Testament not all sicknesses are attributed to demons,[55] nor are sickness and demon possession always synonymous,[56] but there are many references to demons and evil spirits in

[51] ODP, III, II, 6 (ANCL, I, 234-235).

[52] OAC, VIII, LIV (ANCL, II, 538).

[53] The exceptions, none of which are as explicit as Lk. 13:16, are found in the following passages: Acts 10:38; I Cor. 5:5, II Cor. 12:7; I Tim. 1:20. These references to illness, of course, are to be distinguished from the physical and mental tortures of martyrdom to which Satan is directly linked.

[54] An extensive review of the demonology of the early Christian tradition lies beyond the scope of our concern. However a brief treatment of the activities of demons and the origin and nature of demons (cf. below, pp. 45ff.) is necessary to clarify the meaning of the figure Satan.

[55] W. Foerster, after mentioning that sickness cannot always be traced to demons, says: "Nevertheless, it may be said that the existence of sickness in this world belongs to the character of the αἰὼν οὗτος of which Satan is the prince." TDNT, "δαίμων," Vol. II, p. 18. Cf. later discussion of Satan as ruler of demons, below pp. 45ff.

[56] S. Eitrem, *Some Notes on the Demonology of the New Testament* (Osloae: A. W. Brøgger, 1950), pp. 34-35, says that in general the New Testament sources "make a difference between θεραπεύειν and δαιμόνια ἐκβάλλειν,"

the early Christian texts which are associated with illness and infirmity,[57] which in turn are seen as the devil's work of oppression. In the New Testament story of the Gerasene man (Lk. 8:26ff.), e.g., a "legion" of demons possessed this man, who "for a long time ... had worn no clothes, and he lived not in a house but among tombs" (v. 27). Besides this reference to what appears to be mental illness, physical infirmities are attributed to "spirits of infirmity" and "unclean demons," and Jesus' healing is described as a driving out of demons.[58]

In addition to causing a variety of illnesses, demons also spread false doctrine (I Tim. 4:1), work miracles (Jn. 10:21; Rev. 16:14), and sometimes become objects of worship (I Cor. 10:20; Rev. 9:20).[59] Thus demonic activities are varied and similar in nature to Satan's, although demons most characteristically are seen as tormenting spirits who cause illness and possess people rather than deceiving and lying.

The other selected writings basically follow the same type of description as to their activities. Among the Apostolic Fathers, the *Shepherd of Hermas* refers to the entrance of the evil spirit ill-temper into the inner life of a person, which causes the Holy Spirit "to depart out of the place, for it is choked by the evil spirit."[60] Justin says that

---

between healing and exorcism. "Sometimes, however, the distinction fluctuates, the demonology overspreading all anomalies of life ..." Cf. e.g., Mt. 4:24.

[57] NT passages, e.g., that associate evil spirits with illness are: Lk. 7:21; 8:2; 11:26 (evil spirits): Mt. 12:43 (unclean spirit); Lk. 13:11 (spirit of infirmity); Lk. 4:33, 6:18 (spirit of unclean demon). Cf. BAG, "πνεῦμα," p. 682.

[58] Mt. 7:22; 9:34; 10:8; Mk. 1:34,39; Lk. 9:49, 11:14ff., 18ff.; 13:32. Cf. BAG, "δαιμόνιον," p. 168.

[59] For a summary of the chief demonological ideas that underlie the NT, see F. C. Conybeare, "The Demonology of the New Testament," *Jewish Quarterly Review*, VIII (1896), 576-608. Also Langton, *Essentials*, and M. Ziegler, *Engel und Dämon im Lichte der Bibel* (Zurich: Origo, 1957), pp. 103ff.

[60] HM, 5, I, 3 (AF, II, 87-89). This quote is only a partially correct representation of Hermas' demonology. In as much as the present discussion assumes demons to be independently existing spirits who possess people and thereby cause maladies, the quoted statement of Hermas correctly reflects that aspect of his thought. However, much more predominant in his writings is an understanding of demons not shared by the NT and later Greek writers. Demons, more often than not, are personified vices, not spiritual causal agents. As personified vices, it is misleading to characterize the names of his demons as demonic activities. In a later chapter Hermas' understanding of the nature of demons will be discussed.

> devils (*daimones*) have always effected, that all those who anyhow live a reasonable and earnest life, and shun vice, be hated ... (and) are proved to cause those to be much worse hated who live ... by the knowledge and contemplation of the whole Word, which is Christ.[61]

Like Satan, "they who are called devils (*daimones*) attempt nothing else than to seduce (*apagein*) men from God who made them, and from Christ His first-begotten."[62]

Origen also refers to the demonic efforts to destroy Christians. Demons "stirred up both princes, and senates, and rulers in every place,—nay, even nations themselves ... against the word, and those who believed in it."[63] Again, speaking of demons, Origen says, "to them belong famine (*limoi*), blasting of the vine and fruit trees (*apsoriai stapsylēs kai akrodruōn*), pestilence (*aeros diapsthora*) among men and beasts: all these are the proper occupations of demons ..."[64]

There is a great deal of common ground between demonic activity and the activities of Satan which we have partially investigated up to this point. Ultimately the demonic effort is the Satanic effort to "seduce men from God," and a variety of means is used to accomplish this purpose: as tormentors they cause illness, as deceitful liars they spread false doctrine, as tempters they seek to make themselves objects of worship; they also possess persons and attempt to destroy them. Demonic activity, however, is not only an elaboration but an extension of Satanic activity into the sphere of natural evil.[65] Rarely is Satan directly associated with illness, and there is no mention of his being the cause of natural evils in the geological sense of earthquakes, tornadoes, etc., or in the biological

[61] JAii, VIII (ANCL, 78) and MPG, VI, 457.

[62] JAi, LVIII (ANCL, 57) and MPG, VI, 416.

[63] OAC, IV, XXXII (ANCL, II, 194).

[64] OAC, VIII, XXXI (ANCL, II, 517) and MPG, XI, 1564. For a full account of demonic activities, as conceived by Patristic writers, cf. PGL, "δαίμων," pp. 328-331.

[65] Natural evil, in contrast to moral evil, is manifest on 1) the biological level in the forms of life regarded as venomous, pestiferous, etc., whether among plants, insects, animals, that in some way interfere with human well-being; 2) the geological level in the form of earthquakes, tornadoes, tempests, floods, etc.; and 3) on the psychic level, i.e., mental disorders such as schizophrenia, imbecility, psychosis. This definition has been derived from A. N. Tsambassis, "Evil and the 'abysmal nature' of God in the thought of Brightman, Berdyaev and Tillich" (unpublished Ph. D. dissertation, Northwestern University, 1957), pp. 2ff.

sense of being the source of the pestiferous and venomous. However, it is among the "proper occupations" of demons to cause illness on the physical and mental levels, and also "to them belong famine, blasting of the vine and fruit trees, (and) pestilence among men and beasts." The same power that is operative in temptations, deceit and lies, is also present in tormenting afflictions of disease and other natural evils.[66]

Perhaps the most illustrative way of suggesting this pervasive and threatening power of the demonic as ruled by Satan is to cite the apocalyptic vision of the demonic as it appears in the Book of Revelation. Here it is said the demons number a third part of the stars (Rev. 12:4) and constitute a fearful host who in appearance,

> ... were like horses arrayed for battle; on their heads were what looked like crowns of gold; their faces were like human faces, their hair like women's hair, and their teeth like lion's teeth; they had scales like iron breastplates, and the noise of their wings was like the noise of many chariots with horses rushing into battle; they have tails like scorpions, and stings, and their power of hurting men lies in their tails. They have as king over them the angel of the bottomless pit; his name in Hebrew is Abaddon, and in Greek he is called Apollyon. (Rev. 9:7-11) [67]

D. Satan, Possessor and Instigator

Possession, the ability of evil spirits to live and reign in the inner life of a person, is, as we have noted, a prevalent aspect of demonic activity.[68] Satanic possession, on the other hand, is seldom referred to and later writers speak more in terms of Satanic instigation rather than possession.[69]

In Mk. 3:22 the scribes accuse Jesus of being possessed by Beelze-

---

[66] That the same power is operative in all these activities will be more fully established in the section dealing with the nature and power of Satan. Rom. 8:20ff. speaks of the whole creation being "subjected to futility" and in "bondage to decay" and can be cited as NT evidence for demonic or Satanic power conceived to be operative in the natural world, although there is much controversy about the meaning of this passage, as Emil Brunner points out in *The Christian Doctrine of Creation and Redemption* (London: Lutterworth Press, 1952), p. 128.

[67] Apollyon and Abaddon refer to the "destroyer," Satan. Cf. below, p. 36.

[68] Cf. BAG, "πνεῦμα," p. 682.

[69] The use of the concept "instigation" as distinguished from "possession" has been suggested by the use of the Greek word ὑποβάλλω in MP, XVII, 1-2 (AF, II, 335). There is not, however, prevalent usage of this term among the selected writings. The term does provide us with a concept which properly expresses a distinction made in some of the selected literature.

bul: "He is possessed by Beelzebul (*beezeboul echei*), and by the prince of demons (*archonti tōn daimoniōn*) he casts out the demons."[70] Jesus replies: "How can Satan cast out Satan?" (v. 23). This reply and the verses that follow it indicate first of all, that the term Beelzebul is synonymous with Satan, and secondly, that if Jesus were possessed by Satan, then Satan would be rising up against himself as Jesus' activities are aimed at binding Satan[71] and casting out demons. The possibility of Satanic possession is assumed, though Jesus denies that he himself is possessed by Satan.[72]

Another reference to Satanic possession occurs in Luke 22:3 and John 13:27. The Luke version says: "Then Satan entered into Judas called Iscariot" (*eisēlthen de satanas eis Ioudan* ...); John 13:27 reads: "Satan entered into him [Judas]" (*eisēlthen eis ekeinon ho satanas*).[73] In John 6:70, Jesus calls Judas "a devil" (*diabolos*). John 13:2, however, speaks in terms of the Devil (*diabolou*) who had "put it into the heart (*beblēkotos eis tēn kardian*) of Judas Iscariot ... to betray him." This last reference does not constitute possession proper, but is rather like what Origen calls "wicked suggestion."[74]

Beyond the above mentioned references, the overall tendency in the New Testament is to regard possession as a demonic function and not an activity of Satan. This is also true for most of the other selected writings in the early tradition. Among the Apostolic Fathers, however, the *Shepherd of Hermas* seems to be an exception. The *Shepherd of Hermas* describes the activities of the "angel of wickedness" in such a way as to suggest the traditional concept of spirit possession elaborately applied to Satanic activity:

> There are two angels with man, one of righteousness and one of wickedness .... Now see ... the works of the angel of wickedness. First of all, he is ill tempered, and bitter, and foolish, and his deeds are evil, casting down servants of God. Whenever therefore he comes into your heart (*epi tēn kardian sou anabē*), know him from his works.... When ill temper or bitterness come upon you, know that

[70] In John 7:20; 8:48, 52, Jesus is accused of being possessed by a demon (δαιμόνιον ἔχεις), not by Satan.

[71] Cf. Mk. 3:27, the parable of the strong man.

[72] Satanic possession may also be the assumption in a passage previously noted: Lk. 13:16, the woman bound by Satan for eighteen years. Cf. S. Eitrem's discussion of this passage in *Some Notes on New Testament Demonology*, p. 32.

[73] BAG, "εἰσέρχομαι," p. 232, notes the use of the same verb as applied to demon possession in: Mk. 9:25; 5:12ff.; Lk. 8:30, 32ff. Langton, *Satan*, p. 29, makes note of several parallel conceptions in apocalyptic literature.

[74] ODP, III, III, 4 (ANCL, I, 242).

> he is in you (*hoti autos estin en soi*). Next the desire of many deeds and the luxury of much eating and drinking, and many feasts, and various and unnecessary foods, and desire of women, and covetousness and haughtiness, and pride, and whatsoever things are akin and like to these,—when, therefore, these things come into your heart, know that the angel of wickedness is with you (*estin en soi*)... but keep from the angel of wickedness because his teaching is evil in every act. For though a man be faithful, if the thought of that angel rise in his heart (*anabē epi tēn kardian autou*), it must be that man or woman commit some sin.[75]

As Hermas uses the terms, "angel of wickedness" and "devil" are synonymous.[76] The list of activities of the angel of wickedness is similar to, and often identical with, the list of vices designated by Hermas as demons, the difference being that the outbreaks of ill-temper, bitterness, etc., are the result of the possession of the devil [77] rather than personifications of vices, a subject to be returned to in a later section.[78]

Unlike the *Shepherd of Hermas*, very little or nothing is mentioned about Satanic possession in the other writings of the Apostolic Fathers. Likewise, Justin and Irenaeus have nothing explicit to contribute to this aspect of the discussion. A new characteristic enters the descriptions of Satanic activity in *The Martyrdom of Polycarp*, however, which is elaborated upon by Origen.

The Martyrdom of Polycarp refers to:

> the jealous and envious and evil one, the Opponent of the race of saints, [who] seeing the greatness of his [Polycarp's] martyrdom ... instigated (*hypebalen*) Nicetas ... to petition the magistrate not to give us his body.[79]

Satan did not "possess" Nicetas, but "instigated" (from the verb *hypoballō*) Nicetas to petition the magistrate not to give the Christians Polycarp's martyred body. "Instigate" means "to incite,

[75] HM, VI, II, 1-7 (AF, II, 97-99).

[76] The contrast and conflict is always between the angel of righteousness and the devil or the angel of wickedness, e.g., on pp. 97-99 and 133-135.

[77] The verb form ἀναβῇ appears in Hermas quite often in regard to this subject of possession, although he also uses the verbs εἰσέρχομαι and εἰσπορεύομαι in association with the activity of the devil. Cf. HM, XIII, V, 4 (AF, II, 134-135) and Gokey, *Terminology*, p. 147, nn. 39, 41, for examples and discussion.

[78] A discussion of the *Shepherd of Hermas*' demonology belongs in a later chapter concerned with the nature and origin of demons. Cf. above, p. 29, n. 60 and below, pp. 50ff.

[79] MP, XVII, 1-2 (AF, II, 335). Gokey's translation, *Terminology*, p. 91. K. Lake translates the verb ὑπέβαλεν as "he put forward."

to urge on," in contrast to "possess" which means "to enter into" (*eiserchomai*). "Instigate" is also to be distinguished from "tempt"; the latter means "to put to the test through enticement," the former means "to spur into action by inciting."

Origen makes explicit the distinction between instigation and possession in regard to Satanic activity. The basic question Origen is addressing himself to is that of man's responsibility for his own sin. Man is responsible for his own sin if he maintains the free control of his will. The traditional notion of possession seems to violate the freedom of the will, and hence dismisses man from responsibility in those cases. Origen also wishes to distinguish the devil's work from certain human natural instincts which lead men to sin apart from the devil.

Origen distinguishes between two modes of operation among wicked spirits including the Devil: one is possession and the other is wicked suggestion.

> Now, of wicked spirits there is a twofold mode of operation: *i.e.*, when they either take complete and entire possession of the mind, so as to allow their captives the power neither of understanding nor feeling, as for instance, is the case with those commonly called possessed, whom we see to be deprived of reason, and insane (such as those were who are related in the Gospel to have been cured by the Saviour); or when by their wicked suggestions they deprave a sentient and intelligent soul with thoughts of various kinds, persuading it to evil,[80] of which Judas is an illustration, who was induced at the suggestion of the devil to commit the crime of treason, according to the declaration of Scripture, that "the devil had already put it into the heart of Judas Iscariot to betray Him."[81]

The clearest expression of Satanic possession in the New Testament, namely Satan's entering into Judas (Lk. 22:3, John 13:27), has been reinterpreted by Origen in terms of instigation of Satan, rather than possession.[82] For Biblical reference Origen refers to John 13:2 where the word "*beblēkotos*" appears,[83] meaning to put

[80] The Latin text reads: "vel cum sentientem quidem et intelligentem animum cogitationibus variis et sinistris persuasionibus inimica suggestione depravant ..." (MPG, XI, p. 317).

[81] ODP, III, III, 4 (ANCL, I, 241-242), and MPG, XI, 317.

[82] For Origen it is generally "demons" (*daimones*; MPG, XI, pp. 306-307) who lodge in minds and take "complete possession" of a person's nature. Cf. ODP, III, II, 2 (ANCL, I, 227).

[83] Form of the verb βάλλω. Origen also applies this general idea of instigation rather than possession to the workings of the good spirit, who "stirred and incited to good" (ODP, III, III, 4 [ANCL, I, 242]).

into, rather than John 13:27, which says clearly Satan entered into (*eisēlthen*) Judas.

In this way, therefore, an account can be given which recognizes the reality of Satanic power but does not deny man's responsibility for his own sin. As there are certain human instincts which can lead to transgression, apart from any activity of the Devil, such as our feelings of hunger and thirst leading to intemperance, or the desire of sexual intercourse at the time of maturity [84] so, when we have

> not resisted the first movements to intemperance, then the hostile power, seizing the occasion of the first transgression, incites and presses us hard in every way, seeking to extend our sins over a wider field.[85]

Instigation, therefore, characterizes more accurately this aspect of Satan's activity in the early tradition, possession being applicable only to the New Testament references to Judas' betrayal and the *Shepherd of Hermas'* usage. Satan incites man to sin, an activity which is closely related to demonic possession in the sense of an external force of evil almost manipulating a person's existence, but not to the extent that man becomes blameless in the face of his own sin.

E. Satan as Destroyer

The greatest power Satan holds is the power of destruction and death. In Hebrews 2:14 reference is made to the destruction by Christ of "him who has the power of death, that is, the devil" (*ton tō kratos echonta tou thanatou tout' estin ton diabolon*). Paul speaks of handing a man over "to Satan for the destruction of the flesh" (*tō satana eis olethron tēs sarkos*), (I Cor. 5:5), and as previously noted,

[84] ODP, III, II, 2 (ANCL, I, 225). Origen develops these ideas thoroughly: "... as the devil is not the cause of our feeling, hunger and thirst, so neither is he the cause of that appetency which naturally rises at the time of maturity, viz. the desire of sexual intercourse. ... I am of the opinion, indeed, that the same course of reasoning must be understood to apply to other natural movements, as those of covetousness, or of anger, or of sorrow, or of all those generally which through the vice of intemperance exceed the natural bounds of moderation" (ODP, III, II, 2 [ANCL, I, 225-226]). Hence there are many transgressions which are not committed under the pressure or instigation of malignant powers. Cf. ODP, III, II, 3 (ANCL, I, 229).

[85] ODP, III, II, 2 (ANCL, I, 226). On one occasion Origen refers to the devil entering one's heart (ODP, III, II, 4 [ANCL, I, 232]) but it is in the context of a discussion of Eph. 4:27, "Neither give place to the devil" and the sense is figurative.

Rev. 9:11 portrays the demonic hosts as having "as king over them the angel of the bottomless pit; his name in Hebrew is Abaddon, and in Greek he is called Apollyon." The Hebrew word "Abaddon" is used frequently in the sense of "destruction" in the wisdom literature of the Old Testament. The term "Apollyon" means "destroyer" and is the Greek equivalent to Abaddon.[86]

As in the New Testament, references to Satan as destroyer are found among the other writings of the early tradition. Ignatius, when urging for unity in church faith and worship, states:

> When you come together frequently, the powers of Satan are destroyed, and his destructiveness (*ho olethros autou*) is brought to nothing by the harmony of your faith.[87]

The Shepherd of Hermas refers to those who follow "the angel of luxury and deceit" and "are destroyed (*apollyntai*) by this angel, some to death (*thanaton*), and some to corruption (*kataphthoran*)."[88] Irenaeus quotes I Cor. 15:54-55, when referring to the victory in Christ: "Death (*ho thanatos*) is swallowed up in victory. O death, where is thy sting? O death, where is thy victory?"[89] and later says, "when Satan is bound, man is set free."[90] Likewise Origen refers to the ultimate destruction of the "last enemy ... who is called death (*mors*) ... (whose) mind and hostile will ... are to be destroyed."[91]

What is notable in these many references to Satan as destroyer is that the activity of destruction or death has several overtones of

---

[86] BAG, "Ἀπολλύων," p. 95. The association of Satan with death is implied in Romans 5:12: "... sin came into the world through one man and death through sin, and so death spread to all men because all men sinned ..." One man's sin most probably refers to Adam, whose sin brought death into the world. Adam was deceived by Satan; hence Satan is the author of sin. As sin is the cause of death, Satan is associated with the power of death. This is also the context, most likely, for John's reference to the devil as "a murderer from the beginning," (John 8:44). This conception is also found in Jewish apocryphal literature. *The Book of Wisdom*, (2:24) e.g., states that "through the devil's envy death entered into the world." Cf. *The Book of Wisdom*, trans. and commentary by J. Reider (New York: Harper and Brothers, 1957), p. 71.

[87] IE, XIII, 1 (AF, I, 187). Gokey's translation, *Terminology*, p. 72. K. Lake renders the term ὄλεθρος as "mischief." For a discussion of this term cf. below, p. 37, n. 92.

[88] HS, VI, II, 1-2 (AF, II, 173).

[89] IAH, V, XIII, 3 (ANCL, II, 88).

[90] IAH, V, XXI, 3 (ANCL, II, 114).

[91] ODP, III, VI, 5 (ANCL, I, 268), and MGP, XI 338.

meaning. Destruction and death are not simply references to biological annihilation; this is only one aspect of death. The terms for destruction (*olethros*; *apollymi*) in the above references carry the meaning of "corruption" and "ruin" in the sense of "the loss of all that gives worth to existence."[92] Likewise, the terms *thanatos* and *nekros* which mean "death" are used in the figurative sense of spiritual death, i.e., a depraved life.[93] Hence Paul can speak of those who were "dead (*nekrous*) through ... trespasses and sins" (Eph. 2:1).

Given this meaning, the work of Satan as destroyer is being realized throughout all of his other activities. As tempter, Satan brings men to ruin by enticing them from their faith. As deceiver and liar Satan spreads the spirit of error which effects a loss of the Word, i.e., the spirit of truth that gives meaning to life for the Christian. As obstructor and tormentor Satan is operative in tormenting afflictions of martyrdom, disease, and demon possession. The result of these activities often is that man's faith is weakened, his hopes disappointed, the opportunity to attain to Jesus Christ corrupted. Likewise, the instigations of Satan are intended to accomplish the depravation of sentient and intelligent souls. A vivid expression of the destructive power of Satan is illustrated in the example of the Gerasene demoniac. As the result of demon possession, the normal personality of the man who called himself "Legion" was ruined. Human relationships were broken off as he dwelt among the tombs, and the whole episode conveys a sense of personal desolation to the extent of being sub-human. This is destruction, the loss of all that gives worth to existence. Very often the use of the word "death" (*thanatos*; *nekros*) in reference to Satan's works or power carries this dominant meaning of ruin, and the signification of dying (biological annihilation) simply adds greater force to an already cogent term. There can be victory over death now for the believer, and he can call out "O death (*thanate*) where is thy sting?" He who works the loss of all that gives worth to one's existence has himself been destroyed by Christ. The destructiveness of Satan, who holds the power of death, is brought to nothing in the harmony of faith.

---

[92] Cf. "ὄλεθρος," J. H. Moulton and G. Milligan, *The Vocabulary of the Greek Testament* (1929), p. 445. Cf. also BAG, "ὄλεθρος," p. 566, "ἀπόλλυμι," p. 94, and Gokey, *Terminology*, p. 87, n. 22.

[93] BAG, "θάνατος," pp. 351-352; "νεκρός," pp. 536-537.

CHAPTER THREE

THE NATURE AND POWER OF SATAN

Theorizing about the nature, origin, and cosmological status of Satan occurs among the selected writings, especially among the later ones. However, there is an obvious lack of "speculative" interest in the sense of seeking to work out a complete cosmology of evil. Concepts as to the origin, abode, and ultimate future of Satan are often very diverse, and there are only a small number of references. An analysis and interpretation of the nature of Satan as conceived by the early Christian tradition will be therefore necessarily less comprehensive than a discussion of his activities. There are some basic understandings as to the nature and power of Satan common to most of the selected writers, however, and they are best summarized by the New Testament phrases: Satan, the "prince of the power of the air," "ruler of demons," "ruler of the world," and "god of this age."

A. SATAN: PRINCE OF THE POWER OF THE AIR

1. *Origin of Satan*

For the most part, the New Testament writers make no theoretical assertions as to the origin of Satan. However, a number of passages by choice of words and phraseology seem to reflect the idea of Satan as a fallen angel who is chief among a class of fallen angels, an idea which appears frequently in apocalyptic literature.[1] II Peter 2:4, for example, refers to the angels that sinned and were cast into hell. Jude 6 mentions "the angels that did not keep their own position but left their proper dwelling ..." and Rev. 12:9 makes reference to "... that ancient serpent, who is called the Devil and Satan, the deceiver of the whole world—he was thrown down to the earth, and his angels (*hoi angeloi autou*) were thrown down with him." Satan appears to be an angel [2] who, together with his followers, has been cast from heaven.

[1] Cf., e.g., *The Book of Enoch* (ch. XV), pp. 82ff.

[2] Satan is associated with ἄγγελοι in II Cor. 11:14 where it is asserted that Satan can even transform himself into an angel of light; Rev. 12:7 refers to the dragon (associated with Satan in vs. 9) and his angels; Rev. 9:11 mentions the angel of the bottomless pit which may be a reference to Satan. Paul in II Cor. 12:7 refers to a "messenger of Satan" (ἄγγελος σατανᾶ). Cf. also BAG "ἄγγελος," pp. 7-8.

The reason for Satan's expulsion or the time of the fall is not defined in the New Testament. Luke 10:18 is the only allusion in the Synoptics to the fall of Satan. Jesus said, "I saw Satan fall like lightning from heaven." Although this passage has been interpreted as referring to Satan's original fall, the passage is more properly understood as a reference to the defeat of Satan who is already a fallen angel and an active opponent of God.[3]

Among the Apostolic Fathers there are passing allusions to the angelic origin of Satan but nothing is said about the theory behind these allusions.[4] Justin Martyr, however, is explicit on the question of how and when the angels transgressed and refers to one of several theories also known to apocalyptic literature.[5]

> God, when He had made the whole world, and subjected things earthly to man ... committed the care of men and of all things under heaven to angels whom He appointed over them. But the angels transgressed this appointment, and were captivated by love of women, and begat children who are those that are called demons ..."[6]

[3] The present interpretation follows R. Leivestad *Christ the Conqueror*, p. 49, who says that Jesus' statement is "a dramatic, illustrative way of expressing the certainty of the ruin of Satan." It is not a reference to a theory of the original fall of Satan, but to the defeat of the fallen angel. Cf. also Gustav Aulen, *Christus Victor*, trans. by A. G. Hebert (New York: Macmillan Co., 1956), and below p. 57. A contrary view is expressed by G. B. Caird, *Principalities and Powers* (Oxford: Clarendon Press, 1956), p. 31. Caird says that "... in the main Biblical tradition the fall of Satan from heaven coincides with the ministry of Jesus, and in particular with the Crucifixion (Lk. 10: 18; Jn. 12:31; Rev. 12:10). Up to that point Satan regularly appears in heaven and has every right to be there."

[4] Barnabas refers to an "evil angel" (EB, IX, 4 [AF, I, 371]) and "angels of Satan" (ἄγγελοι τοῦ σατανᾶ), (EB, XVIII, 1 [AF, I, 401]). The *Shepherd of Hermas* often speaks of "the angel of wickedness" (HM, VI, II, 1, 4, 5, 7, 9, 10 [AF, II, 97-99]).

[5] In the *Books of Adam and Eve* (cf. *The Apocrypha*, II, pp. 137ff.) there is an account of Satan's fall after the creation of Adam. Satan, as one of the angels of God, had refused, on the grounds of seniority, to obey Michael's command to worship Adam. The *Book of the Secrets of Enoch* (cf. *The Apocrypha*, II, p. 447) provides an example of a theory of the fall of Satan before the creation of Adam. Satan, or Satanail, as one of the higher angels, "having turned away with the order that was under him, conceived an impossible thought, to place his throne higher than the clouds above the earth, that he might become equal in rank to ... [God's] power." He was thrown from the height with his angels and flies in the air continuously above the bottomless abyss. When man was created Satan envied him and sought to rule that world.

[6] JAii, V (ANCL, 75). Cf. also JD, LXXIX, CXXIV (ANCL, 197, 257). The *Book of Enoch* (ch. 6), pp. 62ff. narrates how "the angels, the sons of the heavens, saw and lusted after" the daughters of men, fell and were punished.

Justin suggests it was the illicit union between angels and the daughters of men that resulted in the fall of the angels, although another interpretion is that such action on the part of angels implies a previous fall, a pre-cosmic event before the creation of man.

Irenaeus only hints at a theory of the fall of Satan. It is not the same as the one referred to by Justin, but is also known to apocalyptic literature. Irenaeus says that the devil is a "creature of God, like the other angels,"[7] but transgressed and became an apostate [8] by "becoming envious of man."[9] Like one interpretation of Justin's theory, the idea of the envy of man being the cause of Satan's fall places the event after the creation of man (post-cosmic) but long before the ministry of Jesus.

Pre-cosmic theories placing Satan's fall before the creation of the cosmos do not appear explicitly in the texts as they do in apocalyptic literature. Origen's comments on this subject, however, do suggest that he believes in a pre-cosmic fall of Satan as such a theory is most often related to Satan's sin of pride,[10] and Origen also holds to a pre-cosmic fall of man. Origen's respect for the difficulty of the subject prevents him from definitely stating a precise theory in the manner of Justin.[11] However, he does say that the devil, having become an apostate angel who fell from heaven, "formerly was Lucifer, . . . who used to arise in the morning" [12] and was the

> first . . . to lose his wings, and to fall from blessedness; he who . . . walked faultlessly in all his ways, 'until iniquity was in him,' and who being the 'seal of resemblance' and the 'crown of beauty' in the paradise of God, being filled as it were with good things, fell into destruction.[13]
>
> . . . he induced as many of the angels as possible to fall away with himself, and these up to the present time are called his angels.[14]

In JD, CXXIV (ANCL, 257) Justin refers to the version of the Seventy (LXX) which accounts for Satan's overthrow "because he deceived Eve," which assumes a different understanding of the fall. Justin's comment on it is "my discourse is not intended to touch on this point . . ."

[7] IAH, IV, XLI, 1 (ANCL, II, 51).

[8] IAH, I, X, 1 (ANCL, I, 42).

[9] IAH, V, XXIV, 4 (ANCL, II, 121).

[10] G. Papini, *The Devil* (New York: E. P. Dutton & Co., 1954), p. 36, says in regard to the reasons for Satan's fall: "It is only with Origen that the idea dominant today appears and is sustained, i.e., the theory of pride . . ."

[11] OAC, IV, LXV (ANCL, II, 231).

[12] ODP, I, V, 5 (ANCL, I, 52). Cf. above, p. 15, n. 16, for reference to Lucifer identified with Satan.

[13] OAC, VI, XLIV (ANCL, II, 385). Cf. also OAC, IV, LXV (ANCL, II, 231).

[14] ODP, Preface, 6 (ANCL, I, 5). Cf. also ODP, I, V, 2 (ANCL, I, 45).

Thus there are no clearly uniform theories as to the origin of Satan in the selected literature of the early Christian tradition. On the contrary, there is a wide diversity of theories, determined on the basis of implication and generally from a limited number of references. What is common throughout these diverse theories, however, is the belief that Satan is a fallen angel, though the time and reason for the fall is a matter of varied opinions. Also there is frequent reference to his angels being thrown down to earth with Satan, and it is implied that Satan is the chief among this class of fallen angels.

2. *Abode of Satan and the hierarchy of evil spirits*

It is with this background of association that Satan and his fallen angels are called by St. Paul "the spiritual hosts of wickedness in the heavenly places" (*ta pneumatika tēs ponērias en tois epouraniois*), (Eph. 6:12) and Satan is titled "the prince of the power of the air," (*ho archōn tēs exousias tou aeros*), (Eph. 2:2).

"Spiritual hosts of wickedness" refers to the fallen angels. Reference to the "heavenly places" suggests that Paul shared the common Jewish opinion of the lower atmosphere being the dwelling place of the fallen angels.[15] The lowest heavens were those nearest the earth, possibly the space between the earth and the moon, and were the "dark" regions, in the double sense of being the lower regions where the clouds gather [16] and the domain of evil where sin, error and death reign in conflict with Christ who is light, life and truth. Origen, emphasizing the latter sense, says

> ... the outer darkness, in my judgment, is to be understood not so much of some dark atmosphere without any light, as of those persons who, being plunged in the darkness of profound ignorance, have been placed beyond the reach of any light of understanding.[17]

[15] *The Book of the Secrets of Enoch* (*The Apocrypha*, II, p. 433), e.g., describes the second heaven where God's apostates dwell as a place of "darkness, greater than earthly darkness."

[16] St. Augustine says: "There are therefore some spiritual beings of wickedness in the heavens, not where the stars twinkle and the holy angels inhabit; but in the shadowy dwelling place of this lower atmosphere where the clouds gather together" (Sermon 222, *Migne Patrologia Latina*, XXXVIII, 1090; translation by Gokey, *Terminology*, p. 52). Jesus speaks of the "authority of darkness" in Luke 22:53 which makes Paul's reference to Satan's ability to transform himself into an angel of light (II Cor. 11:14) even more striking. Cf. also the prologue of the Gospel of John and II Cor. 6:14-15 for darkness vs. light imagery, and references in the Qumran's *Manual of Discipline* to the "angel of darkness" (p. 25).

[17] ODP, II, X, 8 (ANCL, I, 144).

Thus the abode of these fallen angels is the lower atmosphere, the domain of evil, and Satan their leader is properly titled "the prince of the power of the air".

This understanding of the abode of Satan and his hierarchical status is common throughout the early tradition. Irenaeus, for example, who seldom uses any realistic imagery concerning Satan,[18] refers to the Devil as "one among those angels who are placed over the spirit of the air" [19] and associates "spiritual wickedness" with "the angels who transgressed and became apostates."[20]

Besides these references to the abode and hierarchical status of Satan, there are passages which suggest belief in a distinct hierarchy of evil spirits. In Ephesians 6:12, Paul says of Christians

> ... we are not contending against flesh and blood, but against the principalities (*archas*), against the powers (*exousias*), against the world rulers (*kosmokratoras*) of this present darkness, against spiritual hosts of wickedness in heavenly places.

In these references Paul may be referring to different ranks of evil spirit beings which inhabit the lower heavens. "Principalities and powers" (*archas*; *exousias*) are terms frequently used in Jewish angelology to designate two aspects of the ten orders of good spirit powers.[21] Paul's reference would be to their opposites.[22] The term

[18] G. Aulen, *Christus Victor*, p. 26, also notes the scarcity of realistic imagery in Irenaeus.

[19] IAH, V, XXIV, 4 (ANCL, II, 121).

[20] IAH, I, X (ANCL, I, 42).

[21] Cf. Langton, *Essentials*, p. 187. Eph. 1:20-21 states that God raised Christ from the dead "and made him sit at his right hand in the heavenly places, far above all rule (ὑπεράνω πάσης ἀρχῆς) and authority (ἐξουσίας) and power (δυνάμεως) and dominion (κυριότητος), and above every name that is named." Cf. also Col. 1:16. It is not until pseudo-Dionysius (*ca.* 500 A. D.) that a definite classification of a Christian angelic hierarchy is clearly elaborated, states H. L. Pass, "Demons and Spirits (Christian)," ERE, IV, 578. The classification is as follows:

First order:	1) θρόνοι	2) χερουβίυ	3) σεραφίμ;
Second order:	4) κυριότητες	5) ἐξουσίαι	6) δυνάμεις;
Third order:	7) ἀρχαί	8) ἀρχάγγελοι	9) ἄγγελοι.

[22] Langton, *Essentials*, pp. 187-188, states, "There was an evident tendency in Jewish literature, as in the Zoroastrian teaching, to draw up a parallel series of evil spirit powers which form their opposites, though this is not so clearly defined or fully developed. ... Standing alone 'principalities' and 'powers' might well mean 'good angels'; the context, however, indicates that the apostle has in mind their opposites, namely, 'evil principalities' and 'evil powers,' and substantially these are synonymous with 'the world-rulers of this darkness' and with 'the spiritual hosts of wickedness in heavenly places.'" M. Dibelius, however, thinks it irreconcilable that the "Prince of the power

"world rulers" (*kosmokratores*) occurs only in this passage of Ephesians in the New Testament [23] and probably refers to angelic world rulers who according to Jewish belief controlled various departments of the universe and were conceived as subordinate to one great prince of evil.[24] The abode of these "world-rulers" was in the lower heavens nearer the earth, below the heavens in which God and the good angels dwelt. Such a belief probably reflects background influence of gnostic astral belief. According to G. Macgregor, "the seven planets are enthroned as *kosmokratores*, or 'potentates of this world' and arbiters of human fate."[25] In this connection note should also be made of Paul's references to those "elemental spirits of the universe" (*stoicheia tou kosmou*) which enslaved unredeemed man (Gal. 4:3, 9).[26] These *stoicheia* are also "elemental astral and cosmic powers" similar in reference to the *kosmokratores*, according to Macgregor.[27]

Paul is thus using varied terminology in an attempt to compre-

---

of the air above us" be identified with "world-rulers of this darkness . . . the spiritual forces of wickedness on high." For a discussion cf. M. Dibelius, *Die Geisterwelt im Glauben des Paulus* (Göttingen: Vandenhoeck & Ruprecht, 1909), p. 157ff., and Gokey, *Terminology*, p. 52.

[23] Langton, *Essentials*, p. 188, says that the Greek term κοσμοκράτωρ "is found in Orphic hymns, in inscriptions, in gnostic writings, and in Rabbinical literature. A similar conception is also found in the apocalyptic literature."

[24] Cf. Gokey, *Terminology*, p. 52.

[25] G. H. C. Macgregor, "Principalities and Powers: The Cosmic Background of Paul's Thought," *New Testament Studies*, I, 20. In contrast to Macgregor's interpretation of these cosmic forces as actual properties of the universe, Ling, *Satan*, pp. 70ff., interprets these cosmic forces as spirit forces within human society, an interpretation dependent on the meaning of the term *kosmos* as used by Paul and John. Whether or not this is the correct interpretation of the New Testament, it is only a partially correct interpretation for the early Greek tradition. Cf. below, p. 52.

[26] Macgregor, "Principalities and Powers," p. 21, includes in the discussion reference to Col. 2:8, 20.

[27] Macgregor, "Principalities and Powers," p. 22, says that the juxtaposition of these two terms στοιχεῖα and κοσμοκράτορες as found in the *Testament of Solomon* seems to warrant such an interpretation of Paul's usage. In this writing certain spirits come to Solomon and say: "We are some of the thirty-six στοιχεῖα,, οἱ κοσμοκράτορες τοῦ σκότους τούτου." R. Bultmann, *Theology of the New Testament* (2 Vols.; New York: Charles Scribners Sons, 1951-1955), I, 173, says that the "elemental spirits of the universe" are "conceived to be in essence star-spirits," who "govern the elapse and division of time." He cites this as an example of gnostic influence. C. Masson, *L'Épître de Saint Paul aux Colossiens* (Paris: Neuchatel, 1953), pp. 122ff., supports the argument that in Paul's writings the στοιχεῖα are probably not to be thought of as cosmic forces.

hend the spirit world known to contemporary beliefs. His terminology seems to reflect belief in a kind of angelic power which includes or is associated with astral spirits with cosmological functions, namely, ruling over certain domains of the created universe. Most of the terms he uses appear in apocalyptic angelology as well as in some gnostic systems where they designate certain classes within a heavenly hierarchy. For the most part the terms are not important as separate and distinct references (Paul reveals no particular interest in angelology), but rather become a collective concept signifying a kind of "cosmic metaphysical totality" [28] with real existence and authority which is all under the domain of the "prince of the power of the air."

Thus, similar to the references to the origin of Satan, there is no clearly worked out cosmology in which evil spirits are given their place, though some sort of cosmology is implied or assumed in a number of passages in the New Testament. Explicit references to a hierarchy of evil spirits are even fewer among the Apostolic and early Greek Fathers, except as they quote and reiterate New Testament passages.[29]

Origen, e.g., reiterates most of the New Testament ideas mentioned in this section and provides us with a summation of the early tradition's implied understanding of the origin and abode of Satan. Origen refers to "that atmosphere which is between heaven and earth ..." which "is not devoid of inhabitants" but includes "those of a rational kind," among them "the prince of the power of the air, the spirit who now works in the sons of disobedience."[30] Concerning the hierarchy of these rational inhabitants of the atmosphere, he says that "... we find in holy Scripture numerous names of certain orders and offices, not only of holy beings, but also of those of an opposite description ..." [31]

---

[28] Leivestad, *Christ the Conqueror*, pp. 92-93.

[29] Irenaeus, e.g., refers to the devil as "one among those angels who are placed over the spirit of the air" (noted above, p. 42). An exceptional reference is found in Justin. He refers to evil angels dwelling in Tanis, Egypt (JD, LXXIX [ANCL, 198]).

[30] ODP, II, XI, 5 (ANCL, I, 151).

[31] ODP, I, V, 1 (ANCL, I, 44-45). It could be argued that there is an inference to different classes of demons in the synoptics. Gokey, *Terminology*, p. 49, notes that some demons can only be cast out by prayer and fasting (Lk. 7:21; 8:2; 6:18; 11:26), which suggests a higher, more powerful order of demons from those who are easily exorcised.

B. Satan: Ruler of Demons

1. *Origin of demons*

Satan, besides being the "prince of the authority of the air," is also frequently called the "ruler of demons" (*ho archōn tōn diamoniōn*) in the gospels.[32] As has been discussed, demons are a type of evil spirit distinguishable from fallen angels in the general type of activity attributed to them. Unlike the apocryphal literature of the period, however, there is very little theorizing about the origin and nature of demons in the early Christian literature, even though their existence is assumed throughout it.[33] The most explicit theories of the origin of demons are found in Justin and Origen, and a brief summary of their theories will help in determining the relationship between the demons and Satan and add another perspective to the nature and power of Satan.

Justin Martyr furnished this explanation already noted of the origin of demons:[34]

> God ... committed the care of men and of all things under heaven to angels whom He appointed over them. But the angels transgressed this appointment, and were captivated by love of women, and begat children who are those that are called demons (*daimones*) ...[35]

Demons are seen as the offspring born of the illicit union of the fallen angels with the daughters of men. This is very similar to an apocalyptic theory of the origin of demons as the souls of giants who were the offspring of the illicit union of fallen angels and women.[36] Justin simply substitutes "demons" for "giants."[37] Justin's theory

[32] This is a frequent epithet of Satan in the synoptic gospels. Cf. BAG, "ἄρχων," p. 113: Mt. 9:34; 12:24; Mk. 3:22; Lk. 11:15. In Mt. 12:24, 27, and Lk. 11:15, 18, the name for the ruler of the demons is Beelzeboul, but as discussed previously (above, p. 15, n. 10), this is either another name for Satan or the name of one of his underlings who is a prince of demons.

[33] TDNT, "δαίμων," pp. 10-16, says that demonology appears only on the margin of the Old Testament and that basically the New Testament stands in the Old Testament succession in this regard.

[34] PGL, "δαίμων," p. 328, says that Justin's view of the origin of demons was refuted by later tradition.

[35] JAii, V (ANCL, 75) and MPG, VI, 452.

[36] *The Book of Enoch* (partially quoted above, p. 39, n. 6) narrates how the two hundred watchers (angels) descended on Mt. Hermon, lusted after the daughters of men, fell and were punished. From the women were born giants who suppressed men, and fought among themselves. The souls of the giants became the evil spirits who dwell on the earth.

[37] E. R. Goodenough, *The Theology of Justin Martyr* (Jena: W. Biedermann, 1923), pp. 198-199, notes that the Gen. 6:2 reference to the "children of God" (who were attracted by women and in uniting with them begat

also suggests that demons are not only a lower class of evil spirits, but that they were born evil, as demons. Such a distinction between demons and fallen angels, however, appears to be incompatible with Justin's interchangeable use of these two terms.[38]

It is just such an understanding of demons as spirits born originally evil that Origen wishes to challenge. Origen asserts that

> ... it is true of all demons, that they were not demons originally, but they became so in departing from the true way; so that the name 'demons' (*daimones*) is given to those beings who have fallen away from God.[39]

Origen does not wish to deny free will to any being. Hence he uses the word "demon" (*daimōn*) as a general term applicable to "those beings who have fallen away from God." In this general sense of the word, Satan and his fallen angels can also be called demons.[40] Such a definition might also explain Justin's interchangeable use of the terms "demons" and "fallen angels," although such usage remains incompatible with his stated theory of the origin of demons.

Origen's usage of the term "demon" is likewise not always internally consistent. On occasion Origen uses the term "demon" (*daimōn*) in a more specific sense designating the lowest level of rational beings whose origin is different from that of angels and men. At least this is implied when Origen makes mention of a race of Titans and giants who have been guilty of impiety and have fallen from heaven. Origen says:

giants) is translated in the LXX as "angels of God," and so it is stated in Philo, Josephus, and the *Book of Enoch*. Goodenough goes on to say that "Justin is the first to substitute demons for giants, or at least to understand giants to be demons, though Athenagoras and Tertullian both followed Justin later." Goodenough considers Justin's demonology very close "to the mode of thought and the ideas of the synoptic Gospels" (p. 205).

[38] JD, LXXIX (ANCL, 198). Goodenough, *The Theology of Justin Martyr*, p. 204, notes Philo's similar interchangeable usage of these terms. Philo says explicitly "souls, demons, and angels are to be distinguished only in name, for they are all three actually the same."

[39] OAC, VII, LXIX (ANCL, II, 489) and MPG, XI, 1517.

[40] Unlike NT usage, Origen, like Justin, uses the term δαίμων with its stronger suggestion of an intermediary between God and man (fallen angels, e.g.) rather than the common NT term "δαιμόνιον." Cf. TDNT, "δαίμων," p. 16. Origen's whole discussion of demons carries this ambiguity inherent in the terminology (using the term δαίμων to refer to both fallen angels and demons of lower origin) which further enables him to bring together a number of traditionally different theories. Likewise, Origen is unclear as to whether all demons are evil, OAC, VII, XXXIX (ANCL, II, 583-584), or only some demons are evil, OAC, VII, LXIX (ANCL, II, 489).

> In my opinion ... it is certain wicked demons (*daimones*), and, so to speak, of the race of Titans and Giants, who have been guilty of impiety toward the true God, and towards the angels in heaven, and who have fallen from it, and who haunt (the denser) parts of bodies, and frequent unclean places upon earth ... (desire) to lead the human race away from the true God ...[41]

In this statement Origen seeks to conflate various theories of the origin of demons without explicitly reconciling inherent difficulties of such a combination. Demons, according to this statement of Origen's, are of the race of Titans or Giants, suggestive of the apocalyptic and Justinian theories of the origin of demons as souls of giants born of fallen angels and women. But, Origen continues, these demons "have been guilty of impiety ... and have fallen ...," and hence were not born evil as Justin states but became evil through the exercise of free will. Here Origen has returned to his first definition of demons which enables him to use the word as a general term applicable to those beings who have fallen away from God.

Thus there appear to be at least two distinct theories of the origin of demons mentioned in the writings of Justin and Origen.[42] One theory connects the origin of demons with the union of fallen angels and women. Demons are their offspring, born evil, and to be distinguished from fallen angels as a lower class of evil spirits. The other theory regards the term demon as generally applicable to those beings who have fallen away from God. According to this latter definition, Satan can be conceived as an arch demon for he is one of the "fallen" angels. This theory does not necessarily imply the

[41] OAC, IV, XCII (ANCL, II, 259) and MPG, XI, 1169. H. Chadwick, *Early Christian Thought and the Classical Tradition* (Oxford: Clarendon Press, 1966), p. 85, says that Origen regards "the diversity of spiritual entities, stretching downwards from the archangels through inferior angelic powers and saints to men and yet lower still to demonic powers, as constituting a hierarchy of consubstantial rational beings, which is brought about not, as many of the contemporary Platonists said, by an evolutionary process of necessary emanations from above but by free will being exercised in different ways."

[42] G. A. Barton, "Origin of Names," p. 159ff., makes the following observation concerning apocryphal literature: "The conceptions of *Demons* which appear in the Apocryphal literature are of four distinct types ... [one type] regards the arch demons as fallen angels, but with varying emphasis on angelic genesis; the second type speaks of angels in union with the wives of men and having offspring; a third type refers to the demon Asmodaeus and reflects Persian influence; finally, the fourth type speaks of evil spirits which are simply the personification of the evil propensities of man." For discussion of the fourth type, cf. below p. 50.

angelic genesis of all demons. Consequently Origen can speak of demons as "of the race of Titans and Giants," but he refutes any notion of these demons being born evil. The term "demon," in other words, can simultaneously denote a lower class of evil spirits distinguishable from fallen angels and Satan, and be used as a term applicable to Satan.

In this context Origen's statement that the subject of demonology is "both wide in extent and difficult for human comprehension" [43] takes on added meaning. This discussion also underscores the lack of "speculative interest" in theoretical demonology which in turn tends to blur any theoretical distinctions between Satan and demons. What remains constant in the varied theories about demons is that Satan is always regarded as their ruler.

2. *Nature of evil spirits*

Satan's association with "evil spirits" both as "prince of the power of the air" and as "ruler of demons" implies that he shares with these spiritual hosts of wickedness (*pneumatika tēs ponērias*) a common metaphysical nature. Likewise, Justin's and Origen's theories of the origin of demons and their relation to Satan support the assertion of their common nature. Any discussion of the early Christian tradition's understanding of the metaphysical nature of Satan, however, can proceed only by interpretive implication from references to the nature of evil spirits in general rather than from specific statements regarding the nature of Satan.

Although there are only a few explicit references to "*pneumata daimoniōn*" in the New Testament,[44] the New Testament references generally indicate a conception of demons as independent spiritual beings who occupy a position somewhere between the human and the divine but are completely subject to Satan.[45] As spirit (*pneuma*) beings they cannot be perceived by the physical senses, for "... a

---

[43] OAC, VII, LXVII (ANCL, II, 487).

[44] Lk. 4:33; Rev. 16:14. F. C. Conybeare, "The Demonology of the New Testament," *Jewish Quarterly Review*, VIII (1896), p. 579, notes the following terms for evil spirits in the NT: δαιμόνιον is very common; πνεῦμα with the epithets "unclean" (ἀκαθάρτου) and "evil" (πονηρόν) is very frequent; πνεῦμα δαίμονος sometimes occurs; δαίμων is less frequent.

[45] BAG, "δαιμόνιον," p. 168. TDNT, "δαίμων," p. 18, says that in the NT, demons are completely subject to Satan and have no relative autonomy as in later Judaism. This is also true for the later writers. Justin, e.g., continues to refer to the demons as "... the host of the devil" (JD, CXXXI [ANCL, 265] and MPG, VI, 780).

spirit has not flesh and bones ..." (Lk. 24:39).[46] Hence they can live and act in ways impossible to material beings. Their tormenting activities of possession are evidence of such a nature. According to F. C. Conybeare, the New Testament writers believed that the physical constitution of a spirit, whether holy or unholy, was akin to moving vapour [47] and some writers among the Fathers of the church seem to think in terms of the spirits having a certain kind of body, whereas others say they do not possess bodies but yet are given to material lusts.[48] Ignatius, for example, associates "bodiless" with demons,[49] as does the *Shepherd of Hermas*. Yet an implied material nature of demons is not absent. Evil spirits are externally harder and rougher than good spirits, and consequently the former cause pain according to the *Shepherd of Hermas*.[50] Possession, in other words, is conceived quite materialistically, as are most spiritual operations. Origen says that demons are "naturally fine and thin as if formed of air."[51] yet they haunt the denser parts of bodies [52] and their grossness makes them unable "to rise to the purer and diviner region."[53]

---

[46] Cf. BAG, "πνεῦμα," p. 680ff. Cf. also Eph. 2:2; 6:12. Langton, *Satan*, p. 33, says of these Pauline references to spirit powers: "St. Paul is here moving in the realm of familiar Greek conceptions. The Greeks conceived of the departed spirits of men as possessing wings, and thus as having their abode in the air.... They are completely transparent, and are invisible to us even at close quarters. The lower heavens are completely filled with these creatures. These Platonic conceptions were developed by other Greek and Latin writers."

[47] F. C. Conybeare, "The Demonology of the New Testament," p. 580.

[48] PGL, "δαίμων," p. 328. Gokey, *Terminology*, p. 54, n. 2, says in reference to NT demonology, "Their pure spiritual nature is taught universally among the Greek Fathers from the fourth century on; on the Latin side, Augustine would still consider the matter doubtful, a doubt that continued until the time of Peter Lombard." Origen believes demons are spiritual in nature, but not so immaterial that they can do without food (OAC, VIII, XXX [ANCL, II, 515]).

[49] IS, II (AF, I, 255).

[50] HM, V, II, 5-7 (AF, II, 93).

[51] ODP, Preface, 8 (ANCL, I, 6). Origen continues "... for this reason demons are either considered or called by man incorporeal."

[52] OAC, IV, XCII (ANCL, II, 259). Origen also says that demons have affinity with certain species of animals and enter bodies of wicked animals (OAC, IV, XCII [ANCL, II, 259-260]).

[53] OAC, III, XXXV (ANCL, II, 117). In Bk. VIII Origen refers to Celsus' reference to the Egyptian belief that "The body of man is divided into thirty-six parts, and as many demons of the air are appointed to take care of it, each having charge of a different part ..." Origen rejects this as compromising the honour of God (OAC, VIII, LVIII [ANCL, II, 542]).

The common characteristic of all the above mentioned conceptions is that evil spirits are spiritual beings which exist independently of man and have power over him. This basic conception is modified in the rather complicated pneuma concept of the *Shepherd of Hermas*. Unlike the above notions of demons as independent causal agents of maladies, Hermas tends to identify the malady or evil propensity in man with the demon. Demons, in other words, are personified vices rather than spirits that lead independent existences. Slander (*ponēra hē katalalia*) e.g., is a restless demon (*daimoniōn*) [54] as are malice and arrogance.[55] In a more or less systematic list Hermas summarizes the various vices which are demonic, using the symbolism of twelve women clothed in black (in contrast to twelve virgins representing virtues):

> Hear, also, the names of the women who have black raiment. Of these also four are more powerful. The first is Unbelief (*Apistia*), the second Impurity (*Akrasia*), the third Disobedience (*Apeitheia*), and the fourth Deceit (*Apatē*); and those who follow them are called Grief (*Lypē*), Wickedness (*Ponēria*), Licentiousness (*Aselgeia*), Bitterness (*Oxycholia*), Lying (*Pseudos*), Foolishness (*Aphrosyne*), Evil-speaking (*Katalalia*), Hate (*Misos*).[56]

Here we have a demonology quite unlike that of the other selected writings in the early tradition. Yet it is too simple to interpret Hermas' demonology as merely the personification of vices, for he also uses descriptive phrases which suggest a conception of evil spirits as independently existing beings. For example, he refers to demonic possession as the choking of the Holy Spirit and driving it out because there is no room.[57] Hermas also tends to write in terms of the personifications themselves. For example, the earthly spirit (*epigeion pneuma*),[58] "doublemindedness (*dipsychia*) is the daughter of the devil ..." [59] and is the sister of grief (*lypē*) and bitterness

---

[54] HM, II, 3 (AF, II, 73).

[55] HS, IX, XXIII, 3, 5; XXIII, 3 (AF, II, 277, 275). Compare the *Testaments of the Twelve Patriarchs* which also present the vices as demons. Cf. *The Apocrypha*, II, pp. 297ff.

[56] HS, IX, XV, 3 (AF, II, 259). The twelve virtues are: Faith, Temperance, Power, Long-suffering, Simplicity, Guilelessness, Holiness, Joyfulness, Truth, Understanding, Concord, Love.

[57] Cf. HM, V, I, 3 (AF, II, 87-89) and above p. 29, n. 60, and p. 23 where Hermas speaks in terms of Satanic possession. Also: HM, V, II, 5-8 (AF, II, 93-95); HM, X, I, 2 (AF, II, 111-112); HM, IX, II (AF, II, 111).

[58] HM, IX, 11 (AF, II, 111).

[59] HM, IX, 9 (AF, II, 109-111). BAG, "διψυχία," p. 199, gives the meaning

(*oxycholia*).[60] Here the overtones of the more prevalent conception of evil spirits as powers independent of man are also present in the *Shepherd of Hermas*.

Although Hermas can speak of demons as personified vices, he never speaks of the Devil or Satan in this manner. When speaking of these personified vices, Hermas always restricts his terms to *diamoniōn* and *pneuma*, and at no time calls them *diabolos*.[61] Thus in Hermas we find a degree of transformation from a traditional understanding of the nature of demons to a more catechetical, ethical use of the term. However, the traditional role of Satan basically stands unaltered. Satan remains the "ruler of demons" and the demons (vices) are his offspring.

In conclusion, the discussion of the origin and nature of demons provides us with a conception, however limited, of the nature of Satan and his hierarchical status. Satan is an independent spiritual being who occupies a position somewhere between the human and divine, who for the most part is to be distinguished from demons both in his origin and his role in the implied hierarchy of evil spirits. He is a fallen angel who is the ruler of a lower class of evil spirits, i.e., demons. As "ruler of demons" Satan directs demonic activities to the accomplishment of the Satanic goal of leading the "human race away from the true God." His close association with "evil spirits" implies that he shares with them a common spiritual (*pneuma*) nature, which has not flesh and bones and is considered by some incorporeal. Thus it could be said that the very existence of demons, as well as their activities, is an elaboration and extension of the pervasive and threatening spiritual power which is identified as Satanic.

C. Satan: Ruler of this World, God of this Age

The New Testament writers John and Paul refer to Satan as the "ruler of this world" (*archōn tou kosmou toutou*), (Jn. 12:31) and "the god of this age" (*ho theos tou aiōnos toutou*), (II Cor 4:4).[62] The

"indecision, doubt" to this term. Langton, *Satan*, p. 45, translates it "doubtfulmindedness."

[60] HM, 10, I, 2 (AF, II, 111).

[61] Cf. Gokey, *Terminology*, pp. 126-127.

[62] The Revised Standard Version translates αἰῶνος as "world" in II Cor. 4:4. This passage is the only one that uses the word "god" (θεός) as applied to Satan. There are several other references to the "ruler of this world": Jn. 14:30; 16:11.

term *"archōn,"* as applied to Satan, principally denotes rule and authority.[63] As ruler Satan exercises the dominating influence over a kingdom. Satan rules his kingdom with authority (*exousia*), i.e., he has dominion over his kingdom by virtue of his exercising rightful power (*dynamis*).[64] Power is the "ability or capacity" [65] to act in the ways previously enumerated, i.e., as prince and ruler, as tempter, deceiver, obstructor, etc. It is his rightful power, according to several writers, because man has freely chosen to bestow it upon him.[66] Hence Satan is also called the "god of this age." Satan is the one (the *theos*) who wields despotic power over most of the created world.[67]

These terms, *archōn, exousia, theos,* and *dynamis* are thus all closely interrelated in meaning. For purposes of our analysis, however, we shall principally associate the term *exousia* (authority) with *archōn* (ruler) in the first section which follows, and associate *dynamis* (power) with *theos* (god) in the second section.

1. *Ruler of this world and age*

The domain over which Satan reigns encompasses, as we have seen, the power of the air and the demons. Also included in this domain are this world (*kosmos*) and this age (*aiōn*). The term *kosmos* has not only spatial connotations of the earth or universe in this context, thus encompassing the powers of the air, but also refers to the whole "complex of inter-related human individuals and institutions."[68] *Kosmos* is a term which serves as a summary description of

---

[63] Cf. BAG, "ἄρχων," p. 113.

[64] Cf. BAG, "ἐξουσία," p. 277ff., concerning the "exercise of power" as a meaning of "authority."

[65] Although the term δύναμις has broader connotations than "ability" or "capacity" (cf. BAG, "δύναμις," pp. 206-207), our analysis shall specify this denotation in order to distinguish it from ἄρχων and ἐξουσία.

[66] This is continually implied in Origen's thought, e.g., as he is concerned with maintaining the freedom and responsibility of man in regard to sin and evil. Irenaeus is also quite sensitive to this issue but insists that Christ's victory over the devil was won by moral force, by justice not because the devil himself justly "obtained dominion over us" but because God "does not use violent means to obtain what he desires" (IAH, V, I, 1 [ANCL, II, 56]). The question of Satan's power being a rightful one, in other words, is a complex one. However, any affirmation of man's freedom implies some rightful authority to whatever power is allowed to work in and through man.

[67] BAG, "θεός," pp. 357-358, designates the use of this term in II Cor. 4:4 as "figurative" and that is the meaning given here.

[68] Ling, *Satan*, p. 32. This definition is in reference to John's use of the term.

mankind subject to all aspects of earthly conditions,[69] whether this be the "totality of human possibilities and conditions of life, or whether it implies persons in their attitudes and judgments."[70] It denotes "the world of men and the sphere of human activity,"[71] and as such it is the world of sin, a world separate from God and condemned by God (I Cor. 11:32), but also the object of divine plan (II Cor. 5:19). Hence Jesus says "I am not of this world" (Jn. 8:23), "I pray not for the world" (Jn. 17:9), for "the world ... hates me because I testify of it that its works are evil" (Jn. 7:7), and the "world hates you (disciples) ... because you are not of the world, but I chose you out of the world" (Jn. 15:18, 19).[72]

As ruler of this world Satan has authority (*exousia*) over all opposed to Christ. The role of Christ is to turn Gentiles "from the authority (*exousia*) of Satan unto God" (Acts 26:18), for the reign of Satan is diametrically opposed to the reign of God.[73] The "power (*exousia*) of darkness" (Lk. 22:53), which is Satan's, includes the "world-rulers" (*kosmokratores*) of this darkness, the "elemental spirits of the universe (*stoicheia tou kosmou*),"[74] and the world (*kosmos*) as mankind, the sum of the totality of human possibilities and relationships. The terms *kosmos* and *exousia* thus designate the extent of Satan's domain.

The term *aiōn* (age) designates the temporal duration of his reign. Satan's reign of evil characterizes this age as well as this world. This age, in contrast to the age to come (Mt. 12:32) is ruled by Satan (II Cor. 4:4).[75] The wisdom of this age (I Cor. 3:18) is undesirable. Paul says "Do not be conformed to this world (*tō aiōni toutō*)" (Rom.

---

[69] Macgregor, "Principalities and Powers," p. 17.

[70] Bultmann, *Theology of the New Testament*, I, 255.

[71] *Ibid.*, p. 256. According to BAG, "κόσμος," pp. 446ff., the term *kosmos* has eight different meanings in the NT. The NT use of this term is in sharp contrast to the Greek meaning of *kosmos* as orderly and beautiful. In the NT the "world" is condemned by God and yet object of his concern. Cf. James 1:27; 4:4; II Pet. 2:20; Jn. 3:16.

[72] Christians are hated by the world: Jn. 15:18, 19; 17:14; I Jn. 3:1ff. Christians have received not the spirit of the world, but the spirit which is of God (I Cor. 2:12).

[73] Cf. BAG, "κόσμος," pp. 446-448; Jn. 12:25, 31; 13:1; 16:11; 18:36; Jn. 2:15, 4:17; I Cor. 3:19; 5:10; 7:31.

[74] Cf. above, pp. 42ff.

[75] The antithesis between this age and the age to come has foundation in a few passages in the Old Testament, e.g., Dan. 10:13ff. The conception of two ages or world-periods was a contemporary Jewish belief and very prominent in apocalyptic literature such as the *Fourth Book of Ezra* (cf. *The Apocrypha*, II, pp. 561ff.).

12:2), and asserts that through Christ man has been delivered "from this present evil age (*ek tou aiōnos tou enestōtos ponērou*), (Gal. 1:4). It will be noted that Paul's use of *aiōn* is very similar to John's use of *kosmos* and the terms are almost synonymous in that they both refer to orders of existence under the dominion of Satan. The basic etymological distinction remains, however, *kosmos* referring to the domain of the kingdom and *aiōn* to its duration.

These conceptions of Satan's ruling authority over this world and age are reiterated in the early tradition. Ignatius seldom refers to the Devil or Satan directly, but very often refers to the "prince of this world" (*ho archōn tou aiōnos toutou*).[76] Barnabas speaks of the "ruler (*archōn*) of the present time of iniquity"[77] who is at present in power (*exousia*).[78] The *Shepherd of Hermas* associates death with this world,[79] and sin, vanity, and evil with this age.[80] The *Martyrdom of Polycarp* refers to "the unrighteous ruler" (*ton adikon archonta*) who was overcome by Polycarp's faith in the Gospel of Christ.[81] Finally, Origen frequently quotes I Jn. 5:19, "the whole of this world lieth in the wicked one,"[82] a phrase suggestive of the vast power and authority held by Satan over this world and age.

2. *"God of this age"*

Irenaeus, in an explicit effort to combat the above tendency of granting Satan complete authority over the world, reminds us that "it is not ... [the Devil] who has appointed the Kingdoms of this world, but God ...."[83] Irenaeus says it is incorrect to interpret the phrase "god of this age" as a reference to Satan; it refers not to another "god" but to the God of this world who has blinded the

---

[76] IR, VII, 1 (AF, I, 235). This phrase appears in the following passages: IM, I, 2 (AF, I, 197); IE, XVII, 1 (AF, I, 191); IE, XIX, 1 (AF, I, 193); IP, VI, 2 (AF, I, 245); IT, IV, 2 (AF, I, 217).

[77] EB, XVIII, 2 (AF, I, 401); cf. also "wicked ruler," EB, IV, 13 (AF, I, 353).

[78] EB, II, 1 (AF, I, 343).

[79] HV, I, I, 8 (AF, II, 9).

[80] HS, V, III, 6 (AF, II, 159-161); HS, VI, I, 4 (AF, II, 171); and HM, IX, 4 (AF, II, 109).

[81] MP, XIX, 2 (AF, II, 339).

[82] ODP, I, V, 5 (ANCL, I, 52); also OCP, II, III, 6 (ANCL, I, 86). Note, however, OAC, IV, XCIII (ANCL, II, 260) and ODP, I, V, 2 (ANCL, I, 45-46) where the association between the prince of this world and Satan remains vague.

[83] IAH, V, XXIV, 1 (ANCL, II, 119).

minds of unbelievers.[84] Inasmuch as all the writers in the early Christian tradition assert, in the final analysis, the ultimate power of God over Satan, Irenaeus' explicit rejection of dualism in this passage serves as an important qualification to the meaning of the phrase "god of this age" as conceived by early Christians.

As "god of this age" Satan is the real spiritual source of power (*dynamis*) behind all evil actions and events, including the realm of the demonic. It is Satan's spirit (*pneuma*) that now works "in the sons of disobedience" (Eph. 2:2). This spiritual power of Satan is suggested in the New Testament by the use of prepositional phrases. He who does sin is "of the devil" (I Jn. 3:8) just as Cain was "of the evil one" (I Jn. 3:12). The sorcerer is the "son of the devil" (Acts 13:10) and in 1 John 5:19 the author says "the whole world lies in the evil one."[85]

As previously noted, there are a number of New Testament references to "powers" which are themselves subject to "the prince of the power of the air" (*ton archonta tēs exousias tou aeros*).[86] In the context of the present discussion it must be added that it is the *dynamis* of Satan that inspires "all rule (*archēs*) and authority (*exousias*) and power (*dynameōs*)" (Eph. 1:21) to oppose the Spirit of God. The *dynamis* of Satan is the spiritual force operative in his rule and authority over this world and age; it is also the source of power behind the lawless one, the anti-Christ (II Thess. 2:9).

This notion that Satan inspires the *kosmos* and *aiōn* with a spiritual power (*dynamis*) opposing the Spirit of God is frequently stated among the Apostolic and early Greek Fathers as well. The importance of the victory of Christ, for Ignatius, is that "the powers of Satan (*hai dynameis tou Satana*) are destroyed" in Christ.[87] Ignatius also writes of the heavenly and earthly enemies and of war between good and bad *dynameis* which is suggestive of Paul's references to the principalities and powers and world-rulers of darkness which are all subject to the prince of the power of the air.[88]

---

[84] IAH, III, VII, 1 (ANCL, I, 273). It is interesting to note that in the *Lost Writings of Irenaeus* (ANCL, II, 179) this contradictory statement appears: " 'The god of the world'; that is, Satan, who was designated God to those who believe not."

[85] Cf. also Rev. 13:11; II Thess. 2:7; Heb. 2:14-15.

[86] Cf. above, pp. 41ff.

[87] IE, XIII, 1 (AF, I, 186-187).

[88] Cf. also Gokey, *Terminology*, pp. 85-86, n. 20: "the δυνάμεις of Ignatius are the Principalities, Powers (ἐξουσίαι), the Worldrulers of this darkness

Polycarp's reference to heretics is that they are "the first born of Satan" or "of the devil,"[89] and the *Shepherd of Hermas* speaks of the Devil losing his power against a Christian "for there is no power in him against you."[90]

Justin Martyr refers to "that power (*dynamis*) which is called the serpent and Satan"[91] and Irenaeus refers to the anti-Christ as "... being endued with all the power of the devil."[92] Origen, while seeking to determine the extent of the "pressure of malignant powers" [93] upon the actions of man, affirms the reality of those "... apostate and refugee powers which have departed from God" and "invent ... errors and delusions of false doctrine."[94]

Thus the power of Satan, his authority over this world and age, allows him to be called the "god of this age." Satan is not, however, a god on an equal but opposing status to the God of creation, as Irenaeus points out, for in origin and nature Satan remains a fallen angel, a creature of God. Yet the Devil wields great power and authority, and is like a god in that he is understood to be the spiritual source of all evil that pervades the entire world (*kosmos*) and age (*aiōn*).

D. The Defeat and end of Satan

1. *Satan's defeat*

Jesus' victory is the dominant idea regarding the defeat of the Devil in the selected writings in the early tradition.[95] In the gospels

---

and the spiritual forces of the air of Paul, Eph. 6:12 ... and the Satan of Ignatius is the Prince of the Power of the air above us of Eph. 2:2."

[89] PP, VII, 1 (AF, I, 293); cf. above, pp. 23ff.

[90] HM, XII, IV, 6 (AF, II, 133).

[91] JD, CXXV (ANCL, 258), and MGP, VI, 768.

[92] IAH, V, XXV, 1 (ANCL, II, 121), and MGP, VII, 1189.

[93] ODP, III, II, 3 (ANCL, I, 229).

[94] ODP, III, III, 4 (ANCL, I, 241); powers = Lt. virtutes.

[95] G. Aulen, *Christus Victor*, p. 39, says "... the classic idea of the Atonement is the dominant view of the Western as of the Eastern Fathers." Aulen distinguishes the classic idea of atonement from the Latin and moral theories of atonement. Briefly, the Latin theory of atonement (Tertullian, Cyprian, Anselm) conceives of Christ as discontinuous from God, satisfying the justice of God by his merit and thus changing God's attitude toward man. In contrast, the Moral theory of atonement (Abelard, Schleiermacher, Ritschl) understands the atonement to be a conversion or amendment on man's part as he responds to the meaning of the life and death of Jesus Christ. The classic theory (Irenaeus, Augustine, Luther), unlike the other two, portrays as a cosmic drama the Christ event as a victory over evil. It is God's activity from the outset, in contrast to the Latin theory; God is the

the strongest expressions of the triumph of Jesus over the Devil have to do with exorcisms.[96] At his baptism the Spirit of God (*pneuma theou*) descended upon him (Mt. 3:16), and being "full of the Holy Spirit" (*plērēs pneumatos hagiou*), (Lk. 4:1), Jesus cast demons out with a word (Mt. 8:8), commanded them and they obeyed. The writers of the gospels judged these actions as demonstrations of Jesus' divine *dynamis* and *exousia* (Mk. 3:15; Lk. 4:36; 9:1; 10:19). Jesus himself, after the return of the seventy and their success in casting out demons, saw in this a decisive sign of the complete overthrow of the demonic source of power, i.e., Satan. Jesus says: "I saw Satan fall like lightning from heaven" (Lk. 10:18).[97] In John 12:31 the author identifies the opponent against whom Jesus' spiritual power is directed as "the ruler of this world (*ho archōn tou kosmou toutou*) ... [who is] cast out (*ekblēthēsetai exō*)," just as demons are cast out (*ekballō*) in the synoptics.[98] "The reason the Son of God appeared was to destroy the works of the devil" (I Jn. 3:8). Jesus heals all oppressed by the Devil (Acts 10:38) and opens their eyes and turns them from darkness to light, from the "power of Satan unto God" (*exousias tou satana epi ton theon*) (Acts 26:18).[99] Christ took on flesh in which the principalities and powers could lodge, divested himself of that flesh "that through death he might destroy him who has the power of death, that is, the devil" (Heb. 2:14), and broke the dominion of powers. God in Christ has freed man from servitude to the Devil.

Christ's death set the *hagion pneuma* free, and he imparts this power (*dynamei tou kuriou*) to disciples and believers as a community of faith (I Cor. 5:4). The *dynamis* and *exousia* of Jesus continue to be effective in his community. Even his name is a "mighty name." Disciples say "Lord, even the demons are subject

reconciler and the reconciled. In contrast to the moral theory the change effected by the Christ event is not simply a subjective change on man's part. It is a complete change in the objective situation of man and his world. As Irenaeus asserts, God Himself is the deliverer and has freed man from servitude to the Devil.

[96] For further information cf. R. Leivestad, *Christ the Conqueror*, pp. 40ff. Leivestad notes on pp. 63-64 that in the gospels "Christ's death and resurrection are nowhere explicitly interpreted as a triumph over the devil, death, or cosmic powers ...," but it is understood "his death is the crowning fulfilment, the glorious consummation of his mission."

[97] Cf. above, p. 39, n. 3.

[98] Mt. 12:28, e.g., quotes Jesus as saying: "... I cast out demons by the Spirit of God" (ἐν πνεύματι θεοῦ ἐγὼ ἐκβαλλω τὰ δαιμόνια)

[99] Cf. also Col. 1:13; 2:15.

to us in your name" (Lk. 10:17). The coming of the anti-Christ is viewed with confidence, for "when the lawless one will be revealed ... the Lord Jesus will slay him with the breath of his mouth and destroy him by his appearing and his coming" (II Thess. 2:8).[100]

The Apostolic and early Greek Fathers express the same confidence in the power of Christ now and in the future. Ignatius refers to the prince of the world being brought to nothing when God appeared in the likeness of man [101] and affirms the community of faith as the continuing victor of Satan: "For when you gather together frequently the powers of Satan are destroyed, and his mischief is brought to nothing, by the concord of your faith."[102] Justin says the Son of God became man "for the destruction of the demons."[103] "The Power of God (*dynamis tou theou*) sent to us through Jesus Christ ...," Justin continues, "rebukes him, i.e., the Devil, and he departs from us."[104]

Irenaeus offers a slightly different emphasis from the preceding "dynamistic" view of Christ's victory over Satan as a manifestation of God's power which utterly overthrows all principalities and powers. Irenaeus says Christ conquered the Devil by justice (*justitia*), by moral force, not simply by power.[105] What is of interest here is that Satan is conquered, and continues to be, for even in Irenaeus and Origen we still find the claim that Christians "in his name perform [miracles] ... and truly drive out devils ...."[106] Origen adds, "... the Christian, the true Christian, I mean —who has submitted to God alone and His Word, will suffer nothing from demons, for He is mightier than demons."[107] Irenaeus summa-

---

[100] Cf. also: Barnabas, EB, XV, 5 (AF, I, 395); Justin, JD, CX (ANCL, 236ff.); Irenaeus, IAH, V, XXVIII, 1ff. (ANCL, II, 130ff.); and Origen, OAC, VI, XLVI (ANCL, II, 387).

[101] IT, IV, 2 (AF, I, 217).

[102] IE, XIII, 1 (AF, I, 187); the *Shepherd of Hermas* likewise says: "I know that you will break down all the power of the devil, and we shall master him, and have power against all his deeds" (HM, XII, VI, 4 [AF, II, 137]).

[103] JAii, VI (ANCL, 76); cf. also: JD, LXXVI (ANCL, 193); JD, LXXXV (ANCL, 205); JAi, XLV (ANCL, 45).

[104] JD, XCVI: (ANCL, 245); cf. also JD, XCIV (ANCL, 218).

[105] IAH, III, XVIII, 7 (ANCL, I, 342ff.); cf. also IAH, V, I, 1 (ANCL, II, 56).

[106] IAH, III, XXXII, 4 (ANCL, I 245-246); OAC, I, VI (ANCL, I, 402).

[107] OAC, VIII, XXXVI (ANCL, II, 521-523); cf. also OAC, VII, XLIII (ANCL, II, 528); OAC, XIII, LXIV, (ANCL, II, 548).

rizes the role of Christ and the Devil and the relation each has to man in the following way:

> For if man, who had been created by God that he might live, after losing life, through being injured by the serpent that had corrupted him, should not any more return to life, but should be utterly (and for ever) abandoned to death, God would (in that case) have been conquered, and the wickedness of the serpent would have prevailed over the will of God. But inasmuch as God is invincible and long-suffering, He did indeed show Himself to be long-suffering in the matter of the correction of man and the probation of all, ... by means of the second man did He bind the strong man, and spoiled his goods, and abolished death, vivifying that man who had been in a state of death. For at the first Adam became a vessel in his (Satan's) possession, whom he did also hold under his power, that is, by bringing sin on him iniquitously, and under colour of immortality entailing death upon him. For, while promising that they should be as gods, which was in no way possible for him to be, he wrought death in them: wherefore he who had led man captive, was justly captured in his turn by God; but man, who had been led captive, was loosed from the bonds of condemnation.[108]

Jesus not only has authority over death, but over life; Jesus is ruler and savior (*archēgos kai sōtēr*), the author and prince of life (*ho archēgos tēs zōēs*); thus Christ defeats Satan.

2. *End of Satan*

The victory over Satan is a decisive one, but will not be fully consummated until the end-days. Hence the followers of Christ must be constantly aware "to keep Satan from gaining the advantage ..." over them (II Cor. 2:11), though his designs are well known to Christians. Paul promises his congregation that the end of Satan will come and "... the God of peace will soon crush Satan under your feet" (Rom. 16:20).

Ideas common to apocalyptic literature appear in the New Testament in regard to the final end of Satan. Mt. 25:41 says that there is "eternal fire prepared for the devil and his angels ..." [109] Paul reminds us that "the last enemy to be destroyed (*katargeitai*) is death" (I Cor. 15:26), and the Book of Revelation proclaims that Satan, reduced to impotence on a fixed day, will on the final day

---

[108] IAH, III, XXIII, 1 (ANCL, I, 362-363).

[109] Cf. also the apocalyptic *Sibylline Oracles* (*The Apocrypha*, II, p. 380) which speak of the burning up of Beliar.

be hurled into a pool of fire and sulphur (Rev. 20:1-3, 10). Among the Apostolic and Greek Fathers Barnabas looks to the day when the Son returns and "... will destroy (*katargesei*) the time of the wicked one ..." (*tou anomou*) [110] and Justin and Irenaeus speak of the eternal fire prepared for Satan and his host, and for the men who follow him.[111]

Whether this destruction of Satan means annihilation, or less strongly, dethronement and ruin, is a question generally open to interpretation,[112] although two of the selected writers suggest a position on the matter. Ignatius speaks of the destruction of Satan [113] in a way which Gokey interprets to mean the "ruin" of Satan, not annihilation.[114] Origen more explicitly states that the end of Satan is ruin rather than annihilation: "The consummation of all things is destruction of evil" [115] and "the last enemy ... who is called death" will be destroyed, but "its destruction ... will not be its non-existence, but its ceasing to be an enemy, and ... death."[116] Origen's interpretation implies that Christ's struggle with Satan is ultimately not against but for the sake of the Satanic powers,[117] and that possibly the evil spirits "will in the future world be converted to the righteousness because of their possessing the faculty of freedom of will ...."[118] Origen does not state this will

---

[110] EB, XV, 5 (AF, I, 395).

[111] JAi, XXVIII (ANCL, 31); IAH, IV, XLI (ANCL, II, 50); IAH, V, XXVI, 2 (ANCL, II, 127-128); IAH, I, X, 1 (ANCL, I, 42) and IAH, III, III, 3 (ANCL, I, 262).

[112] In the case of Paul the question depends on how one translates the verb καταργέιν. Hans-Ruedi Weber, in an article "Christ's Victory over Satanic Power," *Study Encounter*, II, 3 (1966), p. 164, says of this Greek verb in the context of this same discussion: "In its strongest use it can indeed mean 'annihilate,' and there is a tendency among Bible translators and exegetes to regard it in this way when speaking about what happens to the powers through Christ. But this verb often means to overthrow, dethrone and devaluate, especially when it refers to something which, before Christ, had a certain value. Thus understood, the Satanic powers are not annihilated but only unmasked in their false part as world rulers, and dethroned from their usurped position as God's rivals. A number of scholars ... think that this is what Paul is saying. Christ's struggle is then ultimately for the sake of, and not against, the Satanic powers."

[113] IE, XIII, 1 (AF, I, 187).

[114] Gokey, *Terminology*, p. 87, n. 22.

[115] OAC, VIII, LXII (ANCL, II, 555).

[116] ODP, III, VI (ANCL, I, 268); and MPG, XI, 338: "Destruetur ergo non ut non sit, sed ut inimicus non sit et mors."

[117] H. Weber, "Christ's Victory over Satanic Power," p. 164.

[118] ODP, I, VI, 2 (ANCL, I 56); cf. also ODP, I, VIII, (ANCL, I, 68).

happen, but leaves the judgment to the reader who is reminded that the alternative view implies an eternal cosmic dualism. Origen also asserts that "... nothing is impossible to the Omnipotent, nor is anything incapable of restoration to its Creator: for He made all things that they might exist, and those things which were made for existence cannot cease to be."[119]

[119] ODP, III, VI, 5 (ANCL, I, 268).

CHAPTER FOUR

SUMMARY AND COMMENTS

The portrait which emerges from the references to Satan in the early Greek Christian literature is essentially as follows. Satan was believed to be a fallen angel who was the chief of a class of fallen angels. The reasons for his fall or the time of his fall are not defined in the earliest selected writings and not agreed upon among the later writers. But as a fallen angel he was the "prince of the power of the air" who had authority over the "spiritual hosts of wickedness in the heavenly places." There is the suggestion in the writings of Paul, though it is never systematically developed, that these spiritual hosts included such cosmic realities as the "elemental spirits of the universe," the "world rulers of this present darkness" and the "principalities," "powers" and other spirit orders of the universe. Within this cosmic totality, Satan's vast power and authority extended over the world of men and into almost every sphere of human activity. Hence Satan was not only the "prince of the power of the air," but the "ruler of this world" and the "god of this age."

The early Christian believed that Satan was the real spiritual source of power behind all evil actions and events including the realm of the demonic. Satan was the "ruler of demons" who, presumably like him, were believed to be spirit beings existing independently of man and not perceivable by the physical senses. Though the demons were under the authority and power of Satan, they were considered distinguishable from Satan for the most part both in status and origin and in their activities. As a lower class of evil spirits who, according to one theory, were the offspring of an illicit union between fallen angels and the daughters of men, demons sought to realize the Satanic goal of "seducing men from God." Demons had a wide range of activities but were known to the early Christians most characteristically as tormenting spirits who, by possessing persons, caused illness and various natural evils. Possession was not a characteristic activity of Satan himself.

A number of different kinds of experiences were considered deeds of Satan by the early Christians. Satan sought to tempt men from their faith, the most notable example being his tempting of

Jesus. Satan also promoted heresies through deceit and lies, and thereby disrupted the unity of the church, its doctrine and discipline. The torments of martyrdom as well as a variety of obstructions which would prevent one from growing in the faith, such as the mental attitudes and emotional states of sloth, anger, or irreligious sentiments, were believed to be the direct result of Satan's prompting.

The early Christian perceived the essential character of the various activities of Satan to be death and destruction. "Death" meant not only the termination of life, but also the depraved life, the ruin and personal desolation which come with spiritual death, the loss of all that gives worth to existence. This kind of destructiveness, the early Christians believed, had been operative from the beginning of time (the serpent) and would continue to the end-days of time (the anti-Christ).

Satan was known by that name which means "adversary," and was referred to by early Christians as "the Opponent of the race of Saints," "the enemy," etc. Satan was the "evil one," "evil" (*ponēros*) meaning, in the physical sense, that which is sick, painful, spoiled, or in poor condition, and in the ethical sense that which is base, vicious, degenerate. The early Christian experienced such physical and ethical conditions of life as evil and believed them to be the result of a singularly great power, the evil spirit Satan.

Yet as pervasive and overwhelming as the power of Satan was, the early Christian found hope in the victory of Christ over Satan. In Christ Satan had suffered a decisive defeat. Furthermore, the power and authority of Christ the conqueror continued to be effective in his community and would be completely manifest in the end days when Jesus would slay the anti-Christ "with the breath of his mouth." That would mark the end of Satan's power and domain.

This summary portrait of Satan, in that it understands Satan to have an existence independent and external to man, would be disputed by some interpreters of the New Testament who seek to existentialize the Christian mythology of evil. The basic interpretive problem stems from a characteristic feature of the early Christian materials. As this study has revealed, when it comes to defining the ontological status of Satan, the early Christian writers provide so little explicit information that one often has to proceed by interpretive implication. One type of reaction to this fact is to claim, essentially, that this limiting feature of the Satan symbol must be taken at face value and that there are no metaphysical assumptions of the real externality of Satan operative in the New Testament. The claim is that in the New Testament the reality of Satan is only explicitly spoken of in terms of individual and collective human experiences, and therefore the meaning of the symbol should be confined to the experiential level. This is the general interpretive tendency of such writers as Gordon Rupp (*Principalities and Powers*) [1] and Trevor Ling (*The Significance of Satan*).[2] Because T. O. Ling has also done a comparative study between Satan and the Buddhist figure of evil, Māra, we shall cite his work on the Satan mythology as representative of this existential perspective.

Ling writes that "the New Testament writers, in speaking of Satan, were in general speaking of the spirit of society, a society alienated from God."[3] Previous to this statement, in a discussion of several synoptic gospel passages, Ling asserts that "*personification* of a hostile evil force should not necessarily be taken to imply real personality ...."[4] Later in summary, Ling states that

> when a careful consideration of the whole range of New Testament references to Satan has been made, the outline which emerges is that of the spirit of a society, rather than an individual local spirit being.[5]

Ling is suggesting that for the New Testament writers Satan is the "personification" or "representation" of the evil forces generated by unredeemed man in his collective life. Satan's power is derived from man; it is man's acceptance of the malign pressures of societary life that makes Satan "god of this world."[6] To support this general thesis that evil is essentially moral corruption, Ling argues that on the basis of New Testament evidence human sin can be conceived as prior to Satan and he states that there is no clear evidence in the belief of a "Satanic sin" prior to man.[7] Rather Satan derives his evil power from human sin.

---

[1] (Nashville: Abingdon-Cokesbury Press, 1952).

[2] (London: SPCK, 1961). Cf. also the World Council of Churches document, *The Lordship of Christ over the World and the Church* (Lausanne: La Concorde, 1956).

[3] Ling, *Satan*, p. 84.

[4] *Ibid.*, p. 24, Cf. also Ling's article "Personality and the Devil," *Modern Churchman*, 5 (Jan. '62), pp. 141-148.

[5] Ling, *Satan*, p. 84.

[6] *Ibid.*, pp. 60ff.

[7] *Ibid.*, pp. 81ff.

The angelic powers and elemental spirits and principalities that Paul speaks of are also interpreted by Ling as spirit forces within human society, "pressures from various social collective ... [and] religio-cultural systems" that wield despotic power over man.[8] They, like Satan, are "probably not to be thought of ... as cosmic forces, in the sense of being properties of the physical universe."[9] Nor should it be understood, Ling adds on the basis of New Testament evidence, that this hostile force which Satan symbolizes is operative in the world of nature, i.e., at the subhuman level.[10]

Not only differences in conclusions, but also differences in methodological approach separate us from Ling's work. Having acknowledged that among early Christians there is an obvious lack of speculative interest in such matters as the ontological nature and cosmological status of Satan, we have gone on to explore the implied metaphysic because of our basic view that the New Testament, and other early writings, must be understood within their historical context.[11] Comparisons with literature contemporary to the period were cited which were more explicit on these matters and which illuminated and gave coherence to many aspects of the Satan mythology, especially as it appears in the New Testament. Upon studying the historical context of early church writings it becomes difficult to believe that early Christians had no cosmological beliefs (with attendant metaphysical assumptions) in a world shot-through with cosmological beliefs in externally real demonic powers. That these beliefs are not always explicit, though they surface in a number of passages, does not require the conclusion that they are absent. Rather it can be argued that they are truly assumptions, matters which the contemporary world of that period took for granted, hence dealt with only infrequently.

But besides approaching the New Testament as a group of writings that stand within a *Weltanschauung*, we have also viewed the Satan mythology over a wide range of literature covering four centuries. The primary reason for making this broad selection of literature ranging from the New Testament to the early Greek

[8] *Ibid.*, p. 71.

[9] *Ibid.*, p. 70.

[10] *Ibid.*, pp. 78ff.

[11] Robert M. Grant, *After the New Testament* (Philadelphia: Fortress Press, 1967), p. xii, states the position clearly and simply: "... behind the written documents lies a situation (or group of situations) out of which and for which the documents were written."

Fathers rests on the premise that the more inclusive one's view of the Satan mythology the better one's perspective for clarifying basic structures of meaning that give form to it. Clarification of these basic motifs which structure the Satan mythology is possible only in the broader historical context. As Rudolf Bultmann, the major figure in the contemporary demythologizing movement himself says, in order "to clarify the motifs governing the New Testament way of thinking and to uncover the problems that lie within the thinking," one must have "a more inclusive . . . view of the total development . . ." of the literature.[12] Hence in his study of the "Theology and Cosmology" of the New Testament he often refers to the Apostolic Fathers.[13] In addition, Bultmann definitely sees New Testament references to the demonic world-rulers ("angels," "principalities," "authorities," "powers") as figures of Gnostic mythology which brought further development to the cosmological thinking of early Christians.[14] The question is not whether or not there are cosmological beliefs in early Christianity, but what is the content of those beliefs.

This is not to suggest that we are assuming a uniform meaning of the Satan mythology common to all writers in the tradition, or that we are not aware of the risk this methodological approach has of interpreting New Testament writers, for example, *in terms of* other early Christian writers or other religious traditions. Hence we have attempted to note the diversities of viewpoint and emphasis among the particular writers. And very often it has been just those diversities which have helped clarify the basic motifs of the Satan mythology itself. The portrait of Satan which has emerged, based on a broad selection of literature, hopefully, is free of misinterpretations which are not applicable both to particular writings as well as to the larger historical context.

The basic endeavor of most "existentialist" interpreters of the Satan mythology has been to give an interpretation relevant to the contemporary mind. Such an approach is very often extremely cogent, but it is not without its own risks. That is to say, the cogency

---

[12] Rudolf Bultmann, *Theology of the New Testament* (New York: Charles Scribner's Sons, 1955), II, p. 145.

[13] Ling would apparently not agree with the broad use of selected literature to derive a portrait of Satan, for he occasionally labels materials that post-date the New Testament as "sub-Christian" and "sub-apostolic reversions," Ling, *Satan*, pp. 54-55.

[14] Bultmann, *Theology*, I, p. 173.

of much contemporary interpretation of traditional Christian concepts is due to its basic pre-occupation with questions concerning the meaning of human existence, i.e., an "existential" or, in a broader sense, an "anthropological" point of reference. Such an orientation is to be contrasted with questions of the nature of ultimate reality of deity (theology) or questions concerning the origin, structure, or destiny of the world (cosmology).[15] As evident in certain schools of contemporary Christian theology, there appears to be a basic indifference to "theological" or "cosmological" questions, except perhaps as they are related by implication to the primary question concerning man's existence. Such an interpretive bias, as it must be called, runs a high risk when engaged in the interpretation of historical materials, namely, the danger of imposing this "anthropological" interest on the materials in such a way as to exclude or ignore cosmological or theological references in the material, or simply reduce them to the anthropological level. Ling's effort, e.g., to interpret the Pauline references to the world-rulers, elemental spirits, and Satan as the prince of the power of the air, etc., as references to spiritual forces within human society and not as references to cosmic forces which are in some way metaphysical properties of the universe whose existence is not dependent on human society, 1) leads to a denial of aspects of the historical meaning of the mythology in the early tradition, and 2) reduces the full meaning of the mythology. The result is a loss of essential elements of meaning which are necessary for an adequate and cogent contemporary interpretation even with its self-conscious anthropological bias.[16]

[15] J. Kitagawa, makes this three-fold distinction in "Primitive, Classical, and Modern Religions: A Perspective on Understanding the History of Religions," *The History of Religions: Essays on the Problem of Understanding*, ed. J. K. Kitagawa, M. Eliade, C. Long (Chicago: University of Chicago Press, 1967), pp. 58ff.

[16] For a recent and vigorous work supporting our general interpretive position see James Kallas, *The Satanward View: A Study in Pauline Theology* (Philadelphia: Westminster Press, 1966). Also see the well-balanced and thoughtful exegesis of Heinrich Schlier, *Principalities and Powers In the New Testament* (New York: Herder and Herder, 1962).

PART TWO

ANALYSIS OF THE MĀRA FIGURE IN THE EARLY INDIAN BUDDHIST TRADITION

ABBREVIATIONS

Pali Sources

DN	*Dīgha-Nikāya,* Pali Text Society edition (PTS), I-III, cited by volume and page.
DB	*Dialogues of the Buddha,* Parts I-III, The Sacred Books of the Buddhists (SBB), II, III, IV, cited by part and page.
MN	*Majjhima-Nikāya,* PTS edition, I-III, cited by volume and page.
ML	*The Middle Length Sayings,* PTS edition, I-III, cited by volume and page.
SN	*Saṃyutta- Nikāya,* PTS edition, I-V, cited by volume and page.
KS	*The Book of the Kindred Sayings,* PTS edition, I-V, cited by volume and page.
AN	*Aṅguttara- Nikāya,* PTS edition, I-V, cited by volume and page.
GS	*The Book of the Gradual Sayings,* PTS edition, I-V, cited by volume and page.
Dh	*The Dhammapada,* PTS edition, cited by verse.
DhM	*The Dhammapada,* 2nd ed.; The Sacred Books of the East (SBE), X, cited by verse.
DhR	*The Dhammapada.* Translated by S. Radhakrishnan, cited by verse.
Ud	*Udāna,* PTS edition, cited by verse; prose by page.
UdW	*Udāna: Verses of Uplift,* SBB, VIII, cited by verse; prose by page.
It	*Itivuttaka,* PTS edition, cited by page.
ItW	*Itivuttaka: As It Was Said,* SBB, VIII, cited by page.
Sn	*Sutta-Nipāta,* PTS edition, cited by verse; prose by page.
SnH	*Woven Cadences of Early Buddhists,* SBB, XV, cited by verse; prose by page.

Sanskrit Sources

AKP	*L'Abhidharmakośa de Vasabandhu,* translated by L. de la Vallée Poussin, I-VI, cited by chapter and page.
AP	*Ashṭasāhasrikā,* edited by R. Mitra, cited by chapter and page.
APC	*Aṣṭasāhasrikā Prajñāpāramitā* (*The Perfection of Wisdom in Eight Thousand Slokas*), translated by E. Conze, cited by chapter and page.
BA	*The Buddha-Carita of Aśvaghosha,* edited by E. B. Cowell, cited by book and page.
BAC	*The Buddha-Carita of Aśvaghosha,* translated by E. B. Cowell, SBE, XLIX, cited by book and page.
LV	*Lalita Vistara,* edited by S. Lefmann, cited by chapter and page.
LVF	*Le Lalita Vistara,* translated by Ph. Ed. Foucaux, cited by chapter and page.

LVM	*Lalita Vistara*, translated by R. Mitra (Chapters I-XV), cited by chapter and page.
MPL	*Le Traité de la grande vertu de sagesse de Nāgārjuna* (*Mahāprajñāpāramitāśāstrā*), I-II, translated by E. Lamotte, cited by volume and page.
Mv	*Le Mahāvastu* (*Texte Sanskrit*), edited by E. Senart, I-III, cited by volume and page.
MvJ	*The Mahāvastu*, translated by J. J. Jones, I-III, SBB, XVI, XVIII, XIX, cited by volume (I-III) and page.
SBW, *Studies*	*Śrāvakabhūmi of Asaṅga*, translated by Alex Wayman in an article "Studies in Yama and Māra," *Indo-Iranian Journal*, III (1959), cited by page.
SBW, *Analysis*	*Analysis of the Śrāvakabhūmi Manuscript* by Alex Wayman, cited by page.
SP	*Saddharmapuṇḍarīka-Sūtram*, edited by U. Wogihara and C. Tsuchida, cited by chapter and page.
SPK	*Saddharma Puṇḍarīka* (*The Lotus of the True Law*), translated by H. Kern, SBE, XXI, cited by chapter and page.

Other sources frequently cited

BHSD	F. Edgerton, *Buddhist Hybrid Sanskrit Dictionary*, II, (1953).
CESD	Manfred Mayrhofer, *A Concise Etymological Sanskrit Dictionary* (1962).
DPPN	G. P. Malalasekera, *Dictionary of Pali Proper Names* (1960).
ERE	*Encyclopaedia of Religion and Ethics*, edited by J. Hastings, IV (1912), VIII (1916).
Ling, *Buddhism*	T. O. Ling, *Buddhism and the Mythology of Evil.*
MA	*Papañcasūdanī*; *Commentary to the Majjhima-Nikāya* (4 vols., 1933).
MWSD	Monier Williams, *A Sanskrit-English Dictionary* (1872).
PTSD	Pali Text Society, *Pali-English Dictionary* (1959).
Windisch	E. Windisch, *Māra und Buddha.*

CHAPTER FIVE

TERMINOLOGY CENTERED AROUND MĀRA

The terminology designating an evil personage in the early writings of the Buddhist tradition is, like the Christian tradition, widely varied. The term Māra, however, is the dominant reference throughout the selected literature, and most other names and phrases which refer to an Evil One (*pāpimā*) [1] are understood to be references to Māra.

Etymologically the term Māra is related to the Pali *maccu* and the Sanskrit *mṛtyu*, which mean "death." More specifically, whereas *maccu* (Skt. *mṛtyu*) indicates "death itself," " 'Māra' is the *nomen actoris* to the causative *mārayati*;" [2] Māra therefore etymologically means the one who kills or causes death.[3] Often the name "Maccu" is retained as a synonymous reference for Māra,[4] as well as the epithet "Antaka" which means "being at the end, or making an end."[5]

"Pāpimā" (the Evil One) is the term most commonly applied to the name Māra.[6] Like the term Māra itself, "pāpimā" is a word familiar to the religious vocabulary of ancient India. There is the

---

[1] The rendering of the Pali and Buddhist Sanskrit term *pāpa* as "evil" is not done without hesitation, for though the English term "evil" is an accepted rendering (cf. PTSD "Pāpa," p. 453; MWSD, "pāpa," p. 618b) it runs the risk of retaining implicit Christian meanings which do not necessarily belong to the Buddhist understanding of *pāpa*. Rhys Davids relates the term *pāpa* to the Greek πῆμα which the Liddell & Scott *Greek-English Lexicon*, II (1940), p. 1401, renders "misery, calamity." Cf. below p. 157ff.

[2] Windisch, pp. 185-186.

[3] Windisch's phrase is "der tödtet oder sterben lässt." Cf. also PTSD, "Māra," p. 530, "killing, destroying, bringing death, pestilence ..."; MWSD, "māra," p. 811c ($\sqrt{}$mṛi), "killing, destroying ...," and Ling, *Buddhism*, p. 56.

[4] Māra's army is called *maccusena* (hosts of death), SN, I, 122 (KS, I, 152); Māra himself is given the title *maccurāja* (King of Death), Dh, 46 (DhR, 74-75); the two terms Māra and *maccu* (*mṛtyu*) are used in apposition, as in ML, I, 279 (MN, I, 227) and BA, XIII, 109 (BAC, XIII, 138). Cf. also below pp. 96-99.

[5] PTSD, "Antaka," p. 47. For use of this epithet as applied to Māra see especially the Māra suttas: SN, I, 103-106 (KS, I, 129-133); also Mv, III, 416 (MvJ, III, 417).

[6] To cite only a few examples: MN, I, 326-327, 331, 332 (ML, I, 389, 394, 396); MN, III, 115 (ML, III, 158); SN, I, 103ff., 113, 115 (KS, I, 128ff., 142, 145); LV, XXI, 303 (LVF, XXI, 260).

obvious relation of Māra pāpimā with the Brahamanic figure Pāpmā Mṛtyuḥ "Death the Evil One," notes Windisch.[7] In the older Sanskrit literature *pāpmā* was always used as a masculine noun meaning "evil, misfortune and sin."[8] According to Windisch, the term indicates "not only the morally bad, but more objectively, misfortune, sorrow and pain ...."[9] Also in the older Sanskrit literature *pāpmā* is found personified as a masculine god similar to "Mṛtyu", but in the selected literature of the early Buddhist tradition there is complete identification of *pāpimā* and Māra. *Pāpimā* is never used alone as a reference to an evil personage separate from Māra in the texts. Rather the term always refers to Māra.[10] In the *Majjhima Nikāya*, e.g., Moggallāna says to Māra, "You, Evil One, are Māra" (*Māro tvam asi pāpimā*).[11]

Other reminders of the Indian context out of which the Buddhist Māra symbol was created are the occasional use of the proper name "Namuci" as an alternate way of addressing or referring to Māra,[12] as well as the associations of Māra with "Yama" [13] and "Kāma."[14] In Vedic mythology Namuci (*na-muñcati*) was a drought demon who "withheld the waters" and was smitten by Indra's thunderbolt for the rains to be released. Such a death-dealing activity is easily associated with Māra.[15] Regarding Mṛtyu Yama, the *Atharvaveda* (VI, 93) describes this "death god" as "fearfully destructive, the destroyer" (*Yamo Mṛtyur aghamāro Nirṛtho ...*), concepts which have completely merged with the Māra in the selected Buddhist texts.[16] Kāma, the god of sensual love and worldly enjoyment in the Vedic tradition, when used in the Buddhist tradition as a synonym

[7] Windisch, p. 195.

[8] Windisch, p. 192. Ling, *Buddhism*, p. 56, translates Windisch's phrase "Uebel, Unglück, Sünde" by "(the) ill, disaster, or sin."

[9] Windisch, p. 192.

[10] Windisch, p. 195.

[11] MN, I, 332 (ML, I, 396).

[12] E.g., AN, II, 15 (GS, II, 15); Sn, 426, 439 (SnH, 426, 439); SN, I, 67 (KS, I, 92); Mv, I, 208, 264 (MvJ, I, 165, 219); Mv, II, 10, 238-239 (MvJ, II, 10, 225-226); Mv, II, 254, 381 (MvJ, III, 242, 378); LV, XXI, 302 (LFV, XXI, 259).

[13] E.g., Mv, II, 407 (MvJ, II, 362).

[14] E.g., BA, XIII, 108-109 (BAC, XIII, 137-139); Dh, 46 (DhR, 74-75).

[15] Cf. Ling, *Buddhism*, p. 55.

[16] Cf. Alex Wayman, "Studies in Yama and Māra," *Indo-Iranian Journal*, III (1959), pp. 44ff. and 112ff. Windisch, p. 187, translates the Skt. "*Yamo Mṛtyur aghamāro Nirṛtho* ..." by "Yama, der Todesgott, der schlimme Tödter, der Verderber ..." The term Nirṛthah (*Nirṛtho*) is derived from "nir + √r: break up," i.e., destroy. Cf. CESD, "nirṛtih," p. 166.

for Māra, clearly rests on Buddhist views in which death and world desire are coordinates.[17]

Other names and phrases found in the selected writings which are linked to Māra include: "Kaṇha" (Skt. *kṛṣṇa*),[18] "yakkha" (Skt. *yakṣa*),[19] "Pamattabandhu" (Skt. *Pramattabandhu*),[20] and "kali."[21] Kanha (*kṛṣṇa*) means "the Dark One" especially in the moral sense of "wicked."[22] Yakkhas (*yakṣas*), together with rakkhasas (*rākṣasas*) and pisacas (*piśācas*), are the most common demons found in the Buddhist Pali and Sanskrit sources. The terms are used interchangeably for the most part, and as they appear in the Buddhist texts are nearly indistinguishable from each other.[23] Pamattabandhu (*pramattabandhu*) means "friend (or relative) of the careless or indolent" and usually derives its most effective meaning

---

[17] Cf. Windisch, p. 187. For Vedic references to Kāma see MWSD, "kāma," p. 271c. Other associations of the Buddhist Māra with the Vedic use of language, such as *Kṣudhāmāra* (death through hunger) and *tṛṣṇāmāra* (death through thirst), (*Atharvaveda*, IV, 17, 6, 7), are discussed by Windisch on pp. 187ff.

[18] E.g., DN, II, 261 (DB, II, 293); MN, I, 337-338 (ML, I, 401-403); Sn 967 (SnH 967); BA, XII, III, 115-116 (BAC, XIII, 141, 147); LV, XXI, 301, 303 (LVF, XXI, 258-259).

[19] E.g., MN, I, 338 (ML, I, 403); SN, I, 122 (KS, I, 153); Sn, 449 (SnH, 449); Mv, II, 260, 323 (MvJ, II, 246ff., 301); SP, XXII, 351 (SPK, XXII, 391).

[20] E.g., SN, I, 123, 128 (KS, I, 153, 161); Sn, 430 (SnH, 430); Mv, II, 319 (MvJ, II, 299).

[21] E.g., LV, XIII, 173, 180 (LVM, XIII, 236, 244); SP, XXVI, 389 (SPK, XXVI, 438-439). The terms *adhipati* (ruler, master controller) and *pajāpati* (Lord of Creation) are also infrequently associated with Māra, the latter usually in the commentary tradition, e.g., MA, I, 31. For references to *adhipati*, cf. PTSD, "Adhipati," p. 29, and BHSD, "adhipati," p. 13. A more extensive list of demonic names and phrases is furnished in J. Masson, *La religion populaire dans le canon bouddhique pāli* (Louvain: Bureaux du Muséon, 1942), pp. 103ff. Cf. also G. P. Malalasekera, DPPN, II, 611ff.

[22] Cf. BHSD, "kṛṣṇa," p. 191.

[23] The term yakkha (*yakṣa*) is variously translated "demons," or "fairies" by the Rhys Davids'. Mrs. Rhys Davids says "The English equivalent does not exist. 'Geni' (*djinn*) is perhaps nearest .... In the early records, yakkha as an appellative is, like *nāga*, anything but depreciative.... They have a deva's supernormal powers, and are capable of putting very pertinent problems in metaphysic and ethics. But they were decadent divinities, degraded in the later era, when the stories to the *Jātaka* verses were set down, to the status of red-eyed cannibal ogres" (KS, I, 262, n. 1). In DB, III, 188, n. 6, the Rhys Davids' add, "All these non-human creatures had bodies, hence 'spirits' is not very suitable." Cf. PTSD, "Pisāca," p. 461: "demon, goblin, sprite"; and "Rakkhasa," p. 560: "a kind of harmful (nocturnal) demon, usually making the water its haunt and devouring men."

from the context of the passage in which it occurs.[24] Kali, in the Buddhist texts, means "wicked" or "evil" as seen, e.g., in the *Saddharma Puṇḍarīka*'s reference to the "sphere of the wicked Māra" (*Māra kali cakram*).[25]

The terminology designating an evil personage in these selected writings of early Buddhism is thus quite varied, but the dominant term is Māra. Though most of these terms, including Māra itself, grew out of the context of Vedic, Brāhmaṇa and Upanishadic terminology, nevertheless, Māra is principally a Buddhist symbol. In Indian mythology there is no equivalent conception to the Buddhist Māra.[26] An analysis of Māra's activities, nature, and status in Buddhist cosmology as represented in the selected Buddhist texts will provide a portrayal of this figure peculiar to Buddhism.

---

[24] In SN, I, 123 (KS, I, 153), e.g., Buddha refers to Māra as "Pamatta-bandhu" after Māra has accusingly asked the Buddha: "Why makest thou no friends among the folk? Is there no one with whom thou canst be friends?" Cf. PTSD, "Pamatta," p. 416.

[25] SP, XXVI, 389 (SPK, XXVI, 438-439). "Cakra" means "wheel" and refers to Māra's sphere of influence. R. Mitra, in his English translation of the *Lalita Vistara*, renders *kali* as a proper name, probably in reference to the "Kali" deva of the *Purānas* or *Mahābhārata*. Cf. LV, XIII, 173, 180 (LVM, XIII, 236, 244). Edgerton, however, says that in Buddhist Sanskrit *kali* is regarded as a characteristic of Māra. Cf. BHSD, "kali," p. 172.

[26] Cf. Windisch, p. 197. Windisch, p. 187, remarks that in non-Buddhist Sanskrit literature Māra as a separate name is very seldom found, though, as we have noted, the word itself is not a completely new invention of the Buddhists. That no equivalent conception to Māra is found elsewhere in Indian mythology, see also: L. de la Vallée Poussin, *Indo-Européens et Indo-Iraniens* (Paris: Ancienes Maisons Thorin et Fontemoing, 1924), pp. 312-313; Sir Charles Eliot, *Hinduism and Buddhism*, (New York: Barnes and Noble, 1954), I, p. 337; E. J. Thomas, *The Life of the Buddha* (New York: Alfred A. Knopf, 1927), p. 217, n. 2.

CHAPTER SIX

THE DEEDS OF MĀRA

The activities or deeds of Māra (*mārakarma*) [1] are referred to in abundance in the selected literature. As in the Christian literature, descriptions of Māra's deeds generally refer to the activities of an evil personage who encounters man in various ways,[2] but there is considerably more emphasis on another type of reference to Māra, namely, that in which the identity of Māra as an evil personage is replaced by "doctrinal" or "abstract" terms.[3] This latter type of reference, though often linked with the deeds of Māra, is most appropriately discussed in the following chapter dealing with the nature and power of Māra.[4] The concern of this chapter is a detailed analysis of the various activities ascribed to Māra, the Evil One.

Māra's deeds can be characterized, for the most part, as follows: Māra reviles, inclines toward sense desires, attacks; blinds and perplexes; obstructs and interrupts; possesses and holds in bondage; and kills and destroys. As was the case in Part I, this typology is generally applicable to all the selected writings being investigated, although varying emphases and differences in types of references distinguish individual sources and schools from one another. Wherever possible in the development of each section, the Pali sources will be treated first, followed by the Sanskrit. This is not meant to assert that the Pali tradition *in toto* is older than the

---

[1] Cf., e.g., LV, II, 12 (LVM, II, 24).

[2] Included in this category are what could be termed "Jātaka-type" references. In such references certain animal characters of popular folk stories are identified as Māra at the conclusion of the tale. In the *Mahāvastu*, e.g., the story is told of a crocodile who tricks a monkey to ride on his back across a river and then attempts to eat him. The crocodile in the sea is identified as Māra. This type of reference is best understood as an illustrative way of characterizing some of Māra's activities, in this case his enticing and deceiving activities that lead to death.

[3] In this type of reference Māra is less a personage of cosmological status and more an occasion for listing doctrinal definitions of undesirable conditions that must be overcome as one follows the path of the Buddha. Cf. below, the "Plurality of Māras," pp. 100ff.

[4] In this type of reference active verb forms characterizing the activity of Māra are practically absent.

Sanskrit, but for the most part the Pali does contain much of the earliest writings.[5] Due to the nature of the subject matter, as well as to the difficulties involved in dating the Sanskrit sources, the most convenient and clearest way of developing a given topic will determine the order in which the Sanskrit sources are treated. Individual characteristics of the Sanskrit texts, rather than their place in the historical development of Buddhist thought, will be the by-product of this method of treatment.

Before proceeding with this analysis, however, a few general observations can be made regarding the predominant mode of encounter between Māra and Buddha. Māra much more frequently addresses the Buddha and has discourse with him than does Satan with Jesus.[6] In the "Māra Saṃyutta" of the *Saṃyutta Nikāya*, e.g., Māra approaches the Buddha twenty times and other bhikkhus five

---

[5] It is probably safe to assert that the Nikāyas of the Pali Canon were redacted during the first century B. C., and contain many of the earliest texts. Of the Sanskrit literature, the Prajñāpāramitā texts are thought to have been written about 100 B.C.-100 A. D. The various Sarvāstivādin, Mahāsanghika and Mahāyāna texts dealt with most probably belong to the second or third centuries A. D. Nāgārjuna belongs to the second century A. D. and Asaṅga, who represents the Yogācārins, is probably to be dated about 350 A. D.

For specific discussions regarding the problems of dating these sources as well as information available concerning the chronological relation of the various Buddhist schools to each other, see: a) for general discussions: E. Conze, *Buddhism: Its Essence and Development* (New York: Harper & Brothers, 1951); E. J. Thomas, *The History of Buddhist Thought* (London: Routledge & Kegan Paul, 1949); É. Lamotte, *Histoire du bouddhisme indien* (Louvain: Publications Universitaires, 1958); b) for more detailed discussions of specific problems: G. V. Pande, *Studies in the Origins of Buddhism* (Allahabad: Univ. of Allahabad, 1957); E. Conze, *The Prajñāpāramitā Literature* ('S-Gravenhage: Mouton and Co., 1960); E. Conze, "The Oldest Prajñāpāramitā," *The Middle Way*, xxxii, 4 (1958), 136-141; N. Dutt, "The Buddhist Sects. A Survey," *B. C. Law Volume, Part I* (Calcutta: Indian Research Institute, 1945); A. Bareau, *Les sectes bouddhiques du petit véhicule* (Saigon: École francaise d'extrême-orient, 1955); Walpola Rahula, "Asaṅga," *Encyclopaedia of Buddhism*, II, I (1966), 1-14.

[6] Māra most frequently encounters the Buddha through speech. In the *Sutta Nipāta* e.g., Namuci approaches speaking words of pity (*Namucī karuṇaṃ vācaṃ bhāsamāno upāgami*), Sn, 426 (SnH, 426). In the *Mahāvastu* a frequent phrase is "wicked Māra approached him and said" (*Māro pāpīyām upasaṁkramya vadayati*), Mv, II, 237 (MvJ, II, 224). Of the two passages just quoted the *Mahāvastu* phrase is most common throughout the selected literature. Very seldom are descriptive verbs of action or adverbs used to characterize the nature of Māra's speech. Generally it is what Māra says that indicates the tone or attitude Māra is taking toward the Buddha in each instance.

times.[7] In this text it is stated that Māra "had been dogging the Exalted One for seven years" [8] which the Pali commentary explains as meaning six years before Enlightenment and one after.[9] The nature of the occasion on which Māra challenges the Buddha also varies. In the "Māra-Saṃyutta" Māra approaches the Exalted One at Deer Park in Benares while the Buddha is addressing the bhikkhus.[10] On another occasion Māra appears when the Buddha is meditating alone at Rājagaha,[11] or resting on his side after retiring late in the night.[12] At other times the Buddha is surrounded by a great congregation in Jeta Grove or the village of Ekasālā,[13] or he is entering the brahmin village of Pañcasāla for alms when he encounters Māra.[14]

It is in this context of different places and circumstances in which Māra addresses or encounters the Buddha and other persons that the following activities are most appropriately understood.

A. Māra Reviles, Inclines Toward Sense Desires, Attacks

1. *Reviles, abuses, vexes, annoys*

In the *Majjhima Nikāya* the story is related about Dūsī Māra [15] who possessed (*anvāvisati*) [16] brahmins and householders who in

---

[7] Ling, *Buddhism*, pp. 118ff., has furnished a detailed summary analysis of the "Māra Saṃyutta," including a table listing the place, person(s) approached by Māra, the circumstances and the title or name given Māra in each encounter.

[8] SN, I, 122 (KS, I, 153).

[9] Ling, *Buddhism*, p. 117. Windisch, p. 205, notes that the later texts refer to seven years, the earliest texts to six years during which Māra dogged the Buddha. Windisch, p. 18 and p. 211, n. 2, says that in the texts considered to be later ones, the difference between the titles "Buddha" and "bodhisattva" (Pali: *bodhisatta*) was more strictly observed. The bodhisattva is one who is on his way to Enlightenment (Enlightenment being). The Buddha has attained Enlightenment. Hence later Sanskrit texts always refer to the "bodhisattva's" encounter with Māra during the six years before Enlightenment, whereas the Pali texts often use the term "Buddha" in referring to the same pre-enlightenment period. Cf. e.g., Sn, 408 (SnH, 408). Regarding the terms "bodhisattva" and "Buddha" in the present writing, they will be used interchangeably following the usage of the texts being cited.

[10] SN, I, 105, 112 (KS, I, 131, 141).

[11] SN, I, 106 (KS, I, 133).

[12] SN, I, 107, 110 (KS, I, 134, 138).

[13] SN, I, 110, 111 (KS, I, 137, 139).

[14] SN, I, 114 (KS, I, 143).

[15] Dūsī is the name of a former Māra. Cf. below, pp. 116ff. PTSD, "Dūsī," p. 328, relates *dusin-dusaka*, meaning "corrupting, disgracing."

[16] Cf. below, p. 93, n. 80.

turn "reviled, abused, vexed and annoyed" (*akkosanti paribhāsanti rosenti vihesenti*) [17] the monks. Those monks were of good moral habit and lovely in character, but the Māra-possessed brahmins reviled and abused them by saying "... these little shaveling recluses are menials, black, the offscourings of our kinsman's feet."[18] Such abuse not only characterizes an aspect of Māra's approach to the bhikkhus, but also to the Buddha himself.

When Māra draws near and addresses the Buddha his attitude is often reproachful and even abusive. In the *Saṃyutta Nikāya* Māra corrects the Buddha who has abandoned traditional penitential practices (*tapo-kamma*) by saying degradingly:

> Those penitential tasks abandoning,
> Whereby the sons of men are purified,
> The impure fancieth that he is pure,
> When he hath strayed from path of purity.[19]

Continuing in the role of defender of traditional ascetic forms of religion, Māra is represented as speaking through Baka the Brahma who is affirming a false view, and when the Buddha states as much, Māra denounces the Buddha by saying: "Monk, monk, do not meddle with this, do not meddle with this. For, monk, this Brahma is a Great Brahmā ... there were recluses and brahmans in the world before you [who believed in these views]."[20]

Elsewhere Māra the Evil One urges the Buddha to keep his supernatural knowledge to himself and warns him lest he be reborn in woe.[21] On another occasion Māra, after entering the householders of Pañcasāla who thereby refuse to give alms to Gotama, adds further insult to the offense by subsequently urging Buddha to go back again, for he, Māra, will see to it that Gotama gets alms.[22] Buddha in turn warns Māra of the bad karma or demerit that Māra is generating by such deeds; the Buddha's concern is for the future of Māra.

Māra often interferes with the peace and quiet of the Exalted

---

[17] Cf. PTSD, "Akkosati," p. 2: "Paribhāsati," p. 431; "Roseti," p. 577; "Viheseti," p. 643.

[18] MN, I, 334 (ML, I, 397-398). The allusion to "kinsman's feet" in the phrase relates to the brahmin theory of the origin of the four castes, the lower caste springing from the soles of Brahma's feet.

[19] SN, I, 103 (KS, I, 128). Cf. also Sn, 428 (SnH, 428ff.).

[20] MN, I, 326-327 (ML, I, 389-390). "Brahman" is equivalent to "brahmin."

[21] MN, I, 330 (ML, I, 394).

[22] SN, I, 114 (KS, I, 143). Cf. also BA, XV, 128 (BAC, XV, 160).

One. On one occasion, the Buddha was resting on his side after having walked about for the greater part of the night considering, mindful and deliberate, the idea of rising again. Māra approached him and addressed him in this verse:

> What! dost thou sleep? Now wherefore sleepest thou?
> What! would'st thou like a worthless hireling sleep?
> Deeming the house is empty dost thou sleep?
> What! when the sun is risen would'st thou sleep? [23]

This example of the vexing activity of Māra, together with all the other annoyances he causes, though they sometimes interfere with the peace and quiet of the Buddha's solitude, never succeed in disturbing his equanimity. Māra attempts to degrade the Buddha's teaching and wrong him with words, but these reviling activities of Māra do not succeed in annoying the Buddha or Arhats.[24]

2. *Inclines toward sense desires*

Many of Māra's discourses with the Buddha and bhikkhus are intended to incline them away from the path of Enlightenment back into the world of sense desires. Unlike his reviling attempts, these efforts by Māra compliment and extol the Buddha, but again from a basis of traditional religious and social values. In the *Saṃyutta Nikāya*, e.g., Māra urges the Buddha to become a universal king and establish a great empire of peace:

> Let the Exalted One, lord, exercise governance, let the Blessed One rule without smiting nor letting others slay, without conquering nor causing others to conquer, without sorrowing nor making others sorrow, and therewithal ruling righteously.

Then Māra continues:

> Lord, the four stages to potency have by the Exalted One been developed, repeatedly practised, made a vehicle, established, persevered in, persisted in, well applied. Thus if the Exalted One

[23] SN, I, 107 (KS, I, 134). Cf. also SN, I, 110 (KS, I, 138).

[24] E. Conze, *Buddhism: Its Essence and Development* (Oxford: Bruno Casirer, 1951), p. 93, gives this definition of the term "arhat": "The ideal man, the saint or sage at the highest stage of development is called an Arhat. The Buddhists themselves derived the word 'Arhat' from the two words 'Ari,' which means 'enemy' and 'han,' which means 'to kill,' so that an Arhat would be 'A slayer of the foe,' the foe being the passions. Modern scholars prefer to derive the word from 'Arhati,' 'to be worthy of,' and meaning 'deserving, worth,' i.e., of worship and gifts .... As a technical term in Buddhism ... it is restricted to the perfect saints who are fully and finally emancipated. The Buddha himself is habitually called an Arhat."

were to wish the Himalaya, king of the mountains, to be gold, he might determine it to be so, and the mountain would become a mass of gold.

To which the Buddha replies:

And were the mountain all of shimmering gold,
Not e'en twice reckoned would it be enough
For one man's wants. This let us learn
To know, and shape our lives accordingly,
He that hath suffering seen, and whence its source,—
How should that man to sense-desires incline?
(*Yo dukkhaṃ addakkhi yato nidānaṃ*
kāmesu so jantu kathaṃ nameyya) [25]

As the passage is written it suggests that the Buddha understands both suggestions of Māra, to establish an empire of peace and to turn the Himalayas into a mass of gold, as efforts "to incline (*namati*) man to sense desires." Wide is the spectrum, in other words, and numerous are the ways in which Māra encourages man's inclinations toward the pleasures and philosophies of this world and away from the path of the Buddha.

Unlike the previously mentioned passage in which the construction suggests that Māra's role is primarily to encourage man's internal inclinations toward sense desires, other passages imply more strongly that Māra acts as a causative agent who "entices" man away from the path of Enlightenment to sense desires. For example, in the parable of the herd of deer, the man who does not desire the good of the deer "might place a decoy and might tether a female decoy as a lure" to lead the deer on a "treacherous road" to a "low-lying marshy ground." The marshy-ground is a synonym for "sense-pleasures" (*kāma*), the great herd of deer is a synonym for

[25] SN, I, 115-116 (KS, I, 145-146). The verb *nameyya* is in the optative mood, third person singular of the active verb *namati* (bend down or incline). Hence the meaning of the phrase "kāmesu ... nameyya" carries neither a causative nor passive implication, and refers to man's inclination to sense desires rather than man's being "enticed" to sense desires from some external cause. As far as can be ascertained there is no Pali or Sanskrit term used in conjunction with Māra's activities which is equivalent in meaning to the Greek verb πειράζω, "to tempt" (putting to the test by enticement to sin). Windisch, p. 121, uses the German word "Versuchung" when translating the Pali term *upakkama* (going to, nearing, approach) as it occurs in a passage of the "Māra-Saṃyutta" (SN, I, 125). Apparently the context of the passage (references to the alluring enticements of Māra's daughters) determined his use of this German term. As the subsequent paragraphs above will indicate, there does appear to be some justification for such a rendition.

"beings" (*sattā*), the male and female decoys are synonyms for the "passion of delight" (*nandi rāga*) and ignorance (*avijjā*), and the man not desiring their good is Māra the Evil One (*Māro pāpimā*).[26]

These attempts by Māra to lure one from the path through sense desires are commonly portrayed by Māra's daughters (*māra-dhītaro*): Taṇhā (craving), Arati (discontent) and Ragā (passion),[27] who are usually involved in the two principal assaults Māra makes upon the Buddha, immediately before illumination to prevent his attaining Enlightenment, and four weeks after the Enlightenment to persuade him to enter Nirvana before having preached his doctrine. They come to display their bodies and use all sorts of feminine wiles in order to entice the bodhisattva from the path.[28]

In the above examples there is the implication that man's inclinations toward sense desires are not only promoted by Māra through suggestion, but also that Māra actively "entices" man as an external cause into the sense world. Upon interpretation of the various terms which suggest the latter meaning, however, all can be accounted for in terms of man's own internal inclinations toward the sense world. In the parable, the male and female decoys are synonyms for the "passion of delight" and "ignorance." Māra's daughters are "craving," "discontent," and "passion." The overall emphasis, in other words, is that Māra's role is essentially one of encouraging man's own inclinations toward sense desires rather than actively enticing him as an external agent away from the path.

This is also the emphasis in the Sanskrit literature. The *Mahāvastu* relates one of Māra's many attempts to promote worldly and "religious" values. The encounter occurs when the bodhisattva was still living a life of austerity. Māra says: "What wilt thou gain by this striving? Go and live at home. Thou wilt become a universal king. Perform great sacrifices ... [and] when thou diest thou wilt rejoice in heaven and wilt beget great merit."[29] Māra further urges

[26] MN, I, 118 (ML, I, 151-152). Cf. also DN, II, 262 (DB, II, 293); SN, I, 123 (KS, I, 153); SN, I, 128, 132, 133-134 (KS, I, 160, 165-166, 167-178).

[27] SN, I, 124 (KS, I, 156); Cf. also Sn, 835 (SnH, 835); Mv, III, 286 (MvJ, III, 274): "Tantrī, Aratī and Ratī"; BA, XV, 128 (BAC, XV, 160); "Arati, Rati, Tṛṣṇa." For a thorough description of the various references to the three daughters, grouped according to their role in the two principal assaults by Māra against Śākyamuni, cf. MPL, II, 880-881, nn. 1 & 2.

[28] Māra also uses the fisherman's techniques of casting fleshbaited hooks of "gains, favors, flatteries" (*lābhasakkārasiloko*) SN, II, 226-227 (KS, II, 153-154).

[29] Mv, II, 237 (MvJ, II, 224-225); cf. also Mv, II, 404-405 (MvJ, II, 360).

the bodhisattva to enjoy the pleasures of men, for "He who has sons delights in his sons" [30] and it forever remains a puzzlement to Māra why the bodhisattva has vowed to save all beings before entering Nirvana. Māra asks: "Why go on for the sake of other beings?" [31]

Thus Māra not only promotes traditional social ideas and religious ideals; he also questions the radical nature of the path of the Buddha. Aśvaghoṣa, in the *Buddha Carita*, sums up Māra's efforts to incline the Buddha to sense desires in the following passage spoken by Māra himself:

> ... O thou Kshatriya, afraid of death! follow thine own duty and abandon this law of liberation! ... this mendicant life is illsuited for one born in the noble family of the royal sage ...[32] be a king Tathāgata ... cherish thy father and mother, and delight Yasodharā,—possessed of a thousand sons and able to deliver the world, be successively the supreme lord of every world from Yāma heaven onwards.[33]

To which the Buddha characteristically replies: "I will go to my kingdom gradually, I will bring the world to perfect happiness".[34]

3. *Attacks*

Māra not only seeks to incline one to the sense world; he also desires to make the Buddha and his followers "feel dread and horror and creeping of the flesh" (*bhayaṃ chambhitattaṃ lomahaṃsaṃ*).[35] Māra effects many guises in order so to threaten the Buddha. He turns himself into the likeness of a King Elephant whose trunk is like a huge plowshare and tusks like polished silver, and draws near the Buddha to cause him to feel dread and horror.[36] Māra also

---

[30] Mv, III, 417 (MvJ, III, 418); cf. also Sn, 33, 34 (SnH, 33, 34).

[31] AP, XVII, 328 (APC, XVII, 123).

[32] BA, XIII, 108 (BAC, XIII, 138).

[33] BA, XV, 131 (BAC, XV, 163). Asaṅga uses a striking example of the type of inclinations Māra encourages: "when one who is occupied in engagement to the practice of staying awake in the former and latter parts of the night sinks his thought in the pleasure of sleep, the pleasure of resting, the pleasure of lying on his side—that is known as a deed of Māra" (SBW, *Studies*, 114).

[34] BA, XV, 131 (BAC, XV, 164).

[35] This phrase occurs most often in the "Māra-Saṃyutta" of the *Saṃyutta Nikāya*. Cf. SN, I, 104, 128, 129, 130, 131 (KS, I, 129, 130, 160-164). Ling, *Buddhism*, p. 122, notes that the same phrase is applied to yakkha in Udāna, 5. Cf. also Windisch, p. 200, n. 1, for a résumé of the use of these terms in the Pali texts.

[36] SN, I, 104 (KS, I, 130).

takes on the appearance of a King Snake whose "tongue darted from his mouth like ... forked lightning ...."[37] He causes a landslide of huge rocks [38] and an earthquake which causes so much noise one would think the earth was splitting open.[39] Such are the diverse physical shapes and deeds of Māra which seek to thwart the Buddha with fear.

It is Māra's attack upon the Buddha at the time of his Enlightenment, however, that best exemplifies Māra's efforts to make the Buddha "feel dread and horror and creeping of the flesh." References to Māra's attack upon the Buddha appear in both the Pali and Sanskrit selected texts, but the latter are the most elaborate in both description and emphasis.

The "Padhānasutta" of the *Sutta-Nipāta* sets the scene and refers to the battle in the following verses spoken by the Buddha:

> As by the stream Nerañjara I strove
> Self-resolute, in ardent musing bent ...
> ....
> Māra, high-mounted, legion-girt ... [enters] to fight! [40]

The *Mahāvastu* continues:

> Then Māra, in his chariot drawn through the air by oxen and horses, conjured up his host, including horses and elephants, and advanced to the Bodhisattva's noble seat. Mounting his chariot drawn by thousands of horses and carrying a dazzling bow, he uttered a fearful cry, "Slay him, slay him, quickly seize him."
>
> Terrible hordes of Rākṣasas, with the features of elephants, asses, horses and bulls, armed with clubs surged menacingly against the foe-slaying Bodhisattva.
>
> Some big-bellied snakes rose from the ground and cried, "Slay him, seize him"—a horrible cry of desperation. Others breathed snakes from their mouths, others fire, and others venom. Hordes of Piśācas carrying elephants rushed on foot to the assault.
>
> Some carried mountain-tops as they attacked the Sage. Other hordes of Piśācas rained down from the sky showers of hot embers. Others hovering in the air brandished wheels with blades on their rims. In the sky was the clash of weapons making a frightful thunderous din.[41]

---

[37] SN, I, 106 (KS, I, 133).

[38] SN, I, 109 (KS, I, 137); also SN, I, 113 (KS, I, 142).

[39] SN, I, 113, 119 (KS, I, 142, 149); other disguises include that of a bullock (SN, I, 112 [KS, I, 141]), ploughman (SN, I, 115 [KS, I, 144]), and brahmin (SN, I, 118 [KS, I, 148]).

[40] Sn, 425, 442 (SnH, 425, 442); cf. also SN, I, 103-104 (KS, I, 128-129).

[41] Mv, II, 411-412 (MvJ, II, 365-366).

The *Buddha-Carita* adds that Māra commanded his excited army of demons to terrify (*bhayāya*) the bodhisattva, proceeding with "various scorching assaults on his body and mind."[42] There was a wind of intense violence, the stars did not shine and the moon gave no light and a deeper darkness of light spread around[43] as the attack ensued.

But the bodhisattva does not lose his hold and the victory is his:

> The victory is the prince's. In the sky there were roars of drums, and shouts of "hurrah" re-echoed in the three worlds. The clear firmament was shaken when the Master won his victory.[44]

Māra's encounter with the Buddha is thus many-faceted. His method of diverting the bodhisattva from the path is sometimes characterized by subtle efforts to incline man to sense desires, other times by harsh accusations. Māra not only threatens the Buddha, he reviles and attacks him. Māra's approach to the bhikkhus and bhikkhunis is basically the same.

In general these are the activities that characterize Māra's encounter with the Buddha, and as such represent the Buddhist parallel to the Christian description of Satan's temptation of Christ. Both Māra and Satan have a common goal, to divert their opponents from the faith or religious truth which is such a threat to them. And just as popular messianic expectations played a role in Satan's testing of Jesus, so traditional sacrificial and ascetic forms of Indian religion provided a basis from which Māra challenged Gotama and his followers.

B. Māra confuses and Perplexes

One of Māra's most prevalent activities is his attempt to confuse and perplex (*vicakkhukamma*) the followers of the Buddha and even to "blur the vision" (Skt. *vicakṣukarma*) of the Buddha himself.[45] In the *Saṃyutta Nikāya* Māra draws near to Gotama, who is surrounded by a great congregation, in order "to darken their understanding" (*vicakkhukammāya*). Māra challenges the Exalted One in these verses:

---

[42] BA, XIII, 111-112 (BAC, XIII, 142-143).
[43] BA, XIII, 111 (BAC, XIII, 141).
[44] Mv, II, 413-414 (MvJ, II, 367).
[45] PTSD, "Vicakkhu" (plus *kamma*), p. 615: "making blind or perplexed ... darkening their intelligence." BHSD, "*vicakṣu*" (plus *karman*), p. 483; "making perplexed ... in order to make confused."

How now! why like a lion dost thou roar,
So confident before thine audience?
Lo! here for thee a rival wrestler stands.
Dost deem that thou has overthrown us all? [46]

Māra attempts to undermine the Buddha's confidence and thus cause the congregation of listeners to lose confidence and become perplexed. Elsewhere with the same purpose in mind Māra accuses Gotama of not being suitable for the teaching of others.[47]

In the *Mahāvastu* Māra tries to "blur the vision" (*vicakṣukarmāya*) of Gotama by saying:

> Unfreed, thou thinkest thyself freed. What meanest thou to say thou art freed? In close bounds art thou bound, for from me thou wilt not escape, O Recluse.[48]

Māra continually seeks to make the Buddha perplexed by challenging the authenticity of his Enlightenment. Not only does Māra challenge the Buddha by seeking to undermine his confidence, however. In the *Aṣṭasāhasrikā Prajñāpāramitā* (*Aṣṭa*), Māra seeks to blind (*vicakṣukaraṇāya*) the assemblies of the Tathāgata which consisted of "Gods of the realm of sense-desire and of the realm of form."[49] by conjuring up a fourfold army which advances toward them. This is an overt challenge by armed force to confuse and perplex the followers of the Buddha.

Numerous other activities of Māra could also be classified under the general purpose of darkening the understanding, although the terms *vicakkhukamma* and *vicakṣukarma* are not directly associated with these deeds.

Māra's efforts to promote popular opinions which tend to negate religious premises, for example, or his efforts to conceal the truth of religious teaching, can be understood as basically attempts to darken the understanding of the Buddha's teaching. Māra contra-

---

[46] SN, I, 110 (KS, I, 137-138).

[47] SN, I, 111 (KS, I, 139).

[48] Mv, III, 416 (MvJ, III, 417). Both Windisch and Ling interpret the significance of Māra's claims that the Buddha has not escaped his bonds as indicating that "Māra appears entirely unable to realize . . . (or) accept" the Buddha's immunity from him (Ling, *Buddhism*, p. 121; Windisch, p. 200). It is our opinion that the significance of these assertions by Māra points not to the ingenuousness of Māra but to the far reaching activities of Māra which seek to make the Buddha re-evaluate his own religious claims, i.e., "blur the vision" of the Buddha.

[49] AP, III, 78 (APC, III, 29-30).

dicts the Buddhist assertion about the impermanence of life by asserting a popularly held notion that life is long, that "there is no present coming on of death."[50] Likewise, Māra states that "no man is gladdened at life's decline," thus attempting to conceal by this apparent truth the noble truth of *dukkha*, that life is suffering and one is gladdened at life's decline.[51] Elsewhere Māra seeks to conceal the truth of the Buddha's teachings by calling into doubt recorded sayings. In the guise of a *śramaṇa*, Māra will say to those along the path:

> Give up what you have heard up to now, abandon what you have gained so far! ... What you have heard just now, that is not the word of the Buddha. It is Poetry, the work of poets. But what I here teach to you, that is the teaching of the Buddha, that is the word of the Buddha.[52]

Māra also promotes confusion of thought by causing misunderstanding between teachers and their pupils or teaching misinterpretations of the Buddha's teachings. The *Aṣṭa*, for example, states that Māra disrupts the relations between teachers and pupils, leading the student to misunderstand the teacher's actions or become disheartened over what he says.[53] Māra also causes "flashes of insight" to "come up in bewildering multitude" as the perfection of wisdom is being taught, which "make for confusion of thought."[54] Māra also falls into bad opinions (*kudṛṣṭigata*) such as maintaining "being" where there is only emptiness[55] and on the other hand promotes false understandings of the very teaching of "emptiness" (*śūnyatā*). The *Aṣṭa* relates how Māra appears in the guise of a monk and says:

> The same as space is this all-knowledge. It is a dharma which is not, it is non-existent. Who can anoint himself for it, who fully know it?

---

[50] SN, I, 108 (KS, I, 136).

[51] SN, I, 107-108 (KS, I, 135); Buddha's reply is: "Mourning ariseth through life renewed, and saddened is no man at life's decline."

[52] AP, XVII 328 (APC, XVII, 123).

[53] AP, XXX, 483 (APC, XXX, 202 ff.).

[54] AP, XI, 240 (APC, XI, 87).

[55] AKP, IX, 249; Poussin furnished the Skt. term. Apparently Māra himself is also deluded concerning the nature of his own domain. In the *Mahāvastu* Māra asserts that some of those "who dwell in my domain, though caught in the cage of recurrent birth ... escape the snare of death" (*mṛtyu*). Buddha replies that he is deluded for those in Māra's domain become "slaves of Yama" (Mv. II, 406-407 [MvJ, II, 362]).

> There is no one who could go forth to it, there is no one who could fully know it, nothing that should be fully known, there is no one who would understand, there is nothing that should be understood.[56]

Elsewhere Māra says "the Tathāgata has praised detachment, and that ... means that one should dwell in the remote forest, in a jungle, in mountain clefts." But such detachment, continues the text, may in actuality be contaminated by the mental activities, thus failing to attain the real quality of detachment. Such an exhortation as the above must be seen therefore as the deed of Māra the Evil One.[57]

Thus in the *Lalita Vistara* Māra is linked with heretics when the Lord is hailed as the "destroyer of the works of Māra ... (the one who) has overcome heretics."[58] In the *Aṣṭa* Māra is linked with factiousness and dissension [59] as well as attempting to encourage the reading of sutras which do not contain the full perfection of wisdom.[60]

Māra also engages in speculations (*diṭṭhi*) and conjures up deceiving disguises and visions, both of which have the same purpose in mind of darkening the understanding and misleading one from the path of the Buddha. Māra puts the following speculative questions to the bhikkhuni Selā:

> Who was't that made the human puppet ('s form)?
> Where is the maker of the human doll?
> Whence, tell me, hath the puppet come to be?
> Where will the puppet cease and pass away? [61]

Bhikkhuni Selā is not perplexed by these questions and replies with the Buddha's teaching of conditioned co-production which is a middle position between the speculative extremes of eternalism and nihilism.

By conjuring up visions and disguises Māra once again attempts to undermine the confidence of the Bodhisattva who has attained the stage of irreversibleness along the path, or, just the opposite,

---

56 AP, XVII, 331 (APC, XVII, 125).
57 AP, XXI, 391-392 (APC, XXI, 155-156).
58 LV, II, 12 (LVM, II, 24), i.e., "wicked Tīrthikas" (*kutīrthikā*).
59 AP, XI, 249 (APC, XI, 91).
60 AP, XI, 240-243 (APC, XI, 86-88). Sutras associated with the level of Disciples and Pratyekabuddhas, e.g., "although they teach Emptiness, the Signless and the Wishless, nevertheless they do not announce the skill in means of the Bodhisattvas."
61 SN, I, 134-135 (KS, I, 168-169).

cause him to be over-confident. Māra conjures up a vision of the great hells with many hundreds of thousands of Bodhisattvas in them and then says: "Those Bodhisattvas, described by the Tathāgatas as irreversible, have been reborn in the great hells. Just so you also, since you have been described as irreversible, will fall into the great hells."[62] Or Māra, "in the guise of a monk, or a nun, or a lay brother, or lay sister, or Brahmin, or householder, or mother, father, brother, sister, friend or relative" [63] will tell a bodhisattva that his name is one destined to be a Buddha and then the bodhisattva will feel conceit, a thought "more serious even than the five deadly sins."[64]

The *Saddharma Puṇḍarīka* and the *Aṣṭa* warn of an even greater deceit that Māra can effect, namely, adopting the disguise of a Buddha.[65] Such a possibility not only strikes terror in the follower of the Buddha [66] but can result in the most subtle and far reaching undermining of confidence in the Buddha among his followers.

Thus there is a multitude of ways by which Māra attempts to confuse and perplex the Buddha and the followers of the Path. Māra attempts either to undermine the Buddha's confidence in his own Enlightenment or make bodhisattvas over-confident about their eventual Enlightenment. Māra also promotes bad opinions and interpretative misunderstandings, disrupts relations between teachers and pupils, is linked with dissension and the propagation of inferior sutras and heretical teachings, conjures up visions and disguises, adopting even the disguise of the Buddha, all in order to "blur the vision" of Buddhists. Similar in nature and not to be too strictly distinguished from these activities are the obstructing and interrupting activities of Māra.

C. Māra Obstructs and Interrupts

Closely related to Māra's attempts to confuse and perplex are his efforts to set up obstacles (*āvaraṇa*) and bring about interruption (*antarāyam upasaṃharati*) in order to divert the Buddha or his followers from the path.[67]

[62] AP, XVII, 328 (APC, XVII, 123).
[63] AP, XXI, 338 (APC, XXI, 153).
[64] AP, XXI, 391 (APC, XXI, 155); cf. also AP, XXI, 386-388 (APC, XXI, 152-154).
[65] SP, III, 62 (SPK, III, 63).
[66] *Ibid.*
[67] BHSD, "āvaraṇa," p. 107: "hindrance, obstruction." Cf. MWSD, "antarāya," p. 44: "intervention, obstacle." BHSD, "antarāya," p. 39:

In the parable of the deer of the *Majjhima Nikāya*, previously noted, Māra is likened to the man who blocks (*pidahati*) the good road and opens up a treacherous one that leads the deer to calamity.[68] Another example, which appears in the *Mahāvastu*, relates how Māra attempted to obstruct the Buddha's way to plague-ridden Vaiśāli by filling the path with living things thus intending to prevent him from proceeding.[69] Nāgārjuna cites the three obstacles (*āvaraṇa*) which must be overcome if one is to escape the power of Māra and achieve the "perfection of giving," namely, not to think while performing an act of giving: "*I* am giving *something* to *someone*."[70] These illustrative ways of typifying Māra's obstructing activity are most fully elaborated in the selected texts of the Sanskrit tradition.

The *Aṣṭa* mentions a variety of obstructions which are perhaps less insurmountable than those involved in the perfection of giving but which are far more extensive. These are Māra's efforts "to prevent people from learning, studying, teaching and writing the perfection of wisdom."[71] Of what kind are these obstacles (*antarāya*), asks Subhūti. The Lord replies:

> The Bodhisattvas who teach the perfection of wisdom will understand it only after a long time. Or, after understanding has been generated, it will again be disturbed. Or they will write yawning, laughing, sneering. Or they will study with their thoughts disturbed. Or they will write with their minds on other things. Or they will not

---

"hindrance"; "*upasaṃharati*," p. 142: "... act or process of producing or causing." The distinctions between Māra's efforts to obstruct (*āvaraṇa*), confuse (*vicakṣukarma*), and fetter (*saṃyojana*, cf. next section) are not always discernible in the selected texts. The *Aṣṭa*, e.g., lists a number of undesirable events which occur in a bodhisattva's life and refers to them as Māra's attempts to "cause obstacles (*antarāyam upasaṃhariṣyati*) and confusion of thought (*kariṣyaticittavikṣepaṃ*)." Cf. AP, XI, 241 (APC, XI, 88). Likewise, translators often render the term *saṃyojana* as "obstacles" rather than "fetters." Cf., e.g., MPL, II, 702. These various activities, however, will be differentiated in order to further clarify the various characteristics of Māra's deeds.

[68] MN, I, 117-118 (ML, I, 151-152). Cf. above, p. 82

[69] Mv, I, 270 (MvJ, I, 224).

[70] MPL, II, 707: "C'est *moi* qui donne *telle chose* à ce *bénéficiaire*." Elsewhere Nāgārjuna cites as the three kinds of obstacles (*āvaraṇa*): "1. l'obstacle constitué par la passion (*kleśāvaraṇa*), 2. l'obstacle constitué par l'acte (*karmāvaraṇa*). 3. l'obstacle constitué par la rétribution (*vipākāvaraṇa*)." Although there is no explicit connection made between these obstacles and the activities of Māra, this enumeration follows directly upon a discussion of the "fetters" (*saṃyojana*) of Māra. Cf. MPL, I, 346.

[71] AP, XI, 248 (APC, XI, 91). Cf. also AP, XII, 254 (APC, XII, 93).

> gain mindfulness. Or they will write while deriding one another, or while sneering at one another, or with distracted eyes ... Or their writing will be in mutual discord. "We gain no firm footing in it, we derive no enjoyment from it," with these words they will get up from their seats and take their leave. Their thoughts devoid of serene faith they will think "we are not predestined for this perfection of wisdom," will get up from their seats and take leave. Or, because this book does not name the place where they were born, does not mention their own name and clan, nor that of their mother and father, nor that of their family, they may decide not to listen to the perfection of wisdom, and take their leave. And each time they take their leave, they will again and again have to take to birth-and-death for as many aeons as they had productions of thought ...[72]

What characterizes a good number of these obstacles put forth by Māra is their "interruptive" nature. While the bhikkhus study, their thoughts are disturbed, or after they achieve understanding, they are again disturbed, etc. Asaṅga thus characterizes the activities of the *devaputramāra* [73] as attempts to "bring about an interruption (*antarāyam upasaṃharati*) so as to swerve ... (a) person" from the path.[74] And the *Buddha Carita* refers to Māra as "the great disturber of the minds of living beings."[75] It is Māra who interrupts attentive bodhisattvas concentrating on the study of the perfection of wisdom or attentive bhikkhus listening to the Buddha's sermon.[76] Likewise, Māra is frequently known to interrupt the meditative thoughts of the bhikkhus. For example, Māra, "being desirous of making ... (bhikkhuni Somā) desist from concentrated thought" (*samādhimhā cāvetukāmo*), approaches and speaks to her and thus causes an interruption.[77]

Thus Māra's obstructing and interrupting activities which swerve a person from the path can range from merely trivial nuisances, such as "difficulties ... about gain, honour, robes, alms-bowl, lodging, and medicinal appliances for use in sickness" [78] to almost insurmountable obstacles which must be overcome if one is to achieve the perfection of wisdom and thereby escape the power of Māra.

---

[72] AP, XI, 232-233 (APC, XI, 83). Cf. also AP, X, 221 (APC, X, 78); AP, XXXI, 523 (APC, XXXI, 221).

[73] Devaputra (son of god) Māra has lordship over the world of desire (*kāmadhātu*). Cf. below pp. 111ff.

[74] SBW, *Studies*, 112-113.

[75] BA, XIII, 108 (BAC, XIII, 138).

[76] SN, I, 112-113 (KS, I, 141-142); SN, I, 115 (KS, I, 144); AP, XXX, 496 (APC, XXX, 209); AP, XXXI, 522 (APC, XXXI, 221).

[77] SN, I, 129, 130 (KS, I, 161, 162); cf. also SN, I, 119 (KS, I, 149).

[78] AP, XI, 242 (APC, XI, 88); cf. also AP, XI, 240-248 (APC, XI, 87-91).

D. Māra Possesses and Holds in Bondage

The most prominent example in the Pali literature of the possession of a bhikkhu by Māra is found in the episode concerning Ānanda's failure to urge the Buddha to stay on in this life another aeon. Several times the Buddha gave Ānanda the opportunity to request the Buddha to continue in this life, but "So far was his (Ānanda's) heart possessed by the Evil One" (*yathā taṃ Mārena pariyuṭṭhitacitto*) [79] that he failed to reply properly. Hence the Buddha announced that he would die within three months.

On another occasion Māra possesses a Brahma deity in an effort to rebuke the Buddha. Baka the Brahma was in a discussion with the Buddha. At that time an "evil wrong view" came to him and the Lord rebuked him. Then "Māra the Evil One, having entered one of the Pārisajja Brahmas" (*Māro pāpimā aññataraṃ Brahmapārisajjaṃ anvāvisitvā*),[80] rebukes the Buddha in turn for being meddlesome.

Direct confrontation with serious consequences seems to characterize the occasions in which Māra possesses individuals. Elsewhere, e.g., the story is told how Dūsī Māra entered (*anvāvisitvā*) a young man who commits an act of violence against the bhikkhu Vidhura by splitting his head with a stone.[81] On another occasion previously mentioned Māra entered (*anvāviṭṭha*) the brahmin householders of Pañcasāla and inspired them not to give Gotama alms, and Gotama is aware that this is the reviling work of Māra.[82]

---

[79] DN, II, 104 (DB, II, 111); PTSD, "Pariyuṭṭhita" (Buddhist Skt. "paryavasthita"), p. 434: "biassed, taken up by, full of." Cf. also Ud, 62-63 (UdW, 76); SN, V, 259 (KS, V, 231).

[80] MN, I, 326-327 (ML, I, 389); PTSD, "Anvāvisati" (*anu* + *ā* + *visati*), p. 50: "to go into, to take possession of, to visit." I. B. Horner translates this passage as follows: "Māra the Evil One, having entered a certain company of Brahmas ..." She notes that the commentary to this passage states that Māra "is not able to enter Great Brahmas or any priests of the Great Brahmas." Our translation differs based on the same commentary passage which reads as follows: "*Brahma parisajjaṃ anvāvisitvāti ekassa brahmapārisajjassa sarīraṃ pavisitvā. Mahābrahmānaṃ pana brahmapurohitānaṃ vā anvāvisituṃ na sakkoti.*" *Pārisajja*, *Purohita*, and *Mahā Brahma* are the names of the three Brahma lokas and their inhabitants. The term *ekassa* makes it clear that one of the Pārisajja Brahmas was possessed. The commentary then goes on to explain that Māra is incapable of possessing any of the Brahmas in the two higher Brahma lokas, namely the Mahā (Great) Brahmas and the Purohita (Advisory) Brahmas. I am indebted to Dr. Shanta Ratnayaka for this explanation.

Cf. also MN, I, 330 (ML, I, 393), and above p. 80.

[81] MN, I, 336 (ML, I, 400).

[82] MN, I, 334 (ML, I, 397-398). Cf. above, p. 80.

This type of possession which engulfs the individual's or group's entire mode of thought and action can be distinguished from a related activity of Māra which does not constitute possession proper though at first glance it would seem to be so. Māra engages in a tormenting type of activity when he "enters" (*anupaviṭṭho*) the venerable Moggallāna's stomach and causes severe discomfort.[83] Moggallāna recognizes that this discomfiture is due to Māra, and being so recognized, Māra "departs (*uggantvā*) through the venerable Moggallāna's mouth . . .".[84] This is the only example of illness being directly associated with Māra in the selected writings.[85]

The selected writings of the Sanskrit tradition do not characteristically speak of the possession activities of Māra. Nāgārjuna, e.g., in regard to the Ānanda episode, describes Ānanda's failure to reply properly to the Buddha as due to Māra's "obscuring" his mind. Nāgārjuna has Ānanda say (Lamotte's translation): "Māra me violait l'esprit."[86] More typical types of expression which characterize both the Sanskrit and Pali selected literature have to do with the bondage (*baddhatā*) of Māra or the snares (*pāsa*) and fetters (*saṃyojana*) of Māra.

The *Dīgha Nikāya* quotes Māra's command to his host who are surrounding the Lord and the Great Brahma: "Come on / And seize and bind me these, let all be bound by lust!" (*etha gaṇhatha bandhatha rāgena baddhaṃ atthu ve*).[87] The *Aṅguttara Nikāya* warns that

[83] MN, I, 332 (ML, I, 395); PTSD, "Anupavisati," p. 38: "to go into, enter."

[84] MN, I, 333 (ML, I, 396).

[85] For the most part Māra is not connected with disease either directly or indirectly. Wicked female yakkhas (*yakkhiṇī*) are regarded as harmful. They "eat flesh and blood . . . and devour even men . . . and corpses . . . [and] eat babies . . ." These could be interpreted as references to disease. Cf. DPPN, II, 676. Although yakkhas belong to Māra's army when he attacks the Buddha, yakkhas are not generally regarded as agents of Māra but follow their own yakkha king, Vessavaṇa. One passage which makes explicit reference to disease caused by "demonic agency" is obscure and Jones, Senart and Edgerton find no common interpretive ground concerning the passage: "There are two kinds of disease which are produced by demonic agency (*ārddhā*), *maṇḍalaloka* (disease restricted to a certain area) and *adhivāsa* (affects a whole district), (Mv, I, 253; MvJ, I, 208). Jones (MvJ, I, 208, n. 4) says *ārddhā* is identical in meaning to *amanuṣya*, "not human." He says "demonic is a convenient though not exact rendering." Edgerton disagrees with Senart's interpretation "produced by magic" but has no interpretation of his own to propose. Cf. BHSD, "ārddhā," pp. 104-105.

[86] MPL, I, 96.

[87] DN, II, 262 (DB, II, 293); PTSD, "Gaṇhati," p. 242: "take hold of, grasp, seize"; "Bandhati," p. 481: "to bind."

for a bhikkhu "womanhood is wholly a snare of Māra" (*samantapāso Mārassa*) [88] and "anger's loathsome form" which lurks in the heart is also Māra's snare (*maccupāso*),[89] as are false views.[90] Often it is the simile of a snare or hook that serves as the metaphorical basis to illustrate Māra's deeds. For example, Māra is like a fisherman using a fleshbaited hook (*āmisa* ... *balisaṃ*), namely "gains, favours, flattery" (*lābhasakkāra-siloko*),[91] or is the hunter who shoots the turtle with corded harpoon (*papatā*), i.e., lustful enjoyment (*nandi rāga*).[92] And continually does Māra tell the Buddha:

> Bound art thou in the snares by Māra laid ...
> (*Baddho-si māra-pāsena* ...)
> In Māra's bondage liest thou, recluse!
> (*māra-bandhana-baddhosi*)
> Thou has not won to freedom yet from me
> (*na me samana mokkhasīti*).[93]

In the Sanskrit tradition the *Aṣṭa* frequently refers to persons being "beset by Māra" (*mārādhiṣṭha*) or coming "under the sway of Māra" (*māravaśaṃgata*).[94] For example, one who opposes the perfection of wisdom, "Such a person is beset by Māra" (*mārādhiṣṭha*).[95] Or "if one is unpractised, has planted no wholesome roots, (or) is in the hands of the bad friend," he too "has come under the sway of Māra" (*māravaśaṃgata*).[96] Another common term used in the

---

[88] More correctly, "Womanhood is the all around (on all sides) snare of Māra."

[89] AN, III, 68 (GS, III, 56).

[90] AN, II, 52 (GS, II, 61).

[91] SN, II, 226 (KS, II, 153); and above, p. 83, n. 28.

[92] SN, II, 227 (KS, II, 154). Cf. KS, II, 154, n. 1, for explanation of *papatā*.

[93] SN, I, 105 (KS, I, 131). This passage appears in the section titled "snare" (*pāsa*). Cf. also SN, I, 106 (KS, I, 132). Other phrases of similar meaning are: SN, IV, 128 (KS, IV, 83): *māradheyya* (subject to Māra's sway or realm); SN, IV, 202 (KS, IV, 134), It, 56 (ItW, 158): *bandho Mārassa* (Māra's bondsman); AN, II, 52 (GS, II, 61), It, 50 (ItW, 153): *yogayuttā mārassa* (Māra's bondage).

[94] BHSD, "adhiṣṭha," p. 15: "permanently abiding," MWSD, "vaśaṃgata," p. 929: "subject to the will (of another), being in the power of, obedient."

[95] AP, VII, 184 (APC, VII, 60). It is interesting to note that it is this reference to "opposition" to the Perfection of Wisdom, rather than an earlier reference to "a counterfeit of the Perfection of Wisdom" (to arise in the future) which is directly linked with Māra's activity. Cf. AP, V, 112 (APC, V, 40). Other passages in which *mārādhiṣṭha* appears are: AP, XVII, 338 (APC, XVII, 128); AP, XXI, 338, 389 (APC, XXI, 153, 154).

[96] AP, VIII, 186 (APC, VIII, 62).

selected texts is *saṃyojana*, the "fetters" of Māra.[97] Nāgārjuna says that the reason Māra seeks to prevent a man from entering the holy life (*pravrajyā*) is that the fetters (*saṃyojana*) which keep this man from attaining Nirvana will be thinned out.[98] These fetters may range from "great inconveniences" (*ādīnava*) such as distress, pain and uneasiness,[99] to impure attachments to the world [100] with its good fortunes as well as misfortunes.[101]

Thus Māra not only possesses individuals and groups which often results in verbal and physical acts of disrespect or even violence against the Buddha or his followers, but Māra more pervasively holds in bondage the multitude of beings in the universe. Hence when the bodhisattva put the question to Māra, "Who art thou?" Māra replied boastfully:

> I am the lord who intoxicates (*īśvara madakara*) devas and men. The fair Suras and Asuras who dwell in my domain, though caught in the cage of recurrent birth, are overcome by intoxication, and, drunk with pleasure (*kāma*), escape the snare of death (*mṛtyupāsā*).

To which the Buddha replies:

> Behold how thou art deluded. There is no sovereignty for him who is afflicted by sensual desires. There neither has been nor will be. Of this I am certain.

Such persons, says the Buddha, should rather be called "the slaves of Yama" (*yamadāsabhūtā*).[102]

E. Māra Kills and Destroys

In the midst of a discussion on the activities and nature of Māra, Nāgārjuna posits a question very similar to the bodhisattva's question put to Māra, as cited above. Lamotte renders it as follows: "Pourquoi est-il nommé Māra?" The explanatory response is:

---

[97] BHSD, "saṃyojana," p. 538: "fetter." PTSD, "Saṇyojana," p. 656: "bond, fetter."

[98] MPL, II, 844. "Chez cet homme, les entraves (*saṃyojana*) s'amincironnt; il obtiendra sûrement le Nirvāṇa et grossira les rangs du Joyau de la communauté (*saṃgharatna*).

[99] MPL, I, 346. BHSD, "ādīnava," p. 94: "misery, evil, danger, mishap, wretchedness." MWSD, "ādīnava," p. 137: "distress, pain, uneasiness."

[100] MPL, I, 346.

[101] MPL, I, 345.

[102] Mv, II, 407 (MvJ, II, 363). Cf. above p. 88, n. 55. Suras and Asuras are classes of inferior deities.

Il est nommé Māra, parce qu'il enlève (*harati*) l'Āyuṣmat et parce qu'il détruit la bonne racine des Dharma du Chemin et des qualités (*guṇa*). Les hérétiques (*tīrthika*) l'appellent ... Kāmādhipati [103] ... Mais, dans les textes bouddhiques il est nommé Māra parce qu'il détruit [*naśayati*?] toutes les bonnes œuvres."[104]

It is because Māra "destroys" all good works, qualities (*guṇa*) and the root of the Dharma of the Path that he is called "Māra." The heretics (*tīrthika*) call him "Kāmādhipati" (lord of sense desire) but Nāgārjuna emphasizes that it is the destroying character of Māra's deeds that gives him his name "Māra." Māra removes (*harati*) "l'Āyuṣmat," a term which has several connotations. It is a respectful title for venerable bhikkhus and is a term which means "having life and vitality," thus a reference to one who is long-lived.[105] Māra removes (*harati*) a bhikkhu (*āyuṣmat*) from the Path by destroying his good works and qualities. Thus Māra is also called "le voleur de saints" (*āryacaura*) [106] as well as the destroyer of the root of the Dharma. But besides being called the "thief of saints", Māra is also called "death" (*maraṇa*), namely that which removes "life and vitality" (*āyuṣmat*). Hence his appropriate name is Māra, not Kāmādhipati, for he is more characteristically the destroyer and death.

The *Aṅguttara Nikāya* summarizes it in this way:

Who lives as Dhamma bids him never fails.
He presses on to find the truth, a sage,
He conquers Māra, death he vanquishes,
By striving he has reached the end of birth.
(*Dhammādhipo ca anudhammacārī*
na hīyati saccaparakkamo muni
Pasayha Māraṃ abhibhuyya antakaṃ
yo ca phusī jātikkhayaṃ padhānavā) [107]

Who conquers Māra vanquishes death (*antaka*) and reaches the end of birth (*jātikkhaya*). The term *jātikkhaya* essentially means "the destruction of the chance of being reborn."[108] Hence

---

[103] "Kāmādhipati," "Kusumāyudha," "Pañcāyudha" are the names given Māra by the heretics, all of which are epithets of Kāma. Cf. MPL, I, 345, n. 1.
[104] MPL, I, 345.
[105] PTSD, "Āyuṣmant," p. 106: "having life or vitality." BHSD, "āyuṣmaṃ," p. 102: term of address, "sirs."
[106] MPL, I, 345.
[107] AN, I, 150 (GS, I, 133).
[108] PTSD, "Jātikkhaya," pp. 281-282. Cf. also Dh, 423 (DhM, 423).

the "death" which Māra designates does not simply refer to "the event which terminates the individual life," as Ling notes, but "is rather the preliminary to inevitable further karmic existence."[109] Though death-dealing, Māra's purpose is to perpetuate continued life. Hence Māra sought to prevent Godhika from committing suicide, i.e., sought to prevent the termination of Godhika's life, because Godhika had touched temporary emancipation of mind and thereby vanquished death (Māra).[110] Similarly Vakkali's suicide escapes Māra's embrace.[111]

To conquer Māra's realm (*māradheyya*) is to pass "beyond the fear of birth and death" (*jātimaraṇabhaya*),[112] "beyond the Death King's (*maccurāja*) sight,"[113] beyond "death's realm" (*maccudheyya*) [114] altogether. Failure to dig up the roots of craving, on the other hand, allows Māra to destroy one again and again even as the river continually destroys the reeds.[115] Māra as death thus destroys the good works and qualities of the Path of the Dharma, he removes the Āyuṣmat, those who are long lived, in order to perpetuate continued existence with its repeated deaths. He who reaches full knowledge receives full life, i.e., relief from repeated death. Hence Buddha and his followers proclaim:

> Yon-farers over birth and death
> (*jātimaraṇassa pāragā*)
> Enders of ill will we become . . .[116]
> (*dukkhass' antakarā bhavāmase*)
>
> . . . .
>
> Those folk are they who have left death behind
> (*te janā maccuhāyino*) [117]

Thus the Buddha is the one "whom Māra at no time could overcome any more than the winds can overcome the Himalayas . . .,"

---

[109] Ling, *Buddhism*, p. 112.

[110] SN, I, 121 (KS, I, 149-150).

[111] SN, III, 123 (KS, III, 105).

[112] AN, II, 15 (GS, II, 15).

[113] Ud, 61 (UdW, 74); for *maccurāja* cf. also: Dh, 46 (DhR, 74, 75); It, 58 (ItW, 159); Sn, 1118 (SnH, 1118); for *mṛtyurāja*: Mv, II, 293 (MvJ, II, 244); Mv, III, 373 (MvJ, III, 370).

[114] Sn, 358 (SnH, 358); cf. also Sn, 1146 (SnH, 1146).

[115] Dh, 337 (DhR, 165); Windisch, p. 189, notes that the expression *punarmṛtyu* (repeated death) is older in the Brāhmana and Upanishads than *punarjanman* (repeated birth) and *punarbhava* (repeated existence), which suggests *punarmṛtyu* is a more basic characteristic of the concept of cyclic life.

[116] Sn, 32 (SnH, 32).

[117] It, 62 (ItW, 162).

for the Buddha is "the repeller of [the king of] death" (*mṛtyurāja-praṇudaṁ*), hence "the worlds of devas and men adore" him.[118]

As was the case with the figure Satan in the early Christian tradition, the figure Māra as destroyer and death epitomizes the various activities of Māra. Māra reviles, inclines toward sense desires, and attacks the bodhisattva in order to divert him from the Path and thereby disrupt the possibility of attaining Buddahood. Māra attempts to confuse and perplex the Buddha and his followers in order to darken the clarity of the teachings and confidence in Enlightenment. The interruptions and obstructions brought about by Māra which are intended to swerve a person from the path destroy the possibility of attaining to the perfection of giving and the perfection of wisdom. And Māra possesses and holds man in bondage in order to bind him to continued life which is under the power of death.

118 Mv, II, 241 (MvJ, II, 228).

CHAPTER SEVEN

THE NATURE AND POWER OF MĀRA

A. Plurality of Māras

1. *Māra devas: singular and plural*

When the question of the nature of Māra is raised, an important aspect of the meaning of the symbol Māra appears, namely, a plurality of Māras. In the selected Buddhist literature there are passages, more characteristic of the Pali canonical texts, which can be interpreted as references to a general, often unspecified plurality of Māras, while other passages, more frequently found in the Sanskrit treatises, specify four Māras and designate a name for each.

References to an unspecified plurality of Māras in the Pali and Sanskrit traditions occur most often in formula phrases. These conventionally worded formulas are basically shorthand references to the whole universe and are usually used as ways of amplifying the splendors and powers of the Buddha or bodhisattva. For example, when a bodhisattva issues from his mother's womb, there is an infinite and splendid radiance made manifest throughout the universe,

> including the worlds above of the gods, the Māras and the Brahmas, and the world below with its recluses and brahmins, its princes and peoples.
> (*atha sadevake loke samārake sabrahmake sassamaṇa brāhmaṇiyā pajāya sadevamanussāya*).[1]

---

[1] DN, II, 15 (DB, II, 12). The frequency of this type of formula reference, especially in the Pali, can be seen by the following list:

samārakaṃ: DN, I, 87, 111, 150, 224-225 (DB, I, 109, 145, 197, 289); DN, III, 76 (DB, III, 74); AN, III, 30, 342 (GS, III, 22); MN, I, 401 (ML, II, 69); MN, I, 179 (ML, I, 223); MN, II, 133 (ML, II, 317); Sn, 103 (SnH, 84); Mv, I, 330, 331 (MvJ, I, 277, 279); Mv, III, 254 (MvJ, III, 243); LV, I, 3 (LVM, I, 2).

samārake: DN, II, 12, 15, 127 (DB, II, 9, 12, 138); SN, I, 160, 168, 207 (KS, I, 200, 211, 265); SN, II, 170 (KS, II, 114); SN, III, 28, 59 (KS, III, 28, 50); SN, V, 204 (KS, V, 179); AN, I, 259 (GS, I, 237); AN, II, 24 (GS, II, 25); AN, III, 346 (GS, III, 244); AN, IV, 56, 173 (GS, IV, 32, 48, 118); AN, V, 50 (GS, V, 34); MN, I, 85, 143 (ML, I, 112, 184); LV, VI, 63 (LVM, VI, 101).

samārako: SN, IV, 158 (KS, IV, 159); AN, II, 9, 172 (GS, II, 9, 179);

Or it is said of the Buddha that

> Having realized more knowledge himself, he declares it to this world with its devas and Māras and Brāhmas, to this earth with its recluses and brāhmans, its devas and men. (*So imaṃ lokaṃ sadevakaṃ samārakaṃ sabrahmakaṃ sassamaṇabrāhmaṇiṃ pajaṃ sadevamanussaṃ sayaṃ abhiññā sacchikatvā pavedeti.*) [2]

These formula references may refer to a general plurality of Māras, as the translators have rendered it, although it could be argued that the general content of each passage suggests a reference to Māra in the singular.[3] This problem will be taken up later in this chapter.

In a number of Sanskrit texts there are more definite references. The *Aṣṭa* speaks of the great affliction that Māra the Evil One feels when a bodhisattva courses in perfect wisdom, to which Subhūti inquires: "Is this affliction confined to one Māra, or does it affect

---

AN, III, 54, 57, 148 (GS, III, 45, 48, 114); AN, IV, 83, 259 (GS, II, 48, 175); MN, I, 71, 72 (ML, I, 96).

other forms: It, 121 (ItW, 197); Sn, 147 (SnH, 113); Mv, II, 138 (MvJ, II, 132); Mv, I, 39 (MvJ, I, 33); SP, I, 19 (SPK, I, 21); SP, III, 63 (SPK, III, 64); SP, IV, 111 (SPK, IV, 115); LV, VII, 104 (LVM, VII, 141).

[2] AN, III, 30 (GS, III, 22).

[3] In each of the above examples the translators (T. W. Rhys Davids and E. M. Hare) have rendered the Pali *samārakaṃ* or *samārake* in the plural. Grammatically speaking, it is also possible to translate them in the singular, as the endings are accusative singular and locative singular or accusative plural. These endings are determined by their agreement in case and number with *loka* which is accusative singular in the second example and locative singular in the first. The ending does not necessarily determine the number; hence the legitimate differences in the rendering of this formula phrase by different translators of the Pali texts. I. B. Horner, e.g., translates *samārakaṃ* in the singular in ML, I, 223 (MN, I, 179) and ML, II, 69 (MN, I, 401), and in the plural in ML, II, 317 (MN, II, 133). Mrs. Rhys Davids translates *samārake* in the singular in KS, I, 265 (SN, I, 207) but F. L. Woodward translates it in the plural in KS, I, 211 (SN, I, 168), KS, II, 114 (SN, II, 170), KS, III, 28, 50 (SN, III, 28, 59), and KS, V, 179 (SN, V, 204). E. M. Hare translates *samārake* as well as varying forms such as *samārako, mārena*, etc., in the plural in his translations of the *Aṅguttara Nikāya* and the *Sutta Nipāta*. The fact of the matter is there are two types of references to Māra, singular and plural, and the grammar itself does not determine the proper translation of these formula passages, although the analogy of this Māra reference to *sadevakaṃ* (devas) could suggest that *samārakaṃ* should also be in the plural. Thus admitting the ambiguity of the grammar, Ling's thesis that these formula references are singular in number and that there is no other direct evidence in the Canon of a belief in a multiplicity of Māras (Ling, *Buddhism*, p. 96) is called into question. There is such evidence in the Pali Canon as well as in the Sanskrit tradition as the following section will illustrate. The problem is to determine the meaning of this type of reference.

many Māras (*mārāḥ*) or does it extend to all the Māras in the great tri-chiliocosm?" The reply is "all the Māras in the great tri-chiliocosm feel struck with the dart of great sorrow" when bodhisattvas dwell in perfect wisdom.[4] The *Mahāvastu* refers to "kotis of Māras" (*mārāṇa kōṭī*)[5] and the *Buddha Carita* refers to the Lord as the conqueror of "the kleśas and the Māras (*mārāśca*) together with ignorance and the Āsravas."[6]

In contrast to these references to an unspecified plurality of Māras there also appear, particularly in the Sanskrit sources, references of a more specific nature. The most precise and succinct examples of this type of reference are found in the works of Nāgārjuna and Asaṅga. The *Mahāprajñāpāramitāśāstra* states:

> Il y a quatre sortes de Māra: a. le Māra-passion (*kleśamāra*), b. le Māra-agrégat (*skandhamāra*), c. le Māra-mort (*mṛtyumāra*), d. le Māra-fils de Dieu (*devaputramāra*) ...[7]

The *Śrāvakabhūmi* states:

> ... there are four Māras (*tatra catvāro mārāḥ*), ... the *skandha-māra*, the *kleśa-māra*, the *maraṇa-māra*, and the *devaputra-māra*. The *skandha-māra* is the five grasping personality aggregates (*skandha*). The *kleśa-māra* is the corruptions (*kleśa*) that range in the three worlds. The *maraṇa-māra* is what fixes the time of the various sentient beings for death (*maraṇa*) ... (As to the *devaputra-māra*:) When someone is applied to the virtuous side for the purpose of transcending the personality aggregates (*skandha*), corruptions (*kleśa*), and death (*mṛtyu*), a "Son of the Gods" (*devaputra*) born in the world of desire (*kāma-dhātu*) who has attained lordship brings about an "interruption," so as to swerve that person. This is called *devaputra-māra*.[8]

There appear to be two different contexts in which these general and specific references to a plurality of Māras occur, one cosmological in nature and the other doctrinal. The cosmological context refers

---

[4] AP, XXVIII, 471 (APC, XXVIII, 195-196). Cf. also: AP, XXIV, 416 (APC, XXIV, 168), AP, XXVII, 447 (APC, XXVII, 183).

[5] Mv, II, 319 (MvJ, II, 299). Jones says this reference is to "Māra's followers." Cf. also: Mv, II, 408 (MvJ, II, 363), Mv, III, 273, 281 (MvJ, III, 261, 268).

[6] BA, XV, 128 (BAC, XV, 160). Cf. also SP, III, 63 (SPK, III, 64) and AKP, II, 119-120.

[7] MPL, I, 339-340.

[8] SBW, *Studies*, pp. 112-113. Cf. also: AKP, II, 124; SP, XIII, 247 (SPK, XIII, 275); Mv, III, 281 (MvJ, III, 269); SBW, *Analysis*, p. 105 and above, p. 92.

either to this "small universe" with its Brahma and deva heavens, the earth, etc., or to the "tri-chiliocosm," a system of a thousand million universes which extend infinitely in every direction beyond this small universe.[9] In such a context any reference to a plurality of Māras most probably is a reference to Māra devas of cosmological status like Māra the Evil One. The term "deva" is a "title attributed to any superhuman being or beings regarded to be above the human level."[10] The *Aṣṭa* clearly states a belief in a plurality of Māras, traditionally understood to be devas, throughout the tri-chiliocosm, and this may also be the meaning of the *Mahāvastu*'s reference to "*kotis of Māras.*"[11]

Whether or not there is belief in a plurality of Māra devas in this "small universe," however, is more difficult to ascertain from the selected texts. The commonly occurring formula references may or may not refer to a plurality of Māra devas in this universe with its Brahmas, its recluses and brahmins. It is most likely that the reference is to one Māra deva in this small universe, for a number of reasons. The composite legend surrounding the Māra figure refers to one Māra deva ruling the Kāmadhātu (realm of Kāma) at a time. If the formula reference is to a plurality of Māras it is possible to interpret this as a reference to the succession of devas who hold the title Māra, a title held by a single deva at a time.[12] Dūsī Māra is a predecessor of the present Māra, and his relation to the present Evil One is clearly established in the Pali texts,[13] the implication definitely being that there is only one Māra Pāpimā at a time. Likewise, the Pali commentary tradition as well as the Sanskrit tradition's references to the four Māras specifically designate only one "devaputramāra," the other names reflecting a different

---

[9] Cf. L. de la Vallée Poussin, "Cosmogony and Cosmology (Buddhist)," ERE, IV, 129ff.

[10] PTSD, "Deva," p. 329. Though devas are superior to man in the powers and pleasures they enjoy, they are inferior to man in their ability to follow the Path of the Buddha.

[11] It may also refer to "Māra's followers," i.e., the host of Māra that attacks the bodhisattva, in which case the term "Māra" is given a general usage similar to the term "demon" in the early Christian tradition. Cf. above, p. 48.

[12] Ling, *Buddhism*, p. 125, suggests "that Māra is an office which is held successively by beings who are of appropriate ... *karma*. As a personal being Māra has no eternal existence." Māra is a title; the proper name of the present Māra is not stated in any of the texts.

[13] Cf. discussion below, p. 116.

terminology and context. These reasons, together with the accepted traditional Buddhist view,[14] lead us to conclude that when the context is this small universe, the reference is to one Māra deva.

2. *Association of Māra with terms of analysis*

The other context in which the references to a plurality of Māras occur consists of abstract terms reflecting Buddhist teaching. This type is illustrated in the above mentioned *Buddha Carita*'s association of "Māras" with three doctrinal terms designating types of defilement: *kleśas* (impurity, defilement), *avidyā* (ignorance) and *āsravas* (depravity, passions). Even more directly this kind of reference is seen in the four-Māras formula of the *Mahāprajñāpāramitāśāstra* and the *Śrāvakabhūmi*: *kleśamāra, skandhamāra, mṛtyumāra* and *devaputramāra*. Except for the reference to *devaputramāra*, the use of the term Māra in this formula does not signify a cosmological deva.

The meaning of the term "Māra" in this context can be determined by an examination of the various Pali and Sanskrit passages in which this type of usage occurs. Sometimes abstract doctrinal terms are used as the names of the followers of Māra. At other times they are identified with Māra himself. Māra's daughters are named "Craving" (*taṇhā*), "Discontent" (*arati*) and "Passion" (*ragā*)[15] and three of his sons are "Confusion" (*vibhrama*), "Gaiety" (*harṣa*) and "Pride" (*darpa*).[16] Māra's armies are divided into two kinds and defined in the following way:

> D'ailleurs, la faim, le soif, le froid et le chaud sont l'armée extérieure de Māra (*mārabāhyasenā*); les entraves (*saṃyojana*) et les passions (*kleśa*) sont l'armée intérieure de Māra (*mārādhyātmikasenā*).[17]

The interior army is then described in detail as composed of:

> 1) *kāma* (désirs), 2) *arati* (tristesse), 3) *kṣutpipāsā* (faim et soif), 4) *tṛṣṇā* (cupidité), 5) *styānamiddha* (langueur-torpeur), 6) *bhaya*

---

[14] The commentary tradition refers to one Māra, living "in the Paranimmitavasavatti heaven ... like a rebellious prince in a frontier province." Cf. below, p. 111, n. 33.

[15] SN, I, 124 (KS, I, 156). Cf. also Sn, 835 (SnH, 835). For the Skt. *tantrī, aratī, ratī*, cf. BA, XV, 128 (BAC, XV, 160); Mv, III, 286 (MvJ, III, 274); also *ragā, aratī, tṛṣṇā*, MPL, II, 880-881, n. 1, cited above, p. 83, n. 27.

[16] BA, XIII, 108 (BAC, XIII, 137). Cf. below, p. 115, for reference to Māra's two virtuous sons, Sārthavāha and Vidyupratiṣṭha.

[17] MPL, II, 906.

> (crainte), 7) *vicikitsā* (doute), 8) *krodha* (colère) et *mrakṣa* (l'hypocrisie), 9) *lābha* (cupidité) et *mithyāyaśas* (vaine gloire), 10) *ātmotkarṣa* (exaltation du moi) *parāvajñā* (le mépris d'autrui).[18]

Fetters (*saṃyojana*) and defilements (*kleśa*) characterize the interior armies of Māra as well as the names of his sons and daughters. Hunger, thirst, cold and heat mark the exterior armies of Māra.

This type of language is also frequently identified with Māra himself. The venerable Rādha raised the question about the nature and power of Māra to the Buddha in this manner:

> Māra! Māra! they say, Lord. Pray, lord, what is the nature of Māra? (*katamo nu kho bhante Māradhammo ti*). Body, Rādha, is Māra. Feelings, Rādha, is Māra. Perception, the activities, consciousness, Rādha, is Māra. (*Rūpaṃ kho Rādha Māro vedanā Māro saññā Māro saṅkhārā Māro viññānaṃ Māro*).[19]

Here the Buddha identifies the five skandhas (personality aggregates) with Māra.

On another occasion near Rājagaha, in the Bamboo Grove, the venerable Samiddhi came to the Exalted One and asked:

> Māra! Māra! is the saying lord. Pray, lord, to what extent is there Māra or the symptoms of Māra? (*kittāvatā nu kho bhante Māro vā assa Mārapaññatti vā ti*)

The Buddha replies:

> Where there is eye, Samiddhi, objects, eye-consciousness, and things cognizable by the eye, there is Māra and his symptoms. (*Yattha kho Samiddhi atthi cakkhu atthi rūpā atthi cakkhuviññāṇaṃ atthi cakkhuviññānaviññātabbā dhammā atthi tattha Māro vā Mārapaññatti vā*).[20]

---

[18] MPL, II, 907-908. These ten armies of Māra are enumerated exactly in the same order in the *Padhāna-sutta* of the *Sutta-Nipāta*. The *Mahāprajñāpāramitāśāstra* list is based on this canonical text. A more accurate translation of *kāma* is "sense pleasure," which is just one aspect of *tṛṣṇā*, "desire" or "craving"; *lābha* is more correctly rendered "acquisition."

[19] SN, III, 195 (KS, III, 160). Rādha also asks: "Pray, lord, what is Māra" (*katamo nu kho bhante Māro ti*), to which he receives the same answer as above. Cf. also SN, III, 198-200 (KS, III, 162-163).

[20] SN, IV, 38-39 (KS, IV, 19). PTSD, "Paññatti," p. 390: "making known, manifestation, description, designation, . . ." F. L. Woodward (KS, IV, 19, n. 3) notes that the commentary explains *paññatti* as a reference to "the realm of Māra." The English term "symptoms" is an inadequate translation. *Paññatti* in this context means "command" and the question being asked is, essentially, what is the extent of the "realm of Māra's command."

Buddha then continues to list the five other faculties (ear, nose, tongue, body, mind), their objects, consciousness and things cognizable by this consciousness, all of which are identified with Māra and the realm of Māra. Such a listing, similar in purpose to the skandha references, is a scheme by which Buddhists analyze the whole of sensory existence to realize its non-substantiality ("emptiness"). Māra is identified with all of these analyzed aspects of samsara.

Likewise, Nāgārjuna in the course of a discussion on the nature and power of Māra identifies the five aggregates (*skandha*), the eighteen elements (*dhātu*) and twelve bases of consciousness (*āyatana*) with Māra.[21] Nāgārjuna attempts to summarize the many types of reference identified with Māra in the following way:

> Enfin, on appelle encore Māra les passions (*kleśa*), les entraves (*saṃyojana*), les liens du désir (*kāmabandhana*), l'enveloppement de l'attachement (*rāgaparyavasthāna*), les agrégats, les bases de la connaissance et les éléments (*skandhāyatanadhātu*), le dieu Māra (*māradeva*), le peuple de Māra (*mārakāyika*), les gens de Māra (*mārajana*) . . .[22]

Māra is here identified with all defilements (fetters, bonds of desire, i.e., *kleśa*) as well as with the skandhas, the sense-fields, the elements, the totality of the conditions of sensory existence. There is in addition the reference to the god Māra and to his followers.

These references which identify Māra with analyzed conditions of existence as well as with all kinds of defilements that lead to those conditions possibly serve as the theoretical basis for references to an unspecified plurality of Māras. The precise meaning of this identification of the term "Māra" with a plurality of conditions and defilements, however, needs to be clarified, as does the relation of this type of plurality reference to the conception of a Māra deva and his followers.

The *Saṃyutta Nikāya* provides us with a means of classifying these various references to Māra when it quotes the Buddha's answer to a question raised by Rādha. Rādha asked: "Pray, lord, how far is there Māra?" The Buddha begins his reply in this manner: "Where a body is, Rādha, there would be Māra or the things of the nature of Māra, or at any rate what is perishing" (*Rūpe*

---

[21] MPL, I, 343.
[22] MPL, I, 340.

kho Rādha sati Māro vā assa māretā vā yo vā pana mīyati).[23] The Pali term *māretā* literally means "that which kills, the destroyer," and *mīyati* means "that which is passing away or dying."[24] These two terms, like the word "Māra," are derived from the root √mṛ, which means "to die." The meaning of this passage then is as follows. Where there is body, or any of the five skandhas, there is Māra or "that which kills" or "that which is passing away." It is because there is *rūpa* (body) that there is something which is subject to death, namely, the body. Likewise, because there is *rūpa* (body) there is something which "kills" or "destroys," in the sense that *rūpa* is one of the many interrelated factors which eventually leads to or results in birth, decay and death (*paticcasamuppāda*).[25] Both these active and passive aspects of "death" are identified with Māra by the Buddha.

Beyond the specific meaning of this passage, however, the terms *māretā* and *mīyati* provide us with two broad classifications in which to group all the various types of preceding references to Māra, including those which refer to Māra as the Evil One, the cosmological deva of this universe. All conditions which are impermanent and subject to death constitute *mīyati*, that which is passing away or dying. And all defilements, fetters and interruptions that cause death are *māretā*, that which kills, the destroyer. Remembering that this is not a strict distinction, and that skandhas, for example, are both *mīyati* and *māretā*, the broad classification can still prove helpful. The conditions of samsara such as the skandhas, the sense fields, the elements, etc., could be classified as *mīyati*, that which is subject to death. Sense desires and the fetters of impure attachments to the world, and all other defilements resulting from a person's karma-producing activities can be classified as "internal *māretā*," that which kills. The references to the deva Māra and his followers, so prominent in the chapter on the deeds of

---

[23] SN, III, 189 (KS, III, 155).

[24] *Māretā* is an active verbal noun, and *mīyati* an intransitive verb. Windisch, p. 187, says of these two terms: "Die Beziehung des causativen *māretā* zu *Māra* ist evident, während *yo vā mīyati* das Wesen bezeichnet, an dem das Sterben zur Erscheinung kommt."

[25] The final formulation of *pratītya-samutpāda* (Skt.) in terms of the twelve links (or *nidānas*) is as follows: ignorance (*avidyā*), karma-formations (*saṃskāra*), consciousness (*vijñāna*), name and form (*nāmarūpa*), six (inner and outer) sense fields (*ṣaḍ-āyatana*), contact (*sparśa*), feelings (*vedanā*), craving (*tṛṣṇā*), grasping (*upādanā*), becoming (*bhava*), birth (*jāti*), decay and death (*jarā-maraṇa*).

Māra, signify another aspect of *māretā*, namely, a reference to some external causal agent, force, or event "that kills." It is external in that this aspect of *māretā* appears to lie outside the powers an individual has to control his immediate environment, such as the interruptions that occur in meditation and discourse or the great inconveniences (*ādīnava*) such as distress, pain, uneasiness (fetters of Māra) or hunger, thirst, cold, heat (exterior armies of Māra).[26]

Both the conditions of samsara (*mīyati*) and the internal and causative aspects that lead to bondage to samsara (*māretā*) are identifiable with Māra in that Māra means "death." As we have seen, the term Māra is etymologically related to the Pali *maccu* and the Skt. *mṛtyu* which mean "death." It has also been noted that the essential characteristic underlying all of Māra's activities is that of death and destruction, for which reason Nāgārjuna argues that he is to be called Māra and not Kāmādhipati as the heretics call him. It is this basic understanding of Māra as meaning "death," both in its passive sense of "that which dies" and its active sense of "that which kills," that Māra can be identified with the conditions and defilements of samsara.

In such identifications, however, the figure Māra as a cosmological deva, i.e., an evil personage whose activities are varied and extensive, is not being referred to. Hence there are no separate and distinct legends of a number of different Māras who are devas of this cosmological order,[27] though an inherent ambivalence results from the double usage of the term. Māra can connote both the proper name of a deva in this universe and the name of vast numbers of devas in the tri-chiliocosm as well as being a term meaning "death" and thus associated with all that is impermanent or leads to impermanence.

3. *Four-Māras formula*

The purpose of the four-Māras formula, apparently, is to clarify the usage of the term Māra as it came to be used in these varied

---

[26] In this context the "fetters of Māra" can be classified into two types: internal *māretā* such as impure attachments, and external *māretā* such as distress, pain and uneasiness, i.e., "ādīnava" which the BHSD, p. 94, defines as "misery, evil, danger, mishap, wretchedness."

[27] Cf. J. J. Jones, MvJ, III, 261, n. 3. Ling, *Buddhism*, pp. 66ff., cites the lack of several distinct legends about a plural number of Māras as evidence for his interpretation of the Māra symbol representing a "monistic understanding of the demonic."

ways in Buddhist thought. By specifying and designating each of the Māras with a name that characterized it, the general usage of the term Māra was summarized and the relation of a plurality of Māras to the figure Māra the Evil One was clarified. Of the four Māras,[28] the *skandhamāra* epitomizes all conditions of samsara that are subject to death (*mīyati*). *Kleśamāra* epitomizes the internal causative aspect of "that which kills" (*māretā*), namely one's own karma-producing acts of defilements. The *devaputramāra* refers to an external aspect of "that which kills" (*māretā*) seemingly unrelated to the products of one's own volitional life, and as the title suggests, this particular Māra is most appropriately associated with the deva figure of this universe, Māra Pāpimā.[29] Finally, *mṛtyumāra* (*maraṇamāra*) marks the essential character which is basic to all types of reference to Māra, whether in the singular or the plural, and whether referring to the Evil One (*pāpimā*) or to the impermanent conditions of samsara and the defilements that lead to bondage to samsara, namely, *mṛtyu*, "death" itself. "Death" is both the essential meaning of the concept *māra* and the essential character of all conditions and defilements of samsara. The whole of samsara is characterized by *mṛtyumāra*.

Asaṅga's explanation of the meaning of the four-Māras formula substantiates this analysis. In the *Śrāvakabhūmi* Asaṅga explains the meaning of the four Māras as four metaphorical values of death.

---

[28] That the numerical reference is "four" in the selected texts is not of significant importance in itself. The Pali commentary tradition often refers to 5 Māras: *kilesamāra, khandamāra, maccumāra, devaputtamāra* and *abhisaṃkhāramāra*. Cf. BHSD, "Māra," p. 430; DPPN, "Māra," II, 611ff.; R. C. Childers, *Dictionary of the Pali Language* (1909), "Māra," pp. 240-241. *Abhisaṃkhāra* refers to the accumulation of karma (cf. PTSD, "Abhisankhāra," p. 70), hence is simply a broader reference for that which is designated in the Buddhist Sanskrit tradition by *kleśamāra*, namely the internal aspect of *māretā*. References in both the Pali and Sanskrit traditions range from one, three, four to five of the above mentioned Māras. Edgerton says that there is sometimes reference to a sixth Māra, but apparently he has in mind not an additional name to be added to the formula phrase, but the name of a previous Māra deva, Suvarṇaprabha, of the same status as Dūsī Māra. Cf. above, p. 103, and below, p. 116.

[29] According to S. Levi in an article titled "Devaputra," *Journal Asiatique*, CCXXIV (Janvier-Mars, 1934) 1-21, the term *devaputra* in Buddhist literature took on the meaning of a reference simply to a male deva, and lost any special sense derived from its grammar, i.e., "son of god(s)." PTSD, "Deva," p. 330 says that the Pali *devaputta* refers to yakkhas but also is applied "to the four archangels having charge of the higher world," i.e., Yāmā, Tusitā, Nimmānaratī and Paranimmitavasavattī. BHSD, "deva," p. 270, renders both terms *deva* and *devaputra* as "god" and treats them as synonyms.

He identifies the *skandhamāra* as the tenement of death: "one dies among the five personality aggregates (*skandha*) that, having been born are present." The *kleśamāra* defines the "whereby" one dies: "one generates corruption (*kleśa*), and having been subsequently born [thereby] one dies." The *devaputramāra* is the "interruptive element" which prevents one from transcending "the true nature of death." The *maraṇamāra* (*mṛtyumāra*) is death itself. It is what "fixes the time of the various sentient beings for death (*maraṇa*) from the various classes of sentient beings..., the decease and passing away of sentient beings is cessation of the life organ; and death is precisely the intrinsic nature of fixing the time [of that]."

Hence when Asaṅga says there are four Māras (*tatra catvāro mārāḥ*) and lists the four (*skandhamārāḥ kleśamārāḥ maranamārāḥ devaputramārāḥ*), one could properly render the Sanskrit meaning in the manner of Wayman's translation: "there are four 'deaths,' as follows: the personality-aggregate 'death,' the corruption 'death,' the death 'death,' and the son-of-the-gods 'death.' "[30]

In summary, there appear to be at least two distinguishable types of reference in the use of the term "Māra" when it comes to the question of a plurality of Māras in the selected literature. Asaṅga typifies one usage, namely, a strict employment of the etymological meaning of the term *māra* itself. This usage seems to underlie the references which identify analyzed conditions and defilements of samsara with Māra, thus allowing for a projected plurality of innumerable Māras. This usage is also characteristic of the identification of doctrinal terms with Māra's family and armies. Yet there remains an ambivalence in this usage, for the very employment of the name "Māra" signifies another type of reference, namely, an evil personage, Māra the Evil One, who as a deva of cosmological status commands armies, has daughters and sons, is one in a succession of beings who have held the same position, and is one among innumerable Māras of other universe systems.

Apparently the purpose of the four-Māra formula was to summarize and clarify the varied usage of the term "Māra," thereby reducing but not eliminating the ambivalence of its meaning. Three of the Māras in this formula epitomize either the conditions of samsara that are subject to death or conditions which cause death. The fourth Māra, the *devaputramāra*, is a reference to a deva of

[30] SBW, *Analysis*, p. 105.

cosmological status who reigns in this small universe.[31] It is the nature and power of the devaputramāra that is of chief concern in the following sections, which deal with his cosmological status, domain, and followers. Though the possibility of a plurality of Māra devas in the small universe exists, only one Māra, the *devaputramāra* of this cosmos, receives attention in the selected literature, except for a few references to one of his predecessors, Dūsī Māra.

B. Māra: Chief of the Paranirmitavaśavartin devas and Lord of the World of Desire

1. *Cosmological status and abode*

The *Saṃyutta Nikāya* makes this reference to Māra's pervasive influence:

> The Three and thirty Gods,
> And gods who govern in the realms of shades
> They of the Blissful Heav'ns, they who rejoice
> In fresh creations, they who hold control
> Over what others have created:
> All they come evermore 'neath Māra's sway
> For all are bound by bonds of sense-desire.
> (*Tāvatiṃsā ca Yāmā ca | | Tuṣitā cāpi devatā*
> *Nimmānaratino devā | | ye devā Vasavattino . . .*
> *kāmabandhanabaddhā te | | enti Māra-vasaṃ puna*) [32]

Māra controls all who are bound by sense desires, including the gods of the various heavens in the Kāmaloka, the worlds of sense desire. In terms of fixing the cosmological status of one who has such pervasive influence, the various selected texts are not in total agreement. The tendency throughout the early tradition as a whole, however, is to classify Māra as Lord of the Kāmaloka which, in cosmological terms, belongs to the chief of the Paranirmitavaśavartin devas who occupy the highest heavens of the Kāmaloka.[33]

---

[31] MPL, I, 605. Cf. also MPL, I, 340.

[32] SN, I, 133 (KS, I, 167). Cf. also AN, IV, 239-241 (GS, IV, 164-165). The *Aṅguttara Nikāya*, AN, II, 17 (GS, II, 17), refers to Māra as "chief of those who lordship own" (*ādhipateyyānaṃ*) which is most likely a reference to Māra's position among the Vasavattin devas. *Vaśavartin* (*vasavattin*) means literally "having control over" (BHSD, "vaśavartin," p. 473). *Paranirmitavaśavartin* (*paranimmitavasavattin*) means "controlling (enjoyments) magically created by others" (BHSD, "Paranirmitavaśavartin," p. 319). Cf. also Ling, *Buddhism*, pp. 112-113.

[33] The definite cosmological position Nāgārjuna ascribes to Māra is not as clearly defined in most of the selected texts. Also the Theravādin and

Several Sanskrit sources confer this cosmological status upon the *devaputramāra*. Asaṅga refers to the *devaputramāra* as the one "born in the world of desire (*kāmadhātu*) who has attained lordship" (*aiśvaryaprāptaḥ*).[34] Nāgārjuna defines this lordship as being the "chef des dieux Paranirmitavaśavartin,"[35] and as such

> Le roi Māra [*mārarāja*] est le chef des six classes de dieux du Monde du désir ou Kāmadhātu ...[36]

The six classes of devas are:

> Cāturmahārājika, Trāyastriṃśa, Yāma, Tuṣita, Nirmāṇarati et Paranirmitavaśavartin.[37]

Māra is thus the "Lord of the world of desire" (*māraḥ kāmadhātvīśvaraḥ*) [38] which comprises six classes of devas as well as "the world below with its recluses and brahmins, its princes and peoples...." [39]

Sarvāstivādin schools differ from this Mādhyamika classification of Māra's cosmological status to a certain extent. The original difficulty apparently arose when it became necessary to place Māra within the cosmological hierarchy. As the Lord of all that is bound by sense-desire Māra is most appropriately classified as the Lord of the Kāmaloka (world of sense-desire). However, the established cosmological hierarchy with which the Buddhists were apparently working already had that position filled. "Vaśavartin" ("vasavattin") is the name of the chief of the Paranirmitavaśavartin gods, the highest class of devas in the Kāmaloka (cf. BHSD, "paranirmita," "vaśavartin," pp. 318, 473, and DPPN, II, 613, 844). The Theravādin commentary tradition, represented by Buddhaghosa, fused the two traditions by retaining the position of Vasavatti as the king of the Paranimmitavasavatti world and granting Māra the status of a rebellious prince controlling the subjects of a part of this world. The *Papañcasūdanī* (MA, I, 31) states: *Māro ekasmiṃ padese attano parisāya issariyaṃ pavattento rajjapaccante dāmarikarājaputto viya vasatīti vadanti* (It is said that Māra dwells in one part of that land [the paranimmitavasavatti world] just like a rebellious prince [dāmarikarājaputto] overpowering his own subjects and ruling a bordering section of the kingdom). The *Abhidharmakośa*, on the other hand, as a text representative of the Sarvāstivādin tradition, is conspicuously silent on this matter of the cosmological status of Māra. According to L. de la Vallée Poussin, Māra "has no fixed abode, no heaven of his own, in the official cosmology of the Sarvāstivādins," Vaśavartin being the sovereign over kāmadhātu. Cf. "Māra," ERE, VIII, 407. Poussin's statement, however, raises the question of the meaning of such references as "demeures des dieux du Kāma" in AKP, III, 170.

[34] SBW, *Studies*, pp. 112-113.

[35] MPL, I, 340. Cf. also MPL, I, 608.

[36] MPL, I, 605. Lamotte does not furnish the Skt. *mārarāja* but this is most probably what is rendered by "le roi Māra" which frequently occurs in the text: MPL, I, 341, 343, 433; MPL, II, 683, 707, 856.

[37] MPL, I, 405, 605.

[38] BA, XV, 130 (BAC, XV, 163).

[39] Cf. above p. 100.

Together these realms are variously called "Kāmadhātu" (realm of Kāma), "Kāmaloka" (world of Kāma), or the "Kāmāvacara" worlds (sphere of Kāma). And the king Māra is the chief of the highest class of the gods in the Kāmāvacara worlds, the Paranirmitavaśavartin devas.[40]

Concerning the abode of these various classes of devas and of Māra, Nāgārjuna says:

> La montagne du Sumeru contient les demeures de deux classes de dieux: celle des Cāturmahārājika et celle des Trāyastriṃśā. Le reste, résidence des dieux Yāma, etc., ... sont des terres formées des sept joyaux (*saptaratna bhūmi*) et causées par leurs mérites.[41]

Thus the abode of the Paranirmitavaśavartin devas is one formed from seven jewels, the result of their merits. The abode of Māra is described by the *Mahāvastu* as "covered with a canopy of jewels and crowded by throngs of Apsarases," in the midst of the mansions of the Paranirmitavaśavartin devas.[42]

As the deva who rules the world of desire (*kāmadhātu*) Māra can boast of "great magic, power, influence, majesty and splendour."[43] As head of the Kāmāvacara worlds,[44] Māra could boast of similar and even greater attributes than the lowest class of Kāmāvacara devas who comprise part of his deva host,[45] namely, the Cāturmahārājika devas who are described as

> virtuous, mighty, long-lived, beautiful, enjoying great well-being. They have the devas' span of life, their bliss, their sway, their retinue, and their form, voice, smell, taste, touch, garments and ornaments. The ornaments they wear in front are seen from behind, those they wear behind are seen from the front. They cast no shadows. They are self-luminous. They travel through the air, going wheresoever they wish. In the bejewelled mansions (*vimāna*)

---

[40] Wayman (SBW, *Studies*, pp. 114-115) notes that Māra as king of the Paranirmitavaśavartin gods fills a position which in Epic times in the general Indian tradition was held by Indra.

[41] MPL, I, 449.

[42] Mv, II, 360 (MvJ, II, 327); MWSD, "ap-sarās," p. 59: a class of female divinities (sometimes called 'nymphs'; they inhabit the sky, but often visit the earth; ...)."

[43] Mv, II, 268-269, 276-277 (MvJ, II, 252, 260).

[44] AN, II, 17 (GS, II, 17); cf. also LV, XXI, 300 (LVF, XXI, 257) and DPPN, II, 613, 618-619 for usage of the term "Kāmāvacara." For the association of "Kāmāvacara" with Cāturmahārājika, cf. BHSD, p. 227.

[45] For references to the "deva host of Māra," cf. Mv, I, 220 (MvJ, I, 175); Mv, II, 22, 286 (MvJ, II, 19, 269).

of the devas they have plenty of food, abundant meat and drink. They are endowed and gifted with the five modes of sensual pleasure, and disport, enjoy and amuse themselves.[46]

The same sort of description is given of the Trāyastriṃśa devas as well as being suggested of the Yāma, Tuṣita, Nirmāṇarati and Paranirmitavaśavartin devas,[47] each class enjoying the "maturing of their good karma."[48]

Hence Māra can say to Gotama, with disdain,

Thou art a human being, Recluse, while I am a deva; thou wilt not escape from me.

A recluse's body is born of a mother and father, is a heap of boiled rice and sour milk, is subject to rubbing, massaging, sleep, dissolution, disintegration and destruction; while my body, Recluse, is made of mind (*manomayaḥ kāyo*).[49]

Māra is a deva with a mind-made body, who in the region of desire (*kāmadhātu*) is, as the *Lalita Vistara* says, "le seigneur et maître (*adhipatirīshvaro*) qui exerce l'empire."[50]

But there is another aspect to this glory which is Māra's, for Māra, and his abode, and all else that is in saṃsara, "is impermanent, and liable to sorrow and change."[51] For example, "when the self luminous ones pass away from the realm of Cāturmahārājika devas, they are reborn in hell and in the world of brutes, ghosts, or Asuras."[52]

---

[46] Mv, I, 30-31 (MvJ, I, 25-26); Mv, II, 404 (MvJ, II, 360) refers to Māra as flying through the air, thus connecting him with the same kind of attributes.

[47] Mv, I, 32-33 (MvJ, I, 26-28).

[48] Mv, I, 33 (MvJ, I, 28).

[49] Mv, II, 269 (MvJ, II, 253); cf. also Mv, II, 277-278 (MvJ, II, 260).

[50] LV, XXI, 299 (LVF, XXI, 257). S. Levi, "Devaputra," pp. 14-15 defines *devaputra* (*deva*) as follows: "le *devaputra* est un être céleste, de type divin, mais qui ne possède pas intégralement tous les caractères de la divinité soit en degré, soit en qualité: Māra qui emploie ces pouvoirs au mal, Māra le méchant . . . tout puissant qu'il est, reste un devaputra . . . ."

[51] Mv, I, 33 (MvJ, I, 28).

[52] Mv, I, 31 (MvJ, I, 26). PTSD, "Asura," p. 89 refers to asuras as a class of "inferior deities" similar to nagas and yakkhas. Ling, *Buddhism*, p. 21, states that asuras are a more exalted class of evil spirits than yakṣas and piśācas, which are generally referred to collectively as an asura-host, and the idea of a fall from former glory is associated with them. In AN, IV, 434ff. (GS, IV, 291ff.) battles between asuras and devas are described (cf. also SN, I, 215, 222) which the PTSD sees as reflecting a fight between Gods and Titans. Hence another definition of "asura" as "fallen angel" or "Titan." There is an etymological connection between "asura" and "ahurō Lord, ahurō mazdā" of the Avesta, according to PTSD. The change of meaning from a good connotation to an evil one took place in India, according to

Like all else, "the devas are transient, unstable and subject to change."[53]

Hence Māra, the "Lord of desires,"[54] though an exalted deva of great power, majesty, influence and splendor, also experiences sorrow and dread [55] and is subject to death. The present Māra is but one of a succession of Māras. When Māra and his hosts "cut all the roots of previous virtue" [56] they are subject to reaping their own bad karma. The *Abhidharmakośa* recalls that

> Le Māra nommé Dūṣin [,ayant frappé la tête de Vidura, le disciple de Krakucchanda,] tomba, avec son corps même (*svaśarīreṇaiva prapatitaḥ*), dans le grand enfer Avīci."[57]

And Gotama says of the present Māra: "Māra hath generated evil force," i.e., produced bad merit (*apuññaṃ pasavī Māro*) [58] by assailing the Tathāgata. Thus a Māra is capable of acquiring bad karma, i.e., demerit, and the fruits of his grave acts against the Buddha and his disciples will ripen.

Yet the future of Māra and his hosts is not eternally bleak no more than their glory as devas is permanently secure. The *Mahāvastu* notes that "the Bodhisattva saw in Māra's host many who had the roots of virtue...."[59] Two of Māra's own sons, Sārthavāha and Vidyupratiṣṭha, are well disposed toward the Bodhisattva. The former seeks to dissuade Māra from attacking the bodhisattva [60]

A. B. Keith, *Religion and Philosophy of the Vedas* (Cambridge: Harvard University Press, 1925), pp. 231ff.

In the selected literature there is no reference in which Māra is called an asura. Ling, *Buddhism*, p. 98, notes that the name Namuci occurs among a list of asuras in DN, II, 259 (DB, II, 289). After examining the passage Ling concludes that this reference "is evidence of a tradition which regarded Namuci as another spirit-being originally separate from Māra, a tradition having its roots in Indian mythology."

[53] Mv, I, 31 (MvJ, I, 26).

[54] LV, XI, 130 (LVM, XI, 191).

[55] MPL, I, 433; cf. below, pp. 122ff.

[56] LV, XXI, 300 (LVF, XXI, 257).

[57] AKP, III, 41. Cf. also MN, I, 338 (ML, I, 401) and above, p. 93. In Mv, III, 26 (MvJ, III, 25) there is a jataka-type reference to a previous life of Māra as a king.

[58] KS, I, 143 (SN, I, 114).

[59] Mv, II, 315 (MvJ, II, 295).

[60] Mv, II, 327, 330 (MvJ, II, 304-305). In LV, V, 44 (LVM, V, 78) Sārthavāha considers accompanying the bodhisattva in his descent from Tuṣita as "It would be unbecoming and ungraceful in us, ... to allow the Bodhisattva to depart alone without a second." Cf. also BHSD, "Sārthavāha," p. 593, for further references.

and the other, "moved by noble impulse," gives the Lord garments and extols him.[61] As for the future possibilities of Māra himself, Dūsī Māra provides an excellent illustration. Dūsī Māra, the previous Māra who went to Avici Hell, became a great disciple of the Buddha. In the *Majjhima Nikāya*, Moggallāna, a great disciple of the Buddha, identifies himself as being one and the same Dūsī Māra in a former existence. Mogallāna addresses Māra:

> Once upon a time, I, Evil One, was the Māra called Dūsin; as such Kāḷī was the name of my sister, you were her son, thus you were my nephew.
> (*Bhūtapubbāhaṁ pāpima Dūsī nāma māro ahosiṁ, tassa me Kāḷī nāma bhaginī, tassā tvaṁ putto, so me tvaṁ bhāgineyyo hosi*).[62]

That this is a possibility suggests that though Māra "cut(s) all the roots of previous virtue" [63] one who becomes Māra may also become in the future a figure as great as Moggallāna. It is perhaps due to the extreme nature of both possibilities, a Māra and a Moggallāna, that, given the Indian attitude toward women, "it is impossible, it cannot come to pass, that a woman could be a Sakka ... a Māra ... a Brahmā."[64] Such extremes only men are capable of becoming!

Thus the descriptive metaphors which characterize Māra's position in Buddhist cosmology are frequently words denoting splendor and majesty. Very seldom are terms such as "darkness" associated with Māra and his realm,[65] except in descriptive passages of Māra's defeat by the bodhisattva or in passages which seek to extol the light of Enlightenment. The *Mahāvastu*, e.g., refers to the realms of Māra being "eclipsed" and "rendered lustreless and joyless" when a Buddha or a follower achieves Enlightenment.[66]

---

[61] Mv, II, 337-338 (MvJ, II, 310).

[62] MN, I, 333 (ML, I, 396).

[63] LV, XXI, 300 (LVF, XXI, 257).

[64] MN, III, 66 (ML, III, 109); cf. also MPL, I, 134: a woman cannot become a "Māra devarāja"; also AN, I, 28 (GS, I, 26): "That a woman should become a Sakka, a Māra, a Brahmā is a thing impossible. But a man may be."

[65] The chief exception to this is found in the association of "smokiness" and "murkiness" to Māra in SN, I, 122 (KS, I, 152); SN, III, 123 (KS, III, 105). PTSD, "Deva," p. 329, says of the term Deva that it always implies "splendour ... and mobility, beauty, goodness and light, and as such [implies opposition] ... to the dark powers of mischief and destruction (asurā ... petā ... and beings in Niraya [hell])." These connotations are not lost in Buddhist references to "Māra deva."

[66] Mv, I, 41, 230, 240 (MvJ, I, 36, 186, 196). For contrasts of Māra's realm with the light of Enlightenment, cf. SN, I, 113 (KS, I, 142); Ud, 3 (UdW, 3); It, 51 (ItW, 153).

When the epithet "Kaṇha" (Dark One) is applied to Māra, the connotation is principally a moral one, i.e., evil doings, dark deeds. When Dūsī Māra struck the monk, e.g., the Lord's reply was: "Dark One (*Kaṇha*), for striking such a monk you go to suffering."[67] The lustre and joy of the Kāmāvacara worlds and the various classes of devas, rather than the darkness of such a realm, is the basic emphasis in the cosmological descriptions of Māra as the chief of the Paranirmitavaśavartin devas.

2. *Māra's host*

Among the different kinds of assemblies of being in the Kāma worlds (*kāmaloka*),[68] there is a prominent mention of Māra's assemblies (*māra parisā*).[69] Included in Māra's host, according to the *Saddharma Puṇḍarīka*, are the sons of Māra (*māra putrā*), Māra's host of devaputras (*māra-kāyika devaputra*), the daughters of Māra (*māra kanyā*), the followers of Māra (*māra parṣad*) and all other servitors to Māra (*māra pariyuṭṭhito*).[70]

Mention has already been made of members of Māra's family.

[67] MN, I, 337-338 (ML, I, 401ff.).

[68] The *Dīgha Nikāya* (DN, III, 260 [DB, III, 241]) lists the following eight assemblies (*parisā*): "those of nobles, brahmins, householders, religious orders, four-king devas, Three-and-Thirty devas, Māra devas (*māra-parisā*) and Brahma devas." All these assemblies except the Brahma devas belong to the Kāmaloka. The Brahma devas belong to the Rupaloka. Buddhaghosa's explanation of a *Majjhima Nikāya* (MN, I, 72 [ML, I, 97, n. 2]) reference to *māra parisā* is that the meaning is "not (assemblies) of Māras, but an occasion when those in Māra's retinue gather together" (MA, II, 28): "*Mārakāyikā-naṃpana sannipatitvā nisinnaṭṭhānaṃ Māraparisā ti veditabbā; na Mārā-naṃ.*" Ling, *Buddhism*, pp. 97-101, also emphasizes that *mārā parisā* should not be thought of as "assemblies of Māras" but as a conception similar to *mārasena*, the Māra army which is composed of "Agents of Māra," not a plurality of Māras. Ling says: "The beings who compose this assembly or army are ... not thought of as having any identity apart from being agents of Māra; it is the figure of Māra which predominates," and Māra himself is clearly regarded as singular.

[69] In addition to the instances where the Pali phrase *māra parisā* occurs, as cited in n. 68, there are a variety of related Sanskrit phrases: *māra-parisā*: Mv, II, 315 (MvJ, II, 295); *māra gaṇā* (hosts of Māra): Mv, I, 200 (MvJ, I, 159); Mv, II, 4 (MvJ, II, 4); *mārakāyika devatā* (deva host of Māra): Mv, II, 286 (MvJ, II, 269), where it is translated "angels called Mārakāyikas"; SP, XXII, 350 (SPK, XXII, 391-392); AP, III, 49 (APC, III, 22), AP, XXV, 425 (APC, XXV, 172); *mārādhishṭa* (partisans of Māra); AP, XXVI, 436 (APC, XXVI, 178) and above, p. 102; *māraparṣadaḥ* (followers of Māra): LV, XXI, 300 (LVF, XXI, 257), and others quoted from the *Saddharma Puṇḍarīka* in the next sentence of the text above.

[70] SP, XXVI, 385 (SPK, XXVI, 433). LV, XXI, 301 (LVF, XXI, 258) adds Māra's wives.

Māra's daughters have a prominent role in Māra's efforts to entice the bodhisattva from the path. Māra's two virtuous sons, on the other hand, were well disposed toward the bodhisattva, whereas his other three sons are personifications of specific fetters and defilements according to Buddhist doctrine. Reference has been made to the six classes of devas who comprise Māra's host of devaputras, Māra being the Chief of the Paranirmitavaśavartin devas, the highest class of devas in the Kāmāvacara worlds. Note has also been made of the interior and exterior armies of Māra which are essentially listings of various fetters (*saṃyojana*) and defilements (*kleśa*). There is another prominent type of reference to Māra's army, however, which portrays them not as abstract personifications, but as various types of beings who are the followers and servitors of Māra.[71]

In this type of reference Māra is conceived as the great general (*mahā-sena*) who is often described as riding into battle "ready mounted upon his elephant" (*māraṃ savāhanaṃ*) [72] surrounded by his dark hosts (*kaṇha-senaṃ*),[73] the hosts of death (*maccuno senaṃ*).[74] With a "thousand warlike crests the armed hordes of Piśācas, with many a Rākṣasa and many a Yakṣa,"[75] approach the bodhisattva.

---

[71] References to *mārasena* of this type are numerous: DN, II, 261 (DB, II, 293); SN, I, 112 (KS, I, 141); SN, V, 99 (KS, V, 83); Ud, 3 (UdW, 3); Sn. 436-439, 442 (SnH, 436-439, 442); Mv, II, 329 (MvJ, II, 305); SP, VI, 131 (SPK, VI, 143); SP, VI, 143 (SPK, VII, 155); LV, VII, 85 (LVM, VII, 125); MPL, I, 12, 127, 162, 213, 228, 229; MPL, II, 1070. Cf. also *mārakalicakraṃ* (sphere of the wicked Māra): SP, XXVI, 389 (SPK, XXVI, 438-439), cited above, p. 76. Apparently Māra's hosts of devaputras (*māra kāyikāḥ devaputraḥ*) are not active participants in the battle as they are not listed among the members of Māra's army. In addition, their loyalty to Māra is lost in Māra's defeat. At least this is implied in the *Lalita Vistara* passage which describes Māra's vision of his own defeat. Besides seeing himself covered with dust, his palaces collapsing, etc., those "qui sont les chefs des dieux Kāmāvatcharas, tels que Dhrītarāchtra, Viroūṭhaka, Viroūpākcha, Vāiśravaṇa, Śakra, Souyāma, Santouchita, Sounirmita, Vasavartin et les autres, le démon Pāpīyān les vit tous le visage tourné vers le Bōdhisattva et prêts à le servir" (LV, XXI, 303 [LVF, XXI, 259]).

[72] Sn, 442 (SnH, 442), following the rendering by Ling, *Buddhism*, p. 147. Hare translates the phrase more strictly given the context: "Māra, high mounted, legion-girt." Cf. also AN, II, 15, 18 (GS, II, 15, 18); SN, II, 278, 285 (KS, II, 188, 195); It, 153 (ItW, 153).

[73] DN, II, 261-262 (DB, II, 293).

[74] SN, I, 122 (KS, I, 152).

[75] Mv, II, 407-408 (MvJ, II, 363). LV, XXI, 302, 308 (LVF, XXI, 259, 263) adds in addition to Yakṣas and Rākṣasa, "Koumbhāṇḍas et Gandharbas" and "Mahōragas, Prētas."

The demon chief of the army, says the *Lalita Vistara*, is named "Siṃhahanu" [76] and the armies he commands "occupaient en entien les trois mille mondes."[77] The description of Māra's army in the *Lalita Vistara* is long and elaborate:

> le démon Pāpīyān ... fit préparer sa grande armée de quatre corps de troupes, très forte et vaillante dans le combat, formidable, faisant dresser les chevaux, comme les dieux et les hommes n'en avaient pas vu auparavant ni entendu parler; douée de la faculté de changer diversement de visage et de se transformer de cent millions de manières; ayant les mains, les pieds et le corps enveloppés dans les replis de cent mille serpents; tenant des épées, des arcs, des flèches, des piques, des masses, des haches, des fusées, des pilons, des bâtons, des chaînes, des massues, des disques, des foudres; ayant le corps protégé par d'excellentes cuirasses ... Quelques-uns vomissaient du venin de serpent, et quelques-uns, après avoir pris, avec leurs mains, du venin de serpent, le mangeaient ... quelques-uns, portant des montagnes enflammées, s'approchaient fièrement, montés sur d'autres montagnes enflammées. Quelques-uns, après avoir arraché un arbre avec ses racines, accouraient vers le Bôdhisattva.... Quelques-uns, dans leur désir de boire du sang, se coupaient la tête l'un à l'autre; quelques-uns, avec des voix rauques, entrecoupées, altérées, effrayantes, faisaient entendre des grognements tels que: houm houm! pitchout! houlou, houlou! Quelques-uns disaient: empoignez, empoignez! frappez, frappez! liez! saisissez! coupez! brisez! broyez! arrachez! anéantissez le Śramaṇa Gâutama avec l'arbre! [78]

Thus is the fearful host of Māra described as Māra prepared to protect his command over the world of desire.

C. Māra's Realm and Power

Though *devaputramāra* is the Lord of the world of desire (*māraḥ kāmadhātvīśvaraḥ*), being Chief of the highest class of devas in the Kāmaloka, Māra's realm (*māradheyyaṃ*) which is death's realm (*maccudheyyaṃ*) extends beyond the Kāmaloka to the Rūpa and Arūpa worlds.

In the *Majjhima Nikāya* the Lord warns his hearers not to put faith in

> any recluses or brahmans who are unskilled about this world, unskilled about the world beyond, unskilled about Māra's realm

---

[76] LV, XXI, 303 (LVF, XXI, 259).
[77] LV, XXI, 305 (LVF, XXI, 261).
[78] LV, XXI, 305-307 (LVF, XXI, 261-263).

> (*māradheyyaṃ*), unskilled about what is not Māra's realm, unskilled about Death's realm (*maccudheyyaṃ*), unskilled about what is not Death's realm.[79]

The worlds beyond the Kāmaloka consist of the Rūpaloka and Arūpaloka. The higher stages of existence belong to Māra's realm because wherever there is the "fear of birth and death" there is Māra's realm:

> By right exertion they have conquered Māra's realm (*māradheyya*). Freed, they have passed beyond the fear of birth and death (*jātimaraṇa bhayassa pāragū*).[80]

Likewise, it is said of Māra's army that they can hunt and seek "in every sphere of life" (*sabbaṭṭhānesu*).[81] The entire "triple world is assailed by Māra, the Evil one."[82] The whole substrata of rebirth and death, in other words, are within Māra's domain and only "when every base of rebirth is abolished utterly,"[83] when one is freed from becoming again (*punabbhavo*), then is Māra beaten (*abhibhūto Māro*).[84]

Though all "who drift along life's stream" have gone to Māra's realm (*māradheyyānupanna*),[85] the most predominant sphere of Māra's influence is in the Kāmaloka.

> Those pleasures of the sense that are here and now, [and hereafter] ... and those perceptions of pleasures of the senses that are here and now [and hereafter] ... both [the sense pleasures and the perception of them] are Māra's realm (*māradheyyaṃ*); this is Māra's sphere (*Mārass'esa visayo*), this is Māra's crop (*Mārass'esa nivāpo*), this is Māra's pasturage (*Mārass'esa gocaro*).[86]

---

[79] MN, I, 225 (ML, I, 277). The commentary translated by Buddhaghosa (MA, II, 222) says concerning *māradheyyaṃ*: "*Māradheyyaṃ vuccati tebhūmakadhammā ... Maccudheyyaṃ pi tebhūmaka dhammā va.*" The term *tebhūmakadhamma*, which Buddhaghosa applies to both Māra's realm and Death's realm, "refers to the three stages of being, the kāma, rūpa, arūpa existences." Cf. PTSD, "Te," p. 306.

[80] AN, II, 15 (GS, II, 15). E. B. Cowell says that "Māra rules the four heavens from the Yāma to the Paranirmitavaśavartin, Mahābrahman [and] the twenty Brahmalokas above them" (BAC, XV, 163, n. 1).

[81] SN, I, 112 (KS, I, 141).

[82] SP, XIII, 247 (SPK, XIII, 275).

[83] SN, I, 107 (KS, I, 134-135).

[84] Ud, 33 (UdW, 40). Woodward's translation of *punabbhavo* is "no more reborn." Cf. also Ud, 46 (UdW, 55); It, 41, 49-50 (ItW, 145, 153).

[85] Sn, 764 (SnH, 764); cf. also SN, IV, 128 (KS, IV, 83).

[86] MN, II, 261-262 (ML, III, 46); cf. also: MN, I, 160, 173 (ML, I, 203, 217); SN, IV, 158 (KS, IV, 99).

The six spheres of contact are within the central range of Māra's might.[87] If one delights in things cognizable by the eye, for example, one is in Māra's noose (*mārapāsa*).[88] One who clings (*upādiyamāno*) to the *skandhas* in any manner is bound by Māra.[89] Those who hold perverse views, i.e.,

> They who in change perceive the permanent
> And happiness in Ill, and see the self
> In what is not-self, in the foul the fair ...

they also are bond-slaves to Māra.[90]

Passion (*rāga*), hate (*dosa*) and delusion (*moha*) are characteristic of Māra's bondage.[91] Unrest and fluttering of the mind like a fish on dry land are conditions within Māra's realm,[92] and "Māra gets a chance over anyone in whom mindfulness of body has not been developed...."[93]

Given the extent of Māra's realm and the multitude of conditions that come under his influence, it becomes more understandable when the Buddha is quoted as saying:

> I consider no power, brethren, so hard to subdue as the power of Māra (*Māra-balaṃ*).[94]

Namuci's power (*Namucibalaṃ*) [95] is a "force (*senaṃ*) which devas nor the world can crush,"[96] a force that reaches into so many facets of life. "To Māra's power one goes (*vasaṃ Mārassa gacchati*) having his mind unguarded, ruined by view perverse, o'erwhelmed by sloth and torpor."[97]

However, in the final analysis, Māra "is powerless to cause really effective obstacles to a bodhisattva who gives undivided attention to his task" [98] and who is "sustained and seen by the Tathāgata."[99] Hence the bodhisattva resolves:

---

[87] SN, I, 113 (KS, I, 142); cf. also: SN, I, 113, 115 (KS, I, 141, 145); SN, V, 146, 148 (KS, V, 125, 127).
[88] SN, IV, 91 (KS, IV, 56ff.).
[89] SN, III, 73ff. (KS, III, 64ff.).
[90] AN, II, 52 (GS, II, 61); cf. also SN, IV, 202 (KS, IV, 134).
[91] It, 56 (ItW, 158); cf. also It, 92 (ItW, 181); MPL, I, 345-346.
[92] Sn, 967 (SnH, 967); Dh, 34 (DhM, 34).
[93] MN, III, 95 (ML, III, 135).
[94] DN, III, 78 (DB, III, 76).
[95] AN, II, 15 (GS, II, 15).
[96] Sn, 442 (SnH, 442).
[97] Ud, 38 (UdW, 45).
[98] AP, X, 222 (APC, X, 79).
[99] AP, X, 225 (APC, X, 79).

> Je dois donc faire une provocation à Māra Pāpiyān; lui vaincu, tous les dieux Kāmāvatcharās et les autres sont soumis. Et ensuite les assemblées du démon Māra qui ont coupé toutes les racines de vertu antérieure, les fils des dieux Mārakāyikas, après avoir vu mes jeux le lion, tourneront leurs pensées vers l'Intelligence parfaite et accomplie.[100]

D. Defeat of Māra(s)

Buddha's conquest of Māra receives primary consideration in the selected texts, though it is understood that all who follow the Middle Path shall defeat Māra. Buddha is described as the "sage triumphing over Māra" (*Mārābhibhū muni*) [101] and the "crusher of Māra's host" (*Mārasenappamaddano*).[102] In order to attain arhatship a bhikkhu's life is one long battle with Māra.[103] Hence Arhats are called "victors o'er Māra's bondage" (*abhibhuyya Māra saṃyogaṃ*) [104] and are among those who are "neither in Māra's power nor wait upon Māra as servants" (*na te Māravasānugā na te Mārassa paddhagū*).[105]

All the Māras are conquered. The *Saddharma Puṇḍarīka* claims that "the Tathāgata ... exercises his sway with justice, when he sees [that] disciples and Bodhisattvas ... [have] overcome the triple world and conquered all Māras ..." (*sarva-māra-nirghātanaṃ*).[106] In terms less cosmic in scope and more specific in number, the *Mahāvastu* quotes the Exalted One's description of his defeat of each of the four Māras:

> Here at the *bodhi* tree ... I made an end of the jungle and thicket of the round of rebirth and death which has no beginning or end (*anavarāgra*). Here I have broken Māra of the lusts (*kleśamāro*), Māra of death (*mṛtyumāro*), and Māra of the skandhas (*skandhamāro*); I have broken Māra the deva (*devaputramāro*).[107]

---

[100] LV, XXI, 229 (LVF, XXI, 257).

[101] Sn, 545, 571 (SnH, 545, 571); Hare versifies it thus: "Thou, the sage // O'er Māra triumphing." Cf. also: "vanquisher of Māra *(māradamaka)*, Mv, I, 111 (MvJ, I, 88); "vanquisher of Māra's might" *(mārabalaṃ pramathana)*, Mv, I, 149 (MvJ, I, 118); "destroyer of the works of Māra" *(mārakarmājīta)*, LV, II, 12 (LVM, II, 24).

[102] Sn, 561, 563 (SnH, 561, 563); DN, III, 196 (DB, III, 189).

[103] It, 75 (ItW, 170).

[104] Sn, 733 (SnH, 733).

[105] Sn, 1095 (SnH, 1095); cf. also: Mv, II, 23 (MvJ, II, 21).

[106] SP, XIII, 247 (SPK, XIII, 275).

[107] Mv, III, 273, 281 (MvJ, III, 261, 269). SP, XIII, 247 (SPK, XIII, 275) refers to disciples and bodhisattvas fighting against *skandhamāra* and *kleśamāra* in the course of their career.

The *Abhidharmakośa* gives a more detailed account of the defeat of the four Māras by designating the precise time during this stay under the bodhi tree that each was defeated:

> Les Vaibhāṣikas disent: Bhagavat rejette et stabilise afin de montrer qu'il triomphe du Māra que sont les *skandhas* (*skandhamāra*) et du Māra qui est la mort (*maraṇamāra*). Sous l'arbre de la Bodhi, il a déjà triomphé, dans la première veille, du Māra qui est un démon (*devaputramāra*), et, dans la troisième veille, du Māra que sont les passions (*kleśamāra*).[108]

Nāgārjuna also offers a sequence explanation of the defeat of the four Māras, although its emphasis is upon stages of achievement rather than specific times. Nāgārjuna says:

> En obtenant l'état de Bodhisattva, ces Bodhisattva ont détruit le *kleśamāra*; en obtenant le Corps de la loi (*dharmakāya*), ils ont détruit le *skandhamāra*; en obtenant le Chemin (*mārga*) et le Corps de la loi, ils ont détruit le *mṛtyumāra*; en étant toujours de pensée unique (*ekacitta*), en n'adhérant à aucune sphère (céleste) et en entrant dans les concentrations immobiles (*acalasamādhi*), ils ont détruit le Paranirmitavaśavartin Devaputramāra.[109]

Nāgārjuna distinguishes between "the state of a Bodhisattva" which is the first stage of the path (the first thought of Enlightenment) and the *dharmakāya* which is the last stage. The *kleśamāra* is destroyed in the first stage, the *skandhamāra* in the last. *Mṛtyumāra* is destroyed when the Bodhisattva attains the path (*mārga*). The term *mārga* is a very general one and could refer to the whole course of the Bodhisattva's development. Much more specific is the reference to the defeat of the Paranirmitavaśavartin *devaputramāra*. He is destroyed in that advanced stage when a Bodhisattva has one single thought (of *Dharmadhātu*) [110] only (*eka citta*) and does not use his *dhyānas* [111] to be reborn as a deva but has attained the immovable eighth *bhūmi*.[112] Thus at each of these various stages, one of the four Māras is destroyed. The ambivalence of the term "Māra," which can connote both a proper name of a deva of this universe and

---

[108] AKP, II, 124. A. C. Banerjee, *Sarvāstivāda Literature* (Calcutta: Calcutta Oriental Press, 1957), p. 2, states that "the Vaibhāṣika school was at first known as the Sarvāstivāda."

[109] MPL, I, 340.

[110] That is, the sphere (*dhātu*) of dharma, or the sphere of "religion" as rendered by BHSD, "dharma-dhātu," pp. 278ff.

[111] BHSD, "dhyāna," p. 287: "lit. meditation or contemplation; mystic 'trance.' "

[112] BHSD, "bhūmi," pp. 410ff.: "stage, state, condition."

various metaphorical values of "death," leads to this type of descriptive commentary concerning the defeat of the four Māras. Basic to all these descriptions is the common assertion of the defeat of Māra.

As Nāgārjuna has emphasized, following the "path" is the basic means for attaining the conquest of Māra. The *Dhammapada* says: "Those who enter the path and practice meditation are released from the bondage of Māra" (*paṭipannā pamokkhanti jhāyino mārabandhanā*).[113] Specific aspects of the path are often termed ways to conquer Māra and rout his hosts.[114] These numerous references generally constitute an elaboration of the steps of the eight-fold path, the basic aspects of which are *sīla* (morality), *samādhi* (concentration) and *paññā* (wisdom).

The *Dhammapada* makes a general statement that summarizes the basic intent of the many detailed aspects of *sīla*: "He who lives without looking for pleasures, his senses well controlled, moderate in his food, faithful and strong, him Māra will certainly not overthrow."[115] Concentration (*samādhi*) consists of many levels. Simply "quiet thoughts, dwelling on what is not pleasant" enables one to "cut the bonds of Māra."[116] More advanced stages of meditation are called *jhānas* (Skt., *dhyāna*) and one who is able to attain the four *jhānas* in meditation is "Victor o'er Māra and his mount" (*jetvā Māraṃ savahananti*).[117] Also, he who "enters on and abides in" the

---

[113] Dh, 276 (DhR, 276); cf. also It, 49-50 (ItW, 133), Ud, 3 (UdW, 3).

[114] E.g., AN, II, 15 (GS, II, 15) elaborates upon four right efforts (*sammāppadhāna*); 1) avoid evil states not yet arisen, 2) overcome evil states that have arisen, 3) develop good states not yet arisen, 4) maintain good states that have arisen. All such efforts conquer Māra's realm (*māradheyyābhibhuno*). Another general formula linked specifically with the defeat of Māra consists of the seven factors of Enlightenment (*satta bojjhaṅgā*) which are: mindfulness (*sati*), investigation of the Dhamma (*dhammavicaya*), energy (*viriya*), rapture (*pīti*), tranquility (*passaddhi*), concentration (*samādhi*), and equanimity (*upekkhā*). These are ways of crushing Māra's host (*Mārasenappamaddanaṃ*). Cf. SN, V, 99 (KS, V, 83); also AN, IV, 109ff. (GS, IV, 71ff.); AN, IV, 228 (GS, IV, 154); Dh, 104-105 (DhR, 104-105).

[115] Dh, 7, 8 (DhM, 7, 8). The LV, IV, 33 (LVM, IV, 59) refers to "the power of faith" (*śraddhābala*) which exists for the overthrow of the power of Māra. Faith is one of the five powers (*bala*) which are aids to salvation (*mokṣa-bhāgiyā*): faith (*śraddhā*), vigour (*vīrya*), mindfulness (*smṛti*), concentration (*samādhi*) and wisdom (*prajñā*).

[116] Dh, 350 (DhR, 350); cf. also: Dh, 34-35 (DhR, 34-35); SN, IV, 177, 185-186 (KS, IV, 112, 118). "Dwelling on what is not pleasant" refers to the cultivation of the thought of physical repulsion in order to attain detachment from the physical.

[117] SN, II, 279 (KS, II, 189); cf. also DN, III, 79 (DB, III, 76).

nine stages of meditation puts "a darkness round Māra" (*andham'akāsi Māraṃ*) and proceeds unseen by him.[118]

Māra is also conquered by perfect knowledge or wisdom (*paññā*, Skt. *prajñā*). It is urged that "one should attack Māra ... with the weapon of wisdom (*paññavudhena*)" [119] for the bodhisattva through the force of his wisdom (*prajñā*) and his qualities (*guṇa*) defeats the troop of Māra (*mārasenā*).[120] The *Aṣṭa* claims that "Māra and his hosts will be unable to harm those who take up the perfection of wisdom, who bear it in mind, preach, study and spread it."[121]

The *Aṣṭa* provides a good summary of the various aspects of the path which are means of conquering Māra:

> The endowment with two dharmas safeguards a Bodhisattva against all attacks from the Māras, or their hosts: He does not abandon any being, and he surveys all dharmas from emptiness.[122]

When the bodhisattva surveys all dharmas from emptiness (*śūnyatā*) all distinctions which limit man's true freedom have been overcome through the practice of meditation, and the power of perfect wisdom is realized. Not to abandon any being, the vow taken by the bodhisattva, epitomizes the result of such wisdom, namely, a love and compassion directed to all beings, the essence of the perfection of *sīla*. This compassion is unmotivated by distinctions and is directed toward all beings including Māra. As the *Lalita Vistara* says of the bodhisattva at the moment of his conquest of Māra: "Then the bodhisattva was suffused with thought preceded by love (*maitrī*) and compassion (*karuṇā*) toward Māra and the Māra assembly".[123]

The path of the Buddha is arduous and long, so much so that "the realms of Māra will not remain empty" and "the great hells, the animal kingdom, the world of the Pretas, and the assemblies of the Asuras will be overcrowded."[124] The difficulty of the path, however, is offset by the power of the Buddha and his Enlightenment. This power of Enlightenment is expressed in the descriptions of the

---

[118] MN, I, 159-160 (ML, I, 201-203); cf. also AN, IV, 434 (GS, IV, 291).
[119] Dh, 40 (DhR, 40); cf. also Dh, 8, 175 (DhR, 8, 175); Sn, 442 (SnH, 442).
[120] MPL, I, 12.
[121] AP, III, 49 (APC, III, 22); cf. also AP, III, 78-79 (APC, III, 30); MPL, I, 24.
[122] AP, XXVIII, 448 (APC, XXVIII, 183).
[123] LV, XXI, 318. English translation by Alex Wayman, *Studies*, p. 117.
[124] AP, XXIV, 419 (APC, XXIV, 169).

various degrees of conflict between Māra and the Buddha. Generally just the recognition of Māra decides Māra's defeat [125] and the degree of conflict is minimal when a bodhisattva has attained states "beyond the range of the Malign One" (*pāpimā*).[126]

In the *Saṃyutta Nikāya* Gotama sweeps away the daughters of Māra "As down or leaf by (a) wind-god blown,"[127] and destroys Māra's host "as easily as water destroys an unbaked vessel of clay."[128] The *Mahāvastu* narrates how the bodhisattva with a "yawn" or a "cough" inspires terror and routs Māra himself.[129] The bodhisattva also strikes the earth "with hand soft as cotton" and the hosts of Namuci fall into disorder.[130] It was the "elephant" look the Lord gave Dūsī Māra that caused the latter to die and arise again in the great Niraya Hell.[131]

The conflict, therefore, at this stage of the path, is barely perceptible, and as the *Buddha Carita* states after describing the horrible monsters of Māra's army, "the great sage remained unalarmed and untroubled, sporting with them as if they had been only rude children".[132] The resultant defeat of Māra, rather than the degree of conflict, becomes the topic of dramatic description in most of the selected texts.

The *Saṃyutta Nikāya* uses a number of similes to express the extent of Māra's defeat. Māra was like a "crab with all his claws hacked and broken and smashed" or as a crow who had "pecked at what proved to be a rock."[133] Māra took leave of Gotama after his defeat and

---

[125] MN, I, 327 (ML, I, 390): "I, Evil One, know you; do not think that I do not know you. Māra, you are the Evil One," states the Buddha, whereby Māra's arguments are to no avail. Moggallāna also quickly recognizes Māra and thus defeats him (MN, I, 332; ML, I, 395), as does the bhikkhunī, an Ālavite sister (SN, I, 128; KS, I, 160ff.).

[126] MN, III, 215 (ML, III, 258). These states are the ariyan (*ariya*), supermundane (*lokuttara*) states which transcend the three worlds. Cf. also Ud, 33 (UdW, 40); SN, I, 209 (KS, I, 269).

[127] SN, I, 127 (KS, I, 159).

[128] Mv, I, 240 (MvJ, I, 227).

[129] Mv, II, 281, 410 (MvJ, II, 263, 364); cf. also Mv, II, 418, 496 (MvJ, II, 371, 442).

[130] MN, II, 413 (MvJ, II, 336); cf. also Mv, II, 270 (MvJ, II, 253).

[131] MN, I, 337 (ML, I, 400-401). The LV, XXI, 300 (LVF, XXI, 257) names the ray from the ūrṇā tuft of the Buddha, "qui fait la destruction de tous les domaines du démon" (*sarva-māra-mandala-vidhan-sana-kāri*).

[132] BA, XIII, 112 (BAC, XIII, 142).

[133] SN, I, 123 (KS, I, 155); Sn, 447-448 (SnH, 447-448).

> seated himself cross-legged upon the earth ... silent, discontented, with drooping shoulders, and countenance downcast, brooding and at a loss, scratching the earth with a stick.[134]

Gotama had "cut across the stream of the Evil One" who now was "shattered (*viddhastaṃ*) and destroyed (*vinalīkataṃ*)".[135]

The *Mahāvastu* narrates the sixteen great lamentations of Māra after his defeat [136] and the *Lalita Vistara*, in beautifully rich detail, describes Māra's downfall as it had occurred in a dream of Māra before the final conflict:

> Il vit sa demeure enveloppée de ténèbres. Il vit sa demeure enveloppée de poussière et remplie de sable et de gravier. Il se vit, inquiet et talonné par la crainte, courant aux dix points de l'espace. Il se vit avec son diadème tombé et ses pendants d'oreille détachés. Il se vit avant les lèvres, la gorge et le palais desséchés. Il se vit ayant le corps tourmenté. Il vit ses jardins dépouillés de leurs feuilles, de leurs fleurs et de leurs fruits. Il vit les étangs, dont les eaux s'étaient retirées, complètement desséchés. Il vit les cygnes, les cigognes, les paons, les Kalabiñgkas, les Kouṇālas, les Djīvañdjīvas et les autres troupes d'oiseaux qui avaient les ailes coupées. Il vit les tambours, les conques, les tambourins, les timbales, les luths, les guitares, les téorbes, les cymbales et tous les autres instruments de musique mis en pièces et dispersés sur la terre. Il se vit, lui, Māra, abandonné des gens qu'il aimait et de sa suite, avec un visage sombre, retiré a l'écart et tout soucieux. Il vit la première de ses femmes parée d'une guirlande, tombée de sa couche à terre se frappant rudement la tête avec les mains. Et les fils du démon, ceux qui étaient les plus vaillants, les plus forts, les plus brillants, les plus sages, il les vit qui s'inclinaient devant le Bōdhisattva arrivé à Bōdhimaṇḍa le lieu par excellence. Il vit ses propres filles qui criaient en pleurant: Mon père! Ah! Mon père! Il vit son corps couvert d'un vêtement souillé. Il se vit, avec la tête couverte de poussière, pâle, sans force et dépouillé de sa splendeur. Il vit les palais, les galeries, les œils-de-bœuf, les arcades, couverts de poussière et qui s'écroulaient. Et les chefs de l'armée ... il les vit qui, tous, avaient la tête dans leurs mains et s'enfuyaient en pleurant et en criant ... le démon Pāpiyān les vit tous le visage tourné vers le Bōdhisattva et prêts à le servir.[137]

Thus do the assemblies of Māra, having met defeat, turn their thoughts toward complete and perfect wisdom [138] and, it will be

[134] SN, I, 123 (KS, I, 155).
[135] MN, I, 227 (ML, I, 279).
[136] Mv, II, 276-277 (MvJ, II, 260).
[137] LV, XXI, 301ff. (LVF, XXI, 258ff.); cf. also Mv, I, 41, 162 (MvJ, I, 36, 158).
[138] LV, XXI, 299 (LVF, XXI, 257), and above, p. 122. Windisch, pp. 161-

recalled, even Māra the Evil One may become as devoted a follower of the path as the disciple Moggallāna, the former Dūsi Māra.

162, notes that in the Sarvāstivādin text, the *Divyāvadāna*, Māra is converted by the Sthavira Upagupta (a certain love and inclination toward the Buddha formed in Māra's heart), but that in the Tibetan version Māra is not converted. Windisch claims that the earliest form of the story is reflected in the Tibetan version. In the *Buddha Carita*, Māra advises his daughters to "Go to the refuge which he [the Buddha] gives" after they have lost their beauty (BA, XV, 137 [BAC, XV, 163]).

CHAPTER EIGHT

SUMMARY AND COMMENTS

The portrait which emerges from the references to Māra in the early Indian Buddhist literature is essentially the following. On the one hand Māra is the name of a deva of high status within the cosmology of early Buddhists. On the other hand the term "Māra" meaning "death" is identified with the plurality of conditions and defilements of samsara. This ambivalence as well as versatility of the Māra references is summarized in the four-Māras formula. The *skandhamāra* epitomizes all the conditions of samsara that are subject to death (*mīyati*). The *kleśamāra* epitomizes one's own karmic acts of defilement and sense desire that result in "death" (internal *māretā*). The *devaputramāra* refers to some external causal agent, force or event which lies outside one's own control and which also results in "death" (external *māretā*). Finally, *mṛtyumāra* marks the essential character basic to all types of reference to Māra, encompassing all conditions and events of samsara as well as the deeds of the Māra deva, namely *mṛtyu*, "death-itself." "Death" for the early Indian Buddhist refers to continual death after rebirth.

The nature and power of the *devaputramāra* (*Māra pāpimā*) is described in the selected texts in the following way. Māra is a deva with a mind-made body, who together with the six classes of devas in the Kāmaloka, enjoys the maturing of his good karma. Though virtuous and long-lived, Māra is subject to impermanence and sorrow like all beings in samsara. As the "Lord of the world of desire," however, Māra enjoys the splendor and majesty of his cosmological position as Chief of the Paranirmitavaśavartin devas, the highest class of devas in the Kāmaloka. His host of followers includes the six classes of devaputras in the Kāmaloka, his beautiful daughters and virtuous sons, as well as an army of *piśācas*, *rākṣasas* and *yakṣas* of inconceivable number and ugliness. Māra's realm, which is death's realm, extends beyond the Kāmaloka to the Rūpa and Arūpa worlds. The entire triple world, in other words, is assailed by Māra the Evil One, for within samsara one is never freed from the fear of birth and death and continual becoming.

Māra's deeds are concentrated in the realm where he is most effective, the Kāmaloka. Here Māra holds in bondage by sense desires the multitude of beings in this sphere of the universe. On occasion Māra even possesses individuals and groups of the Kāmaloka, which most often results in verbal acts of disrespect toward the Buddha and his followers, i.e., those who threaten Māra's power over the world. Māra seeks to confuse and perplex the Buddha and his followers by promoting bad opinions, sowing discord and undermining their confidence in the truth and power of Enlightenment. Anything he can do to obstruct and interrupt those who are followers of the path of Enlightenment, he attempts. For example, he interrupts the meditations of bhikkhus as well as the solitude of the Buddha, and is thus called "the great disturber of the minds of living beings". In order to swerve the bodhisattva from the path, Māra sometimes encourages man's inclinations toward sense desires, other times speaks harsh accusations attempting to preserve traditional social and religious ideals not in accord with the Middle Path. Māra also resorts to attacking the Buddha with his fearful army. All of this is to assert his power and achieve his purpose of the continuance of life which forever remains subject to death and destruction.

Māra is known by that name which etymologically means "death", or more precisely, "the one who kills or causes death", and is frequently associated with the coordinate to death, Kāma, god of sensual love and worldly enjoyment. Also Māra is the Evil One (*pāpimā*), evil (*pāpa*) entailing not only that which is morally bad but more objectively, all that is essentially miserable and full of suffering, i.e., subject to death. In this sense the Māra deva himself is subject to Māra.

Yet as pervasive and inherent to samsara as the power of Māra is, the early Buddhists believed that Gotama the Buddha and other arhats were able to conquer this Māra deva and his death realm. All who follow the Middle Path, which includes the practice and realization of *sīla* (morality), *samādhi* (concentration) and *paññā* (wisdom), shall defeat Māra. And, it will be recalled, even Māra the Evil One may become in the future as devoted a follower to the Path as was the disciple Mogallāna, the former Dūsī Māra.

On the basis of this summary portrait of Māra, some comments on other interpretations of the Māra figure can be made. J. Masson, in his book *La religion populaire dans le canon bouddhique pāli*, devotes a chapter to an interpretation of the Māra symbol.[1] He groups the

[1] (Louvain; Bureaux du Muséon, 1942), pp. 99-113.

varied references to Māra in the literature into two basic types, the popular *māra* and the monastic *māra*. He refers to Buddhaghosa as giving these two meanings to the term *māra*, the popular reference being the picturesque Māra deva (*maccu*) and the monastic *māra* carrying the sense of *kilesa* (defilements).[2] Masson himself notes that the Pali literature does not always lend itself to this kind of division, but designates such passages as belonging to a stage of transition between the two conceptions of Māra.[3]

On the basis of our analysis it is possible to see how such a distinction can be made, the *devaputramāra* being a presentational symbol whereas the other type of Māra reference is highly abstract and analytical. The presentational symbol would be appealing and useful pedagogically to laymen, whereas the abstract *māras* are more catechetical and less stimulating to the imagination. However, such a distinction between the popular and monastic Māras in the final analysis is quite arbitrary, for the Māra deva is a monastic symbol as well. The *devaputramāra* is retained in the four-Māra formula and is discussed in highly technical "monastic" treatises. There is no real evidence that suggests that even the most learned and intellectual laymen and bhikkhus themselves did not find meaning and value in the Māra deva mythology. On the contrary, men like Asaṅga and Nāgārjuna describe the Māra mythology in detail and apparently consider it an integral part of the Dhamma. We shall attempt to give a more thorough explanation of this fact in the following chapters.

Other than Windisch's work on Māra, the other most extensive and provocative study of the Māra mythology has been done by T. O. Ling in a book titled *Buddhism and the Mythology of Evil*. Ling's study is limited to the Theravadin Pali sources, but the aim of his book is "to draw no conclusions that are inconsistent with the portrait of Māra found in Mahāyāna Buddhism, but only those which may justifiably be said to be representative of Buddhism as a whole."[4]

The main theme of his interpretation is the dual nature of the Māra symbol. Throughout the Pali Canon, Ling asserts, Māra the Evil One serves as a connecting symbol "between popular demonology on the one hand, and the abstract terms of the Dhamma on the

---

[2] *Ibid.*, p. 100.
[3] *Ibid.*, p. 104.
[4] Ling, *Buddhism*, p. 12.

other"[5]. According to Ling, the popular Indian mythologies of evil, from which Māra emerges, are characterized by their animistic demonology which attributes the ills that man experiences to a pluralism of wholly external forces.[6] Buddhist metaphysics, however, offers a monistic understanding of the demonic in that rather than "concentrating on the ills of life and trying to deal with each as it comes (the method of the animist)," the Buddhist system "brought into correlation with one another in a single conception" the various "contingent ills of life and the sources of those ills ...." "Māra is the mythological symbol to which may be conveniently related these various factors of the human situation."[7] The radical insights of Buddhist thought, according to Ling, shape the conception of the mythological figure of Māra into a remarkably integrated symbol which personifies the unitary nature of evil.[8] And thus the Māra image, with its affinities to popular demonology but shaped by Buddhist doctrine into a unified conception, serves the doctrinal function of bridging the frontier between Buddhist metaphysics and popular belief. The unified nature of the symbol represents the Buddhist's comprehensive understanding of what an animist might only see as an incoherent tangle of evil forces.[9]

It becomes essential, therefore, according to Ling's interpretation, that the Māra symbol maintain itself as a singular conception in order to function as a bridge between the frontier of pluralistic animism and the Buddhist monistic understanding of the demonic. Herein lies its pragmatic value.[10] "Even in the Mahāyāna literature," Ling states, "where the idea of Māra's legions is more prominent, the dominant emphasis is still upon the lord of these legions, Māra himself."[11] Hence the unitary focus is maintained. The "subsequent scholasticism which divided the Māra symbol into four aspects: the *khandas*, the *kilesas*, the *devaputta*, and death ...," Ling states, "is doubtful ... evidence of belief in four Māras."[12] Rather there is a unitary nature and function of the Māra symbol in Buddhism.

Ling has pointed out an important function of the figure Māra in

[5] *Ibid.*, p. 77.
[6] *Ibid.*, p. 26.
[7] *Ibid.*, p. 67.
[8] *Ibid.*, pp. 66-69.
[9] *Ibid.*, p. 66.
[10] *Ibid.*, p. 66.
[11] *Ibid.*, p. 60.
[12] *Ibid.*, p. 66.

early Buddhist literature. As we have seen, Māra is not only the name of a deva of high status within the cosmology of early Buddhism who commands a large following of what could be termed popular demons. But the term Māra also connotes "death," both in a passive sense of "that which dies" and an active sense of "that which kills" and therefore "Māra" can be identified with the plurality of conditions and defilements of samsara as well as designate the title of a cosmological deva. Within this context it can be asserted that the Māra symbol has a dual nature and that it serves as a bridge between the frontier of Buddhist metaphysics and popular belief.

Ling has failed to distinguish, however, between the function of the symbol Māra and the meaning of the symbol insofar as it articulates the Buddhist understanding of the nature of evil. Though Māra may bridge popular and doctrinal references in one term, thus becoming a focal symbol of evil for Buddhists, it cannot be said that Māra is an integrated symbol which personifies the unitary nature of evil as understood by Buddhists.

The general impression derived from our analysis of the Māra mythology as it appears in a wide range of literature is not one of the singular importance of one symbol, the *devaputramāra*, but rather an evident plurality of *māra* references with a number of different meanings. Besides the *devaputramāra*, there is the *skandhamāra*, the *kleśamāra*, and the *mṛtyumāra*. Rather than consider this four-Māras formula as "subsequent scholasticism" which tends to destroy the unitary function and meaning of the Māra symbol, it appears to be more appropriate, if one is to consider what is representative of Buddhism as a whole, to view this formula as an effort to make explicit the inherent versatility and also ambivalence of the meaning of the Māra symbol as understood by Buddhists of the early Indian tradition. When one sets out to consider the Buddhist understanding of the nature of evil examining the Māra symbol in all its versatility, what comes to the foreground is not a monistic understanding of the nature of evil, but if anything, an endlessly diverse sense of *pāpa* (evil) throughout all the varied conditions of samsaric existence itself.

The following comparison of the Māra mythology with the Satan mythology will develop more thoroughly each tradition's understanding of the nature of evil. Through comparison, the distinctiveness of each tradition's estimate of evil will be made evident.

PART THREE

A COMPARISON OF THE EARLY CHRISTIAN AND BUDDHIST MYTHOLOGIES OF EVIL

CHAPTER NINE

SIMILARITIES AND CONTRASTS BETWEEN THE TWO MYTHOLOGIES

Having completed an analysis of the historical materials of the early Christian and Buddhist traditions, it is now appropriate to explore some of the more important similarities and contrasts between the two mythologies. Before beginning, however, it is necessary to state the interpretive stance we bring to this comparison.

A. Hermeneutical Position

Among both ancient and modern Christians and Buddhists there are basically two different ways in which their mythologies are understood. Some understand them to be descriptions of actual experiences, personages and events; others "de-mythologize" all or portions of the mythologies and translate the meaning into different terms. We shall refer to the latter as the "reflective mind" and the former as the "non-reflective mind." The non-reflective mind accepts mythological references for what they say they are, stories about the activities of real superhuman beings. The reflective mind, on the other hand, questions the cognitive status of mythological references and alters or reinterprets their meaning and reference. The *Shepherd of Hermas*, for example, regularly demythologized demonological references; that is, he explicitly altered the cognitive status of stories about demons from that of referring to actual external agents of evil to that of personifications of certain vices which man himself committed. Likewise, reflective Buddhists treated references to the *devaputramāra* and his demonic armies as personifications or transparent metaphors of defilements and fetters for which man himself is responsible.

Essentially what the reflective mind does is to treat mythological stories as theories about experience, explanatory overlays of experiences *per se*, and considers it a proper task to translate the mythology's meaning into new interpretive categories—in the above examples, the vices of men. The basic assumption in regard to a general theory of experience upon which this reflective attitude is based is that there is a core of experience which is separable in thought from its interpretations, the latter standing to experience in the relation of form to matter. Hence a variety of interpretations are applicable to the same experience.

Our position in the following comparative analysis of the two mythologies is that of the reflective mind. The underlying theory which argues that there is a core experience separable from interpretation is not our view, however. When it comes to an analysis of the character of the early Christian and Buddhist experience of evil, for example, we will demythologize references to the nature and power of Satan and Māra into interpretive categories more existentially grounded and furnished by Rudolf Otto. In so doing, however, we do not pretend to claim that we are fully rendering or even duplicating the non-reflective Christian or Buddhist experience of evil. Rather, our translation will be only a partial rendering, at best, of those experiences. We would maintain that the reflective mind has no direct experiential access to the non-reflective experience. We can only hope to gain through theoretical interpretations some oblique insight into what is essentially another order of experience.

The reason for maintaining this position is that in terms of a general theory of experience we hold to the view that perception itself is dependent upon belief, that "we bring to the simplest observation a complex apparatus of habits ... accepted meanings and techniques."[1] In addition to the extensive Buddhist thought on this subject, Western philosophers such as Kant, Hegel, Dewey, and more recently Kuhn and Feyerabend,[2] offer substantial support to the theory that experience and interpretation constitute an inseparable matrix. Feyerabend, for example, states that perception "is the result of the reaction of the total organism," that the way one observes an event is not only a response to "sense data clues," but "to knowledge acquired, beliefs held, the emotional condition of the receiver, his fear and his expectations." He offers the following example:

---

[1] John Dewey, *Experience and Nature* (New York: Dover Publications, Inc., 1958), p. 219. Dewey maintains that the mind in itself is "a system of belief, recognitions, and ignorances, of acceptances and rejections, of expectancies and appraisals of meanings which have been instituted under the influence of custom and tradition ...." (p. 219).

[2] Cf. Thomas S. Kuhn, *The Structure of Scientific Revolutions* (Chicago: University of Chicago Press, 1969) and P. Feyerabend, "Problems of Empiricism," Robert G. Colodny, ed., *Beyond the Edge of Certainty* (Englewood Heights, N. J.: Prentice-Hall, 1965), pp. 145-260.

> We are all aware of thoughts, impulses, feelings that run counter to our conscious intentions. Usually we disregard them for they do not occur in a very coherent fashion. They may appear and disappear without any apparent reason. It is quite different with a person believing in the existence of demons. He would perceive a meaningful pattern in such occurrences; they would appear to him as the result of the attempts of some demon to corrupt him. Considering the astounding plasticity of the human mind, this belief *could even bring about a more regular display of such alien occurrences*; ... Demons would have become directly observable.[3]

Such a theory of the dependence of perception upon belief provides the reflective modern mind with an important perspective, especially when dealing with historical mythological materials. The experiential content of a non-reflective mind governed by a powerful mythological belief is not made up of conscious symbolic structures called "mythologies". Rather the stories about Satan and Māra are immediate conceptual means of grasping, enriching and describing experiences as they actually happen. The non-reflective mind *lives* in an observational world which finds its own empirical confirmations relevant to its belief system, just as the reflective mind finds its own empirical support defined by the boundaries of its own interpretive categories. It is primarily the construction of general theories about the experiencing process itself, such as the one just enumerated, and the implication this has for the translation of mythological references into other interpretive categories, that provides the means for the reflective mind of gaining some insight into another order of experience.

Having thus asserted, in brief, that the Satan and Māra mythologies bring enlargement and enrichment of meaning to certain experiences of non-reflective Christians and Buddhists in an immediate way not totally translatable into other terms, let us proceed to our comparative discussion of the two mythologies with the explicit purpose of translating or "demythologizing" them into experiential terms. Those characteristics of each mythology which distinguish one from the other provide an appropriate starting point for the comparison. These general comparisons will lead us into an examination of the kinds of experiences each tradition regarded as evil,[4] the character of those experiences as

---

[3] P. Feyerabend, "Problems of Empiricism," p. 220.

[4] In the following discussion, we will speak of "Christian" and "Buddhist" experiences, i.e., of "collective" as well as "individual" experiences. A

reflected in the mythologies, and the implications all this has for a proper understanding of the Buddhist term *pāpa* in relation to the Christian term *ponēros* (evil).

B. Distinguishing Characteristics

Several general observations can be made at the outset before a more detailed comparison of these mythologies of evil is undertaken. One obvious characteristic which distinguishes the early Christian mythology from the Buddhist is the amount of "demythologizing" that occurs in the Buddhist texts in contrast to the Christian texts. That is, the reflective mind is more characteristic of early Buddhists than early Christians. In the early Buddhist writings Māra is often explicitly viewed as a figurative reference with discernible metaphorical meaning and is equated with or translated into abstract terms as the four-Māras formula illustrates. In the early Christian writings, on the other hand, only the *Shepherd of Hermas* reflects a similar tendency,[5] which is itself an exception to the general type of mythological portrayal of Satan.

The reason for this difference is most likely due to the fundamental difference in the very character and orientation of the two religious traditions. Buddhism is a method of analysis, a highly analytical approach toward all aspects of experience, practiced in order to realize the cessation of *dukkha*, that inherently imperfect, misaligned, ill-at-ease condition of ordinary existence. The cessation of *dukkha* can be accomplished through the realization of Truth (*dhamma*). The path of discipline (*vinaya*; *dhamma*) taught by Gotama the Buddha, the core of which is mental culture popularly called "meditation," affords man a means of attaining Truth.

For early Christians the Holy and True[6] was centered in an historical event, the life, death, and resurrection of Jesus Christ, and it was the proclamation (*kerygma*) of this event and its meaning

particular experience of evil, Bhikkhunī Somā's for example, was certainly an individual one, being realized subjectively by a person. But one can also speak of Bhikkhunī Somā's encounter with Māra as a characteristic "Buddhist experience" in that the expressive content was molded by a Buddhist thought world and conveyed by means of Buddhist terminology. Such an experience is an "early Buddhist experience" in as much as it took its form and was communicated within the Buddhist world of activity and concern.

5 Cf. above, pp. 50ff.

6 The terms "Holy" and "True" refer respectively to the Christian theological and Buddhist philosophical orientations, although both terms are regarded as correlates in each religious tradition.

for man that became the basis of the Christians' doctrine and creed. The predominant orientation of early Christians, in other words, was historical; for Buddhists it was closer to being ideational. Buddhists found what they considered to be the Holy and True not in the *person* of the Buddha, but in his *teaching* of the Path to true freedom (*nirvāṇa*) and Enlightenment.

It is within these differing religious contexts that each tradition's treatment of their mythology of evil is most clearly understood. The Buddhist analytical approach tended to define experiences of evil in abstract rather than mythological terms,[7] whereas the historical orientation of early Christians allowed experiences of evil to be expressed in stories ostensibly related to historical events, i.e., as mythology.[8] It will become increasingly obvious as the comparison of these two mythologies unfolds that important differences between the portraits of Satan and Māra are due to the different orientations resulting from what each considered Holy and True.

Another basic difference between the early Buddhist and Christian mythologies of evil is in the amount of cosmological speculation. The Māra mythology includes a more explicit and clearly defined cosmology than does the Satan mythology. Although there is not total agreement among the early Buddhist schools as to the exact cosmological status of Māra, there are statements in the literature which are definitely cosmological in intent, statements regarding the nature and structure of the universe and Māra's place in it. The early Christian writings only imply such a status for Satan and make no attempt to work out fully a metaphysical cosmology.

The reasons for this are probably historical as well as religious. India gave birth to and nourished the early Buddhists and bequeathed them a wealth of cosmological explanations as to the nature and structure of the universe. The doctrines of karma, rebirth, and samsara tended to promote this kind of speculation. According to

---

[7] Later in this study it will also be maintained that the Buddhists demythologize the Māra mythology in order to more accurately convey the Buddhist understanding of the nature of *pāpa*. Cf. below, pp. 159ff.

[8] The reflective mind is more characteristic of contemporary Christians than early Christians for a number of reasons. One reason is that mythological time and space cannot be coordinated with the time and space of history and geography according to the critical method; another reason is that there are a number of alternative interpretive theories about experience available to the modern, such as psychological, socio-historical, or broad existential categories of explanation, which were not available to the ancient mind.

the moral law of cause and effect (*karma*), one's actions in the past, present, or future not only determined one's state of being in samsara, but carried cosmic implications for the state of the universe. Early Greek Christianity, on the other hand, was nurtured by the Hebrew tradition, which from its origin concentrated on the history of its people rather than on the nature of the universe, and this emphasis together with the general assumption of time as linear and progressive rather than cyclic, oriented early Greek Christians toward the realities of historical events more than cosmological principles. Such cultural predispositions may also at least partially explain why the Christian's relation to the Holy and True was based on an historical event and the Buddhist's was based on the discipline and knowledge of certain teachings which include an explicit cosmology. And these different orientations, in turn, affected the characteristic features of each tradition's mythology of evil.

The separate historical, cultural conditions in which the early Christian and Buddhist lived also account for those different aspects of each mythology which refer to the reactions of their contemporaries. Christians were subject to the "terrible torments" (*deinas kolaseis*) of martyrdom, such as struggling with wild beasts or having limbs mangled. The Buddhists, however, were subject to verbal rather than bodily abuse. Brahmins and householders "reviled, abused, vexed and annoyed" (*akkosanti paribhāsanti rosenti vihesenti*) them, taunting them about their pretended purities or scornfully claiming that greater men than they had respect for traditional views.

The conditions within the Roman Empire during the first few centuries of the Christian tradition frequently resulted in the persecution of Christians. For example, while Trajan was emperor, Ignatius was sent to Rome and put to death.[9] In A.D. 156 Polycarp, Bishop of Smyrna, was burnt alive at eighty years of age. By the time of the emperor Decius, persecution was spread throughout the entire empire. The reaction of Indian contemporaries to early Buddhists, on the other hand, was much more tolerant, though very argumentative. There is only one notable instance of a ruler's persecuting Buddhists in the period of Indian history with which we are dealing, and historians tend to consider accounts of it as

---

[9] Hans Lietzmann, *The Founding of the Church Universal*, trans. by B. L. Woolf (London: Lutterworth Press, 1958), p. 161.

exaggerated by the Buddhist tradition itself.[10] Puṣyamitra (*ca.* 187-151 B. C.), founder of the Suṅga dynasty which marked the return of northern India to Brahminism, is represented by Buddhist legends as hunting down Buddhist monks on whose heads he put a price.[11] Whether or not this was in fact the case, it obviously was not a characteristic experience for early Buddhists, for their mythology of evil speaks of abuse from Brahmins, but not of persecution.

Another difference between these two mythologies lies in the strikingly different portraits of the two chief figures of evil. Whereas Satan is generally conceived as a fallen angel whose domain is in the lower atmosphere and whose power is identified with the "powers of darkness," Māra is portrayed as the highest deva in the heavens of the Kāmaloka, whose meritorious past lives have brought him honor, wealth and prestigious power. That each of these figures are primary symbols of evil raises important questions about each tradition's experience and understanding of the nature of evil. These questions bring us to a closer examination of the similarities and differences between the two mythologies.

C. Kinds of Experiences Regarded as Evil

The descriptions of the activities of Satan and Māra provide a means for identifying those kinds of experiences early Christians and Buddhists considered evil. A comparison of the verb forms or phrases which characterize the activities of the two figures of evil discloses that similarities between early Christian and Buddhist

---

[10] A. L. Basham, *The Wonder That Was India* (New York: Grove Press, 1959), p. 57.

[11] Cf. *Divyāvadāna*, ed. by E. B. Cowell and R. A. Neil (Cambridge: The University Press, 1886), p. 434, where the putting of a price of 100 dinars on the head of a Samaṇa is mentioned: "*Yo me sramaṇasiro dāsyati tasyāhaṁ dīnāraśataṁ dāsyāmi.*" In the *Manjuśrīmūlakalpa*, vs. 532, Gomi-mukhya (Puṣyamitra) is said to have hunted down bhikkhus. Cf. K. P. Jayaswal, *An Imperial History of India*, 1934, as cited by S. Dutt, *The Buddha and Five After Centuries* (London: Lusac & Co., Ltd., 1957), p. 164, n. 3. N. N. Ghosh's article, "Did Puṣyamitra Suṅga persecute the Buddhists?" (*B. C. Law Volume, Part I* [Calcutta: Indian Research Institute, 1945]), pp. 210-217, concludes that there were persecutions. Cf. also É. Lamotte, *Histoire du bouddhisme indien* (Louvain: Publications Universitaires, 1958), pp. 386, 424ff.

Also, the 7th century Chinese traveller Hsuan Tsang refers to Mihirakula, a Central Asian invader of Western India in the early 6th century, as a fierce persecutor of Buddhism. Cf. Basham, *The Wonder That Was India*, p. 67.

experiences of evil are found on the level of general characteristics. Specific aspects of their respective accounts of such experiences, however, show important differences.

Generally speaking, both the early Christians and Buddhists had similar experiences of "evil" when they were urged or felt inclined toward actions which were not in accord with what they regarded as ultimately good and true. For example, in the New Testament gospels Satan tempted Jesus to work miracles, to fly from the roof of the temple, or to seek to be the "prince of the world," all of which would be actions appropriate to popular messianic expectations but not to Jesus' own understanding of his mission. Satan is referred to by St. Paul as "the tempter" who entices men from their faith. Among the Greek Fathers Origen also views Satan's temptations as a means of putting the followers of Jesus to the test.

Likewise, the Buddhist Pali texts record episodes in which Māra urges Gotama to become a universal king and establish a great empire of peace—certainly an acceptable social goal, but not the goal of one on the direct Path of freedom (*nirvāṇa*) and Enlightenment (*bodhi*). The Sanskrit literature also relates how Māra encourages man's inclinations toward worldly and "religious" values which lead away from the Path of the Buddha. The *Mahāvastu*, e.g., quotes Māra as saying to the Buddha (a query applicable to the followers of the Buddha as well): "What wilt thou gain by this striving? Go and live at home ... (and) when thou diest thou wilt rejoice in heaven and wilt beget great merit."

The specific manner in which this type of conflict with traditional religious and social values was described, however, differs between the two traditions. The Christian characteristically spoke of being tempted (*peirazō*) by Satan, whereas the Buddhist referred to man's "inclinations" toward values and desires of this world (*kāmesu namati*) promoted by Māra.

The term "tempatation" (*peirazō*) means, principally, "being put to the test," meeting an external challenge. When used in connection with Satan, "temptation" also connotes "enticement to sin". The Christian experienced a "testing" of his total orientation to life, an enticement away from his faith. The Buddhist term "inclination" (*namati*), on the other hand, as it is developed in the literature, emphasizes one's own inclinations—essentially misdirected natural instincts on the part of man—which remove him from the Buddhist perspective and lead him into the pursuit of alien values.

In these first examples, it is notable that evil, for both the founders of these traditions and their followers, is integrally related to what each considers Holy and True. As faithful followers of Jesus, Christians view as evil that which is disruptive of their desire to realize a full life in Christ. Jesus himself regarded any form of enticement away from his messianic goal as the work of Satan. Those who follow the Path of the Buddha and seek to attain perfect wisdom (*prajñā*) and freedom (*nirvāṇa*), likewise regard whatever inclines one away from this purpose as "evil". In both traditions, evil is essentially a disruptive break in the bond between man and what he considers sacred.[12] However, having once stated this, we must also keep in mind that the difference between "temptation," a term for which there is no exact equivalent in the selected Buddhist literature,[13] and "inclination," is suggestive of differences in the two estimates of evil.

Another kind of experience of evil broadly similar in both traditions concerns problems internal to the religious community. When the religious doctrine or teaching was misrepresented or the unity of the church or sangha challenged, such events constituted evil. The Apostolic and Greek Fathers especially warned against what the New Testament refers to as the spirit of error which seeks to take away the Word that has been sown in men's hearts so that weeds may grow in its place. St. Ignatius of Antioch admonishes the Ephesians: may "no plant of the devil be found in you." He criticizes the Docetists who are inspired by the Devil, and condemns the Judaisers as instruments of the Devil. Irenaeus states even more specifically: "Let those persons ... who blaspheme the Creator, either by openly expressed words, such as the disciple of Marcion, or by the perversion of the sense (of Scripture), as those of Valentinus and all the Gnostics falsely so called, be recognized as agents of Satan."

The Buddhist Māra sought to "blur the vision" and "darken the understanding" of the followers of the Path by various means. The Sanskrit *Perfection of Wisdom* literature, e.g., defines as activities of Māra the disruption of proper relations between teachers and

---

[12] Ricoeur, *Symbolism*, p. 5, defines evil as the "crisis" in "the bond between man and what he considers sacred." I have chosen to use the more general term "disruptive" rather than "crisis" in that the former is applicable to the Buddhist as well as Christian experience.

[13] Cf. above, p. 82, n. 25.

pupils, the promotion of "bad opinions" such as maintaining "being" where there is only emptiness, as well as false understandings of the very teaching of "emptiness" (*śunyatā*). The Pali literature narrates how Māra attempts to undermine the disciples' confidence in the Buddha and seeks to make the Buddha perplexed by challenging the authenticity of his Enlightenment.

The early Christians characteristically spoke of this type of experience as being "deceived by lies" (*planaō, pseudos*), whereas early Buddhists talked of being "confused and perplexed" (*vicakkhukamma, vicakṣukarma*). Again this difference is related, in the final analysis, to different understandings of the Holy and True. The early Christians experienced the Holy in their relation to an historical personage, Jesus, whose life and events could be narrated and their religious significance defined. The error and delusion of false doctrine resulted from the failure of heretical teachings to articulate properly the true religious significance of the Christ event in history. Hence heretics were "deceived by lies." Buddhist language did not become "doctrinal" in the Christian sense, basically because of the Buddhist attitude that language was fundamentally soteriological in function and meaning. Buddhist language is always most correctly understood to be simply a means toward achieving the ineffable truth; conceptual constructs can in no way "contain" the truth itself.[14] The Buddhist experiences a "blurring" of his vision of the Path and finds misunderstandings between teachers and pupils "confusing and perplexing," hence evil, but does not consider them "lies" which misrepresent an historical, definitive truth.

Still another kind of experience of evil relates to illness and natural calamities. Rarely are disease and infirmity directly linked with the primary symbols of evil in either tradition. Satan is seldom cited as the cause of illness and on only one occasion in the selected texts is Māra the direct cause of illness.[15] However, there is an indirect association of Satan and Māra with illness and natural disasters, an association which is stronger among early Christians than among Buddhists. The problems of cold, hunger, thirst, and heat are

[14] For a discussion of this point see Frederick J. Streng, "The Problem of Symbolic Structures in Religious Apprehension," *History of Religions*, IV, I (1964), pp. 126-153.

[15] Lk. 13:16 refers to a woman bound with an infirmity for eighteen years by Satan. ML, I, 395, relates that Māra entered the venerable Moggallāna's stomach and caused severe discomfort.

occasionally cited by the Buddhists as the external armies of Māra, and inconveniences (*ādīnava*) such as distress, pain and uneasiness are termed the "fetters of Māra." Yakkhas are also associated with disease but they are not generally regarded as agents of Māra by early Buddhists. Yakkhas have their own king, Vessavaṇa. The early Christians speak more prevalently of demonic possession as the cause of certain kinds of illness, and understand this possession to be an extension of Satan's effort (as the ruler of demons) to seduce men from God. Physical infirmities are attributed to "spirits of infirmity" and "unclean demons," and Jesus' healing is described as a driving out of demons.

The fact that illness and natural disorders are sometimes regarded in both traditions as evil, though peripherally so, may be due simply to the negative effect illness has upon one's energies and actions which hinder him from pursuing the religious life. The early Christian was more likely to experience illness and natural calamities as disruptive evil than was the Buddhist, however, because of the difference in basic attitudes toward the nature of man's present existence in relation to the Holy and True. From the perspective of the Enlightened Buddhist, life is essentially *dukkha* (suffering and ill); hence illness and disease are manifestations of a basic condition which one must radically break through (*nirvāṇa*). To realize the truth of suffering (*dukkha*) is a step on the path to Enlightenment rather than an obstruction to it. The early Christian's evaluation of this life, on the other hand, is that it is fundamentally good, or at least originally so, as it is the creation of the one true God. Any perversion of this initial condition, such as illness and disease, is unnatural and hence some account has to be given of it, while the Buddhist has no need to give a similar account. He is prepared to take it as a "given," while the Christian is not.[16]

Mental attitudes and emotional states ranging from slothfulness and lustful pleasures to anger and irreligious sentiments are also broadly associated with the experience of evil by followers of both traditions. The *Shepherd of Hermas*, for example, says: "when ill temper or bitterness come upon you ... (or) the desire of many deeds and the luxury of much eating and drinking, ... and desire of women, and covetousness and haughtiness, and pride ... know that

---

[16] Hence, when the early Christian writers did engage in mythological speculations, a dominant concern was the quasi-historical and very problematic question of the *origin* of Satan and demons.

the angel of wickedness [Satan] is with you." Origen in turn refers to those "wicked suggestions" that deprave a sentient and intelligent soul with thoughts of various kinds persuading it to evil, the example par excellence being the suggestion of the Devil to Judas that resulted in his betrayal of Jesus.

Likewise the Buddhists frequently refer to Māra as the fisherman who uses fleshbaited hooks of "gains, favors, flattery," and binds all by lust, anger, or desire. The Pali literature quotes Māra's command to his host who are surrounding the Lord and the Great Brahmā: "Come on / And seize and bind me these, let all be bound by lust!" "Womanhood" and "anger's loathsome form which lurks in the heart" are also understood as Māra's snares. Sanskrit works frequently refer to persons being "beset by Māra," such as those who are unpractised, plant no wholesome roots, or keep bad friends.

The Christian usually speaks of these experiences as "hindrances" and "obstructions" (*egkoptō*) to the realization of a true life in Christ. The Buddhist, similarly, refers to such experiences as "obstacles" (*āvaraṇa*) or "interruptions" (*antarāya*) brought about by Māra so as to swerve a person from the Path, as when thoughts about the teaching or meditational practices are disturbed by internal desires or external nuisances. The Christian, however, also speaks of his being "instigated" (*hypoballō*) by Satan into ill-temper or similar attitudes. That is, in early Christian literature there is an expressed sense of experiencing an emotion, such as lustful pleasure, as an obstacle to a truer life, yet being incited or urged into such a course of action by a power adverse to one's well-being. The Buddhist, on the other hand, though he experiences interruptive, unwholesome attitudes as obstacles to the pursuit of the Path, views them not so much as predicaments into which one is urged, but rather as manifestations of what one is already bound to (*baddhatā*) just by the fact of existing. The intoxicating powers of lust, anger and intemperance are described by the Buddhist as "snares" (*pāsa*) and "fetters" (*saṃyojana*) which bind him to samsaric existence and deny him access to the freedom of Enlightenment.

Again it is the difference in basic attitudes toward the nature of man's present existence as evaluated from the perspective of the Holy and True that explains this difference between early Christians and Buddhists. The Christian considers this present existence as inherently good (cf. the Doctrine of Creation). Actions and attitudes which obstruct or hinder one from the realization of that good are not an integral part of the nature of existence and therefore are accounted for in terms of an external instigating power opposed to the proper course of life. The Buddhist, however, judges ordinary existence as an inherently imperfect mode of being (cf. the Noble Truth of *dukkha*). Actions and attitudes which interrupt one's progress toward Enlightenment are therefore examples of the internal character of samsaric existence itself, further manifestations of the very bondage from which he seeks to free himself. For this reason the Buddhist regards unwholesome states of intemperance, etc., as more serious experiences of evil than does the Christian. Anger, lust, etc., are instances of a more pervasive evil: the desire that intoxicates the human condition and so perpetuates an existence full of suffering. These unwholesome states are not merely external obstructions to an inherently good life. They are symptomatic of an inherently imperfect mode of existence which is the very antithesis of what the Buddhist considers Holy and True.

All of the above kinds of experiences were associated with the activities of a Satan or Māra. The function of these symbolic references to the activities of the two mythological figures was thus to identify the varied kinds of experiences regarded as evil as well as to emphasize their common character as being disruptive of efforts to relate to or attain the Holy and True as perceived by each tradition. The two mythological episodes which are most illustrative of this disruptive characteristic are Satan's temptation of Jesus and Māra's attack on Gotama. These two episodes are frequently referred to throughout the early literature of each tradition and epitomize what each tradition understood to be the fundamental nature of evil, namely, a power opposing and disruptive of what each considered the truest expression of the ultimate—the person of Christ and the insight wisdom attained and taught by the Buddha.

D. Character of Experiences of Evil

The mythological descriptions of the nature and power of Satan and Māra suggest further that the existential character of these varied kinds of experiences of evil is also symbolically portrayed in these two mythologies. Descriptions of the nature and power of Satan and Māra articulate symbolically the general nature and power of the experiences of evil themselves. A comparison of the Buddhist and Christian mythologies discloses a basic similarity as well as difference between them. What might be termed a numinal sense of *mysterium* and *tremendum*, an overplus of meaning eluding conceptual apprehension, is similarly conveyed in both mythologies. First this similarity will be discussed before moving to a consideration of the difference.

The *tremendum* aspect of the experience is mythologically expressed in the great power and influence Satan and Māra have over man and the world. Satan is the ruler of demons and the ruler of this world (*kosmos*), which includes the "world rulers" (*kosmokratores*) of this darkness, the "elemental spirits of the universe" (*stoicheia tou kosmou*) and the world as mankind—the sum of the totality of human possibilities and relationships. The extent and authority (*exousia*) of Satan's reign is vast; hence he is appropriately called the "god of this age" whose power (*dynamis*) inspires all evil "rule, authority, and power" in the heavenly places as well as on earth, from the beginning of this present evil age (*aiōn*) to its end.

The Buddhist Māra, likewise, holds man in his power (*balaṃ*) and commands a fearful host of demons. Māra is the Lord of the world of desire (*kāmaloka*) which is comprised of six classes of devas as well as "the world below with its recluses and brahmins, its princes and peoples ...." His realm, as death's realm (*maccudheyya*), however, extends beyond the Kāmaloka to the Rūpa and Arūpa worlds. The whole substrata of rebirth and death, in other words, are within Māra's domain. The Pali texts say of Māra's armies that they can hunt and seek "in every sphere of life." And not only is the entire "triple world ... assailed by Māra, the Evil One," but a succession of devas filling the Māra position continues this domain throughout the cyclic process of samsara. Thus the Buddha has said: "I consider no power, brethren, so hard to subdue as the power of Māra" (*Māra balaṃ*).

These aspects of the Satan and Māra mythologies express the feeling of encountering a power that precedes, outlives and extends far beyond the reach of an individual's life; a despotic and infectious power of such magnitude that an acute sense of impotence or even captivity to this power is experienced. This is a sense of *tremendum*.[17]

[17] The Pali expresses this sense of *tremendum* vividly in the phrase describing Māra's desire to make the Exalted One "feel dread and horror and creeping of the flesh." Cf. above, p. 84. Likewise, the mythological descriptions of Māra's attack upon the bodhisattva (cf. above, pp. 84ff.) and the apocalyptic vision of the fearful host of demons in the Book of Revelation (cf. above, p. 31) give expression to this dimension of experiences of evil.

A numinal sense of *mysterium* is conveyed in the portraits of the nature and abode of Satan and Māra. Satan is called the "prince of the power of the air," the ruler of "spiritual hosts of wickedness in the heavenly places." This reference by St. Paul to "heavenly places" suggests that he shared the common Jewish opinion of the lower atmosphere being the dwelling place of fallen angels. Irenaeus also refers to the Devil as "one among those angels who are placed over the spirit of the air." In addition to this heavenly abode, Satan is also conceived as a "spiritual" reality which is unlike man's form and mode of existence. Unlike man, Satan cannot be perceived by the physical senses, and he is capable of deeds which are beyond man's capabilities, e.g., possession.

These qualitative differences between man and the chief figure of evil are also characteristic of Māra the Evil One. Māra is a deva (god) of the highest class of devas in the Kāmaloka; he is the chief of the Paranirmitavaśavartin devas who occupy the highest heavens in the world of desire. His abode is far above Mt. Meru, the center of the Buddhist universe. As a deva, Māra has a mind-made body which, unlike that of a human being is not "born of a father and mother," and is superior to the human form which is nothing but "... a heap of boiled rice and sour milk, ... subject to rubbing, massaging, sleep, dissolution, disintegration and destruction." In contrast, Māra's body is self-luminous, long-lived, does not cast a shadow, and like Satan, is capable of deeds far beyond the powers of man.

In other words, there is a dimension to experiences of evil that lends itself to mythological descriptions of realms qualitatively different from man, numinal dimensions beyond the horizon of the usual, the intelligible and the familiar—a sense of *mysterium*. The Satan and Māra mythologies are thus symbolic expressions of the general character of early Christian and Buddhist experiences of evil. So that when St. Paul, for example, speaks of Satan as hindering him from visiting the church in Thessalonica, or when he is kept from being too elated in his work because of the harassments and hindrances placed in his way by Satan, perhaps the reference to Satan is a means of articulating in-depth realities of the experience. In these particular hindrances Paul experienced not simply disappointment and frustration. There may also have been a real sense of his own impotence in the face of a radically unintelligible and profane power which was hostile to him and his efforts to visit fellow Christians. The Satan mythology gave expression to these aspects of an experience distinguishable from more ordinary occasions of failure or dissatisfaction.

Similarly, when bhikkhunī Somā experienced an interruption while attempting to enter concentrated thought, she spoke of it as an activity of Māra. The reference to Māra, likewise, distinguishes perhaps the character of the experience from other simple annoyances. On this particular occasion bhikkhunī Somā may have experienced not only an interruption but also a sense of bondage to an infectious inclination and inexplicable power which constantly sought to cripple her efforts to realize Enlightenment.

That the chief symbols of evil in the two traditions both give expression to the numinous dimension of the experiences of evil may provide a partial explanation for the remarkable similarity in the relation of both Satan and Māra to the activity of "possession." The writers of early texts in both traditions view major crimes or acts detrimental to Jesus or Gotama as deeds resulting from "possession" by Satan or Māra. Early Christians understood Judas' betrayal of Jesus as the result of being possessed (*eiserchomai*) by Satan, and early Buddhists viewed Ānanda's failure to encourage the Buddha to stay on in this life as due to "possession" (*pariyuṭṭhita*; *anvāvisati*) by Māra.

Perhaps what these references to Māra and Satanic possession expressed for the early writers was that in these acts detrimental to the Christ and the Buddha, the numinous realities basic to all experiences of evil were most vividly present. Such explicit opposition and blindness as was manifest in these direct encounters with the Christ and the Buddha did not appear to be solely attributable to human volition. By ascribing these events to possession by Satan and Māra, the early writers pinpointed in terms of their own experience of evil the reality of that power which was the disrupting source of opposition to all efforts to relate to or realize the Holy and True.[18]

It will be recalled, moreover, that in the early Christian tradition, "possession" is principally a demonic rather than a Satanic activity, and in the early Buddhist tradition, Māra does not character-

[18] Likewise, the torments of martyrdom and the woman bound with an infirmity for eighteen years were seen as the work of Satan rather than the work of demons because of the obvious and extreme nature of the disruptive power being manifested.

istically possess, but rather "holds in bondage." Likewise, there is a tendency in both traditions to alter earlier references from "possession" by Satan or Māra to "wicked suggestions" (Origen) or "obscuring of the mind" (Nāgārjuna). One reason for the reluctance of Origen and Nāgārjuna to speak of possession is apparently the result of reflection upon the implications of such a notion in the context of other beliefs. "Possession" tends to deny man's free will and therefore also denies his responsibility for his own sins or karma-producing deeds.[19]

That Satan and Māra give expression to the numinous quality of experiences of evil, however, may be a more basic reason for the infrequency of references to possession by Māra and Satan in the early traditions. "Possession" refers to the ability of spirits to "enter into" and "reign over" the inner life of a person. Perhaps to the early Christian or Buddhist this suggests too strongly, however obliquely, that the numinous power which "possesses" becomes one with a person's mind or will and thus becomes something which, although it remains antagonistic to man's religious interests, begins to border on the explicable and the familiar. The danger of the latter implication is that the element of *mysterium* and *tremendum*, that sense of the uncanny and profane power which is not easily associated with the common and familiar and which is present in the profoundest experiences of evil, is obscured. Hence the frequent occurrence of possession by Satan and Māra would inadequately express the basic character of all experiences of evil. By dissociation from possession, the chief figures of evil retain a primary function as symbols articulating the *mysterium-tremendum* dimension of experiences of evil.

As encompassing and infectious as was this numinous dimension of the experiences of evil, however, it was felt to be derivative and lacking in ultimacy. That is, it was not thought to be as primordial as the experience of the Holy and True wherein ultimate reality and power resided. This is reflected in the mythological portrayals of the limitations and defeat of the chief figures of evil. Satan's status is that of a creature, a fallen angel, who has been decisively defeated by the power and authority of Christ and whose future destruction (*katargein*) is certain. Similarly, Māra, though a deva, is himself subject to death and liable to change and sorrow. Māra is defeated

[19] In addition the Buddhist, unlike the Christian, ultimately denies the possibility of possession by an external power of evil. Cf. discussion below.

by the bodhisattva and his future demise is also certain, for Māra will reap the result of his karma as do all beings in saṃsara.[20]

Next let us look at the basic difference in the experience of evil in the two traditions, as conveyed by their respective mythologies. Whereas a dominant characteristic of the Christian mythology could be referred to as a sense of *horrendum*,[21] the Buddhist experience may more accurately be characterized by *fascinans*. This difference is conveyed by the way in which the two mythologies characterize the chief figures and their realms. Satan's abode is in the lower atmosphere, the "dark" regions where the clouds gather and where sin, error and death reign. Satan is a fallen angel, who, according to some texts, transgressed and became an apostate, hence was cast out of heaven down to earth. Though he is chief of the fallen angels and prince of this world, what is emphasized is the lowliness of his hierarchical status in contrast to what he had been previously. Thus Satan's domain and power are identified with the "powers of darkness" that reign over this present evil age.

Māra, on the other hand, is described as reigning with great power, majesty, influence and splendor. His abode is formed from seven jewels due to previous good merits, is "covered with a canopy of jewels and crowded by throngs of Apsarases," and stands in the midst of the mansions of the highest class of devas. Rather than being linked with the asura-host, with whom there is the association of a fall from former glory, Māra is associated with the devas who are "virtuous, mighty, long-lived, beautiful, and enjoying great well-being."

The dissimilarities are apparent. The metaphorical coloring conveyed by the terms which describe Satan and his realm, as well as the fallen status of Satan himself, suggest that in the final analysis the character of the early Christian experience of evil was "dark" and negative. It was a confrontation with an opposing power which perverted what was initially good and was hostile to

[20] Likewise, the occasional suggestions among Christians that evil spirits will in the future world be converted to righteousness (Origen) or the possibility projected by the Buddhists that Māra may become in the future a figure as devoted as Moggallāna, imply that the reality of evil is not of an ultimate nature.

[21] Rudolf Otto, *The Idea of the Holy*, trans. John Harvey (New York: Oxford University Press, 1958), pp. 106-107, n. 2, suggests that in regard to Satan the *mysterium tremendum* might be intensified to *mysterium horrendum*. In the experience of evil there "is a horror that is in some sort numinous, and we might designate the object of it as negatively numinous."

man's welfare, namely, a sense of *horrendum*.[22] Although there is initially a sense of *fascinans* in the Christian experience of temptation, such an experience ultimately carries a sense of *horrendum* because of the realization that its tendency is toward a violation of the inherent well-being of man. Since man's present existence is inherently good, evil is experienced as that which is externally adverse to such a condition. The term Satan itself means "adversary." As an adversary Satan is the source of "evil" (*ponēros*; *ho ponēros*—the Evil One), a term which means in the physical sense, "sick, painful, spoiled," or in "poor condition," and in the ethical sense, "base, vicious, degenerate." In other words, evil, for the Christian, means essentially a degenerating, spoiling opposition to what is inherently or originally a good and desirable condition of human existence. Evil is a condition of personal desolation or ruin brought about by what is experienced as an actively opposing power hostile to a good and full life. Satan's powers of death and destruction, "the loss of all that gives worth to existence," epitomize evil.

The early Buddhist mythology, on the other hand, though it reflects a sense of meeting an equally pervasive and despotic power which makes what is not really desirable seem desirable, characterizes that power not as essentially dark and negative but rather as splendid and attractive. Māra has the majesty and splendor of a deva who is long-lived and often associated with *kāma*, the expression of love and enjoyment of life in this world. Māra is not the hostile power which brings ruin and end to life; rather he promotes life in samsara and those pleasures that lead to its continuance. The early Buddhist experience of *pāpa* ("evil"), in the context of the Māra mythology,[23] is basically one of being attracted to the pleasures and ideals of this world. Although there is initially a sense of adversity in conflicts the Buddhist had with contemporary religionists (e.g., the reviling abuse of Brahmins), finally even this kind of experience of *pāpa* betrays a sense of *fascinans* because the

[22] We are here comparing the characteristic motifs of each tradition's portrayal of its chief figure of evil. It should be noted, however, that on occasion Satan can appear as an angel of light (Lucifer) and Māra is sometimes called *Kaṇha* (*Kṛṣṇa*), the "Dark One," and on one occasion is associated with "smokiness" and "murkiness."

[23] We are not here discussing the general sense of the Buddhist term *pāpa* ("evil") as it is used in Buddhist ethics, for example, but only as it is given meaning by the Māra mythology.

effect is perceived to be adherence to traditional religious practices which the Buddhist judged as merely another facet of the enticing realm of samsara. Because man's present existence is inherently imperfect, experiences of *pāpa* are characterized by the inherent, seemingly attractive conditions of samsaric existence. The Māra mythology shows that the experience of "evil" in early Buddhism is more adequately characterized by the mood of *fascinans*, than by that of *horrendum*.

The attraction which the Buddhist feels toward samsara is understood as the result of desire conceived in ignorance as to the true nature of phenomenal existence. To emphasize the true character of samsaric existence as fundamentally undesirable, another type of usage of the Māra symbol came into being in the Buddhist tradition. In addition to its symbolical use as the title of a cosmological deva, *māra* came to be used as a concept associated with representative aspects of the whole of samsara. The root meaning of the term *māra* is "death" (*mārayati*: that which kills). Death in the Buddhist context refers not simply to the termination of an individual life, but also to continual death after rebirth. With this conceptual meaning, *māra* became identified with three terms, *skandha, kleśa, maraṇa*, the first two of which point to aspects of samsara, and the third of which the Buddhist considers a general characteristic of the whole of samsara. The *skandhamāra* identified all phenomenal existence with death (*māra*). The *kleśamāra* identified all karmic defilements with death (*māra*) as they are causative factors in the continuation of the death-birth cycle. And *maraṇa-māra*, referring to "death itself," reiterated the meaning of the concept *māra* as it is here being used and identified the whole of samsara with death (*māra*).

By using the title Māra, referring to the Māra deva, the Buddhist acknowledges that samsaric existence has a mysteriously attractive, binding power. At the same time, by identifying representative aspects of samsara with the concept *māra* meaning "death," the Buddhist emphasizes the basic undesirability of ordinary, impermanent existence. It is the latter usage that stresses the essential meaning of the Buddhist understanding of *pāpa*, ("evil").[24] This Sanskrit-Pali term has been linked with the Greek word *pema*,

---

[24] Hence Māra, rather than *Kāmādhipati*, is the proper title of the Buddhist symbol of evil. Cf. above, p. 97.

which means "misery, calamity" [25] as well as with *talaiporos* which means "suffering, distressed, miserable (a hard life)."[26] Etymologically the term *pāpaḥ* has been traced to the sense of inferior social classes often opposed to the superior.[27] The basic meaning of the term *pāpa*, therefore, most probably is: that which is essentially miserable, full of suffering, and inferior. All conditions of samsara which are subject to or cause death (*skandhamāra, kleśamāra, maraṇamāra*) are of the nature of *pāpa*, i.e., constitute an inferior, lowly, essentially miserable form of existence. The attractive life which the Māra deva (*Māra pāpimā*) extols is judged by the Buddhist as inferior and fundamentally full of suffering (*pāpa*) because it is impermanent and can be equated with death (*māra*) in all its aspects.

E. The Meaning of *Pāpa* in Relation to *Ponēros* and "Evil"

We have seen that the fundamental difference in meaning between the Christian *ponēros* and the Buddhist *pāpa* is closely related to their respective doctrines of creation and *dukkha*, which in turn are determined by each tradition's understanding of the Holy and True. The Christian seeks to affirm the basic goodness of ordinary existence through a full life in Christ. His understanding of *ponēros* is essentially that of a mysterious power hostile to and destructive of the intrinsic worth of life. The characteristic experiences of *ponēros* are: being tested, tormented, deceived, instigated into acts of degeneracy, and falling ill or becoming diseased, each of which is a spoiling of the basic worth of existence. Evil (*ponēros*) is an undesirable, often aggressively negative and morally degenerate violation of the human condition. The Buddhist, on the other hand, judges the human condition itself as a "violation" of absolute freedom (*nirvāṇa*), and therefore seeks to break through the ordinary conditions of human existence which are identifiable with suffering and death. His understanding of *pāpa* in the context of the Māra mythology is conceived in a strikingly different way from that of the

---

[25] M. Mayrhofer, *A Concise Etymological Sanskrit Dictionary* (Heidelberg: Carl Winter Universitätsverlag, 1962), p. 255.

[26] PTSD, "Pāpa," p. 453. According to Windisch, p. 192, the term *pāpmā* in older Sanskrit literature signifies "not only the morally bad, but more objectively, misfortune, sorrow and pain . . . ." Cf. above, p. 74.

[27] Wilhelm Rau, *Staat und Gesellschaft im Alten Indien* (Wiesbaden: Otto Harrassowitz, 1957), pp. 32ff., 61. I am indebted to Dr. Mahinda Palihawadana for these references to Rau and Mayrhofer.

Christian *ponēros*: *pāpa* has to do with that mysterious, attractive binding power inherent in ordinary existence itself. Characteristically, the experiences of *pāpa* are: being naturally inclined toward sense desires, bound to the snares and fetters of samsaric existence, and continually interrupted and confused in efforts to release oneself from a state of being which is imperfect, impermanent and full of suffering.

The connotations of the English term "evil" are applicable to the meaning of *pāpa* only if the context is made clear, and careful consideration is given to specific usages. The term "evil," in English, readily reveals its Christian heritage, for it connotes not only that which is undesirable (lowly, miserable, worthless), but also that which is "not morally good" (wicked, sinful) as well as what is "offensive, wrathful, harmful, injurious, and malignant."[28] The moralistic and strong malignant connotations of the term are not applicable to *pāpa* when the latter is associated with the ordinary conditions of samsara. The impermanent (*maranamāra*), non-substantial (*skandhamāra*) conditions of samsara are not intrinsically harmful nor are all human actions, as such, morally wrong; hence they are not "evil" in these two senses. On the contrary, the Buddhist would maintain that samsara constitutes those conditions which enable one to attain Enlightenment. It is only in and through samsara that Nirvana can be realized. What is important is one's attitude toward samsara. Adherence to the attractions of samsara promotes the continuity of samsara with its attendant suffering; adherence to the Path of the Buddha which leads one in and through samsara results in freedom and salvation.

Samsara, in other words, can be associated with *puñña* (good, virtue) as well as with *pāpa*. A more appropriate rendering of *pāpa* in the context of its association with the ordinary conditions of phenomenal existence may be the term "bad" rather than "evil." The English word "bad" in contemporary usage does not as readily carry the moralistic and strong malignant connotations as does the term "evil." Although one does talk of "bad conduct," for example, as morally wrong and possibly harmful (and in this usage the term becomes a synonym for evil), one can also talk of "bad weather" or of "bad food," the former meaning undesirable, troublesome weather, the latter referring to inferior, poor or rotten food. The

---

[28] Cf. Webster's *Third New International Dictionary*, 1966.

meaning of "bad" in this type of usage approximates more accurately than does the term "evil" the meaning of *pāpa* when associated by the Buddhist with samsaric existence. Samsaric existence is *pāpa* (bad) because it is something which is undesirable, troublesome, i.e., ill (*dukkha*), and is inherently inferior to the state of Enlightenment.

The connotations of "evil" and "bad" as that which is morally wrong and injurious are applicable to the Buddhist use of *pāpa*, however, if the reference is to those karma-producing acts of defilement (*kleśamāra*) which ultimately are based on a desire and fascination for an inferior mode of existence. Not only overt conduct such as acts of violence towards others, but also intellectual and emotional attitudes such as anger, hypocrisy, desire, etc., constitute defilements which are harmful and injurious to efforts to follow the path to emancipation. Thus *pāpa* can connote that which is harmful, offensive, and malignant as applied to man's own bad karma. *Kleśa* is not only "bad" ("ill, inferior and undesirable"), it is "evil" ("morally wrong, offensive and malignant," connotations which, as we have stated, are also involved in certain usages of the term "bad"). Because the English term "bad" embraces both connotative levels more readily than does the more forceful term "evil," it appears to be a more appropriate general rendering of the Buddhist meaning of *pāpa*.[29]

A difficulty in interpretation arises when it is noted that the *devaputramāra* mythology suggests not only that *pāpa* is to be understood as a malignant power, but also as an opposing power *external* to man. The mythological portrayal of Māra's attack against the Buddha, for example, expresses strong negative connotations suggestive of an offensive, malignant external force of *pāpa*. This mythological suggestion of the reality of an external *māretā* (that which kills) [30] beyond the harmful results of one's own karma-

[29] That the Buddhists use the same word where we might use different ones (evil and bad) is not to suggest that they were conscious of the different meanings when they used the term. Rather it simply points out the inherent difficulty in attempting to understand experiences structured by one language system in terms of the categories of meaning of another language. The Buddhist use of *pāpa* suggests that they saw resemblances where we require distinctions in meaning. Often those resemblances evade us. For an interesting discussion concerning assumptions in translations which are often misleading, see A. W. H. Adkins, *From the Many to the One* (Ithaca, New York: Cornell University Press, 1970), pp. 1-12.

[30] Cf. above, pp. 106ff.

producing acts of defilement (internal *māretā*) cannot be reconciled with a basic Buddhist premise: the efficacy of the law of karma. The Buddhist follows the Path in order to attain Enlightenment, and insofar as it is true that good actions bear good fruits, one can proceed with confidence in following the path. However, the karmic principle which gives efficacy to the path is jeopardized if one admits of real factors outside the freedom of man's self-determinations that determine his behavior, i.e., if one admits to the reality of a radically *external māretā* that impinges upon man's will rather than being reducible to it.

The traditional Buddhist solution to this interpretive problem has been to limit the meaning of the *devaputramāra* reference through demythologization. This process we have noted throughout early Buddhist literature. Māra's external armies were named hunger, thirst, cold and heat; his daughters "Craving," "Discontent," and "Passion." Likewise, the Māra Pāpimā figure has been traditionally viewed by informed Buddhists as the personification of the three doctrinal *māras* (*skandhamāra*, *kleśamāra*, *maraṇamāra*). The Pali commentary tradition elaborates even further and refers to a fifth *māra*, the *abhisaṃkhāramāra*.[31] *Abhisaṃkhāra* refers to the accumulation of karma, and as a *māra* is simply a broader doctrinal designation for internal *māretā* (*kleśamāra*). The effect of this fifth *māra* is not only one of re-emphasizing the translatable nature of the Māra mythology, but also a re-emphasis on the idea that in the final analysis internal, not external, *māretā* is the true source of injurious *pāpa*. That is, when *pāpa* is experienced, the source lies not in the disruptive external circumstances themselves, but in how man responds to them. Ultimately it is man's own intellectual, emotional, and volitional karmic response that constitutes the active, counter-productive and malignant power of *pāpa*.

The contribution of the *devaputramāra* mythology toward an understanding of the Buddhist estimate of *pāpa* is thus strongly qualified by demythologization. The mythology is not intended to contribute the meaning of externality to the Buddhist understanding of *pāpa*. As we have already noted the connotations of the English terms "bad" and "evil" as wrathful, malignant, and harmful, though they are given expression through the mythology, are applicable to the meaning of *pāpa* only insofar as they can be applied to man's

---

[31] Cf. above, p. 109, n. 28.

own karma-producing activities (*kleśamāra*; *abhisaṃkhāramāra*). The reality of an external *māretā*, other than mundane intrusions such as malicious brahmins or wandering buffaloes, is denied. The problem of "evil" for the Buddhist is to bring about the cessation of man's own internal *māretā* and thus break through the impermanence and suffering of samsara.

In contrast, the Satan symbol is not demythologized by the early Christian writers under study. Even the *Shepherd of Hermas*, who among the selected writers is the only one to consistently demythologize demons as personified vices, never speaks of the Devil or Satan in this manner. When speaking of these personified vices, Hermas always restricts his terms to *daimonion* and *pneuma*, and at no time calls them *diabolos*. The reason for this is that the Satan figure, mythologically portrayed as an external agent of evil, expresses the Christian understanding of the ultimate source of *ponēros* as external to man. Although man contributes to the power of evil through his own sin, the early Christians understood the nature of *ponēros* to be ultimately an extrinsic power foreign and hostile to the rightful conditions of human existence. Furthermore, unlike the Buddhist who "depersonalized" man through dharmic analysis (analyzing all phenomena into its component parts and relations), the Christian's emphasis upon the personal character of man and God lent itself to a personified representation of evil. Consequently Satan was not demythologized. The existential "problem of evil" for the Christian was one of conquering the power of *ponēros*. The theoretical "problem of evil" was one of reconciling the reality of *ponēros* with the Christian understanding of the nature of God and His creation.

This difference between the Christian affirmation and the Buddhist rejection of the externality of the source of "evil" is ultimately a derivative contrast stemming from their separate understandings of what constitutes the Holy and True. The Christian, who understands his present existence to be fundamentally purposeful as the creation of a Holy, transcendent God, also knows evil, in the final analysis, to be an adverse power alien and external to the original created order. The informed Buddhist, on the other hand, understands his present existence as fundamentally imperfect and inferior to the state of complete emancipation (*nirvāṇa*). This state, paradoxically, is a condition immanent in samsara itself. Thus the Buddhist knows *pāpa* and *māra* as intrinsic to samsara itself.

F. The Function and Meaning of the two Mythologies

The retention of the *devaputramāra* reference in the four-Māras formula, and the general use of mythology throughout Buddhist literature, raises the question, in light of the above discussion, of the function or purpose of the Māra mythology in Buddhism. If the meaning of the Māra mythology can be expressed in demythologized form, why its abundant use in the literature? More specifically, why is the *devaputramāra* retained in the abstract, doctrinal four-Māras formula? [32]

The most frequent and important reason given by the reflective Buddhist in answer to these questions lies in the mythology's pedagogical function. As Ling has noted, the Māra symbol served as a bridge between the frontier of Buddhist metaphysics and popular belief. Buddhist doctrine is subtle and difficult; the terms *skandhamāra* and *kleśamāra,* for example, are highly abstract doctrinal concepts. The Māra mythology, however, provided the unskilled laity with a picture-story of the diversities of *pāpa* in a way that discursive teaching was incapable of conveying. This presentational rather than discursive advantage of the Māra mythology made it pedagogically useful to the reflective Buddhists to retain references to the Māra mythology and even elaborate upon them.

There may be additional reasons for the retention of the *devaputra-māra* in the four-Māras formula. In our analysis of the mythologies, we have noted several experiential functions that the Buddhist mythology served. The mythological references to the activities of the Māra deva served as a means of identifying the varied kinds of experiences of *pāpa* as well as emphasizing their common character as being disruptive of efforts to realize Nirvana. In addition, the descriptions of the nature and power of Māra can be viewed as symbolic expressions of the numinal dimensions of experiences of *pāpa*, namely, *mysterium tremendum fascinans.*

In addition to these, there may be another experientially oriented function of the Māra mythology not discussed as yet. It will be recalled that one reason the Māra mythology was extensively de-mythologized, culminating in a list of four or five Māras, was the needed corrective which asserted that the source of *pāpa* was not

---

[32] Cf. also W. L. King, "Myth in Buddhism: essential or peripheral?" *Journal of Bible and Religion,* 29 (July, 1961), pp. 211-218.

external to man (Māra deva) but was of man's own doing (*kleśamāra*; *abhisaṃkhāramāra*). That the mythology was retained, on the other hand, may have been due to the fact that though the reflective Buddhist *understood pāpa* to be something brought about by man, he may also have *experienced* it as something mysteriously attractive and "outside" himself. The attractions of samsara are "already there" and "other than" himself. Not that the source of *pāpa* is in fact external to man. Experientially there is a sense of bondage *to* samsara, but upon analysis the Buddhist realizes this is in fact the result of binding oneself. To express this existential aspect of the Buddhist experience may be another function of the Māra mythology and an additional reason for its retention even among the most reflective Buddhists.

On a more general level, there appear to be additional symbolic functions which both the Satan and Māra mythologies may have served for early Christians and Buddhists, respectively.[33] From the point of view of the reflective mind, each mythology may have had a very immediate, even pragmatic value to Christians and Buddhists. Each mythology provided a means of coping with certain kinds of experiences by providing a conceptual explanation of each event.

To designate interruptions during meditation or obstacles preventing Christians from gathering in community as the work of a Māra or Satan is to give an immediate explanation to the event. The mythological reference provided the early Christian or Buddhist with a conceptual "handle" which helped him from becoming completely disoriented by the experience. *Satan* was behind the terrible torments of martyrdom; *Māra* was the cause of the brahmins' abusive speech. In each instance these mythological figures provided an explanation which perhaps brought some coherence to an otherwise blinding, scandalous, highly equivocal event.

In addition to furnishing a means for immediately coping with each experience as it happened, both mythologies also may have served the purpose of bringing a whole evaluative context to each experience of evil. An individual experience of evil, once viewed as the work of a Satan or Māra, acquired a whole background of

---

[33] The following comments are indebted to Ricœur's discussion of the symbolic function of myths; cf. *Symbolism of Evil,* pp. 161ff. Cf. also his discussion of the concept "servile will," p. 155.

meaning. It was now an experience which was disruptive of the bond between him and what he considered sacred. It became an occasion which, from this larger perspective, was to be resisted with all one's strength. Furthermore, when an experience was linked with the work of a Satan or Māra, it no longer remained an event confined to the individual's present experience. The mythology, when applied to an isolated occasion, "universalized" the experience. This occasion, among many others in the early Christian's or Buddhist's life, became one of a whole series of episodes which constituted man's continual "cosmic" warfare against the unholy.

This pragmatic, evaluative, and universalizing function of the two mythologies has led to some misinterpretations, especially in Buddhist studies. It is probably correct to say, with Ling, that as the Buddhist concentrated on the ills of life, and through dharmic analysis dealt with each one as it came, the Māra mythology provided a means of "seeing things steadily and seeing them whole."[34] That is, the mythology provided the Buddhist with an immediate evaluative means of coping with each experience. The Satan mythology performed the same unifying function for early Christians. But unlike the Satan mythology, this symbolic *function* of bringing a wholeness of perspective to separate experiences of evil must be distinguished from the *meaning* of the Māra symbolism as an expression of the Buddhist understanding of the nature of evil. The Māra deva, unlike Satan, was only one of a plurality of references, all of which must be taken into account when arriving at an estimate of the Buddhist understanding of *pāpa*. The four-Māras make explicit the Buddhist association of *pāpa* with the diversity of all active and passive conditions that constitute samsaric existence. The Satan mythology, on the other hand, not only served the symbolic function of bringing a unified perspective to the early Christian's separate experiences of evil, but also personified the Christian understanding of the unitary nature of evil, namely, that the numerous and diverse powers which disrupt one's religious life are all derived from one fundamental power, which is called "Satan," "the adversary."[35] The Buddhist does not share this "monistic" view of evil; rather his is a pluralistic understanding of the diversities of *pāpa*.

---

[34] Cf. Ling, *Buddhism*, p. 67.
[35] Cf. Schlier, *Principalities and Powers*, p. 16.

G. Concluding Remarks

As a general definition one can agree with Paul Ricœur that "evil" is essentially a disruptive break in the bond between man and what he considers sacred. Such is the broad meaning of the term evil when applied to both the Christian and Buddhist Satan and Māra mythologies. However, we have also seen that the Christian and Buddhist understanding of evil is intimately bound up with the basic orientation of the whole of each religious tradition. It is precisely because the meaning of "evil" is derived from the meaning of the sacred that one must carefully delineate what each tradition means by this general term, for as the traditions differ in their understanding of the ultimate good, they also differ in their understandings of "evil."

The English word "evil" carries Christian connotations and should be used cautiously in any discussion of the Buddhist viewpoint. The popular Western misunderstanding of Buddhism as a pessimistic religion of negation, for example, stems in part from the misuse of the term "evil" when considering the Buddhist experience and evaluation of life. The world is not considered evil by the Buddhist. That is, life is not principally experienced as offensive, malignant and filled with *horrendum*. Quite the contrary, it is precisely life's fascination that makes it so problematic for the Buddhist. That the Buddhist does associate samsara with *pāpa* requires that the meaning of the term *pāpa* be carefully defined to avoid wrong connotations.

Likewise we have noted that the way in which the mythologies develop, i.e., the lack or prevalence of demythologization, also provides an important clue to the basic understanding of evil that governs the use of the mythologies. To demythologize Satan, for example, in such a way as to conclude that the power of evil in this world is ultimately derived from men themselves,[36] is to change the content as well as the form of the early Christian perspective.[37] *Ponēros*, unlike *pāpa*, was understood by early Christians as a power external and hostile to man and ultimately derived from one source—Satan, the adversary. The Buddhist Māra symbol, on the other hand, does not represent a similar understanding of the unitary nature of evil. Such an interpretation of the early Buddhist

[36] Cf. above, pp. 64ff.

[37] Cf. also James Kallas, *The Satanward View*, p. 136.

materials can be made only at the expense of ignoring distinctive features of the Buddhist treatment of its own mythology of evil.[38] The Māra symbol fragments into a number of separate meanings through deliberate demythologization, and the subsequent emphasis is on the intrinsic character of *pāpa* which is as multi-faceted as the very structure of existence itself. In these important ways the two mythologies of evil exhibit some characteristic features which mark each off from the other, features which are highlighted by comparison and are not that clearly seen, perhaps, from within each tradition alone.

To conclude, it is hoped that the data collected in this study will provide others with more information in formulating views not only of the experience and understanding of evil in the early Christian and Buddhist traditions, but also concerning the reality of evil as an aspect of human experience in general.[39] That is, such a discussion as this should also be brought into the arena of religious philosophy. When the two mythologies of evil are brought together as two cultural expressions of the *human* experience of evil, it is possible that a basic structure underlying both traditions may come into view. Both the Buddhist and Christian mythologies disclose that there are "light" as well as "dark" features to various experiences of evil. Satan is sometimes called Lucifer, disguised as an angel of light, and Māra is sometimes called the Dark One and associated with "smokiness" and "murkiness." The Christian can speak of bondage to this world just as the Buddhist does of samsara, and the Buddhist mythologically portrays the cause or source of evil as external to himself just as the Christian does. But whereas the Christian maximizes externality and the sense of *horrendum*, minimizing *fascinans* and man's contribution to the power of evil (as viewed within the limited context of the Satan mythology), the Buddhist maximizes the inherent bondage to samsara and the *fascinans* character of it, while minimizing the externality and *horrendum*

[38] Cf. above, pp. 131ff.

[39] The highly disputed question of the historical influence early Christianity and Buddhism had on each other can also be raised in light of the present study. Not only should ideas such as the Suffering Savior be compared with the Suffering Bodhisattva, the Trinitarian formula compared with the Three Bodies of the Buddha, but also the Christian and Buddhist mythologies of evil should be examined in light of this historically oriented question. Such a study would invariably involve a close examination of the Persian mythology of evil (cf. above, p. 16, n. 21) and deserves to be treated as a separate research endeavor.

features of such experiences. Perhaps each tradition, by illuminating different aspects of the existentially known character of evil, when brought together will help us to a fuller understanding on the generic level of the human experience of evil. In both traditions evil is something more than the privation of the good. There is a *positiveness* to the unholy which is not adequately accounted for by admitting to the deafness in man which resists the ideal.

BIBLIOGRAPHY

PART ONE

Primary Sources

New Testament:

The Holy Bible (Revised Standard Version).

Apostolic Fathers:

Ignatius. "The Epistles of Saint Ignatius." *The Apostolic Fathers.* Translated by K. Lake. The Loeb Classical Library, Vol. I. Edited by E. Capps, T. E. Page, and W. H. D. Rouse. New York: G. P. Putnam's Sons, 1925.

Polycarp. "The Epistle to the Philippians of Saint Polycarp, Bishop of Smyrna and Holy Martyr." *The Apostolic Fathers.* Translated by K. Lake. The Loeb Classical Library, Vol. I. Edited by E. Capps, T. E. Page, and W. H. D. Rouse. New York: G. P. Putnam's Sons, 1925.

Barnabas. "The Epistle of Barnabas." *The Apostolic Fathers.* Translated by K. Lake. The Loeb Classical Library, Vol. I. Edited by E. Capps, T. E. Page, and W. H. D. Rouse. New York: G. P. Putnam's Sons, 1925.

Hermas, Shepherd of. "The Shepherd." *The Apostolic Fathers.* Translated by K. Lake. The Loeb Classical Library, Vol. II. Edited by T. E. Page, E. Capps, L. A. Post, W. H. D. Rouse, and E. H. Warmington. Cambridge: Harvard University Press, 1946.

"The Martyrdom of St. Polycarp, Bishop of Smyrna." *The Apostolic Fathers.* Translated by K. Lake. The Loeb Classical Library, Vol. II. Edited by T. E. Page, E. Capps, L. A. Post, W. H. D. Rouse, and E. H. Warmington. Cambridge: Harvard University Press, 1946.

Early Greek Fathers:

Justin Martyr. "The Writings of Justin Martyr and Athenagoras." Translated by Rev. M. Dods and Rev. G. Reith. *Ante-Nicene Christian Library,* Vol. II. Edited by Rev. A. Roberts and J. Donaldson. Edinburgh: T. and T. Clark, 1867.

Irenaeus. "The Writings of Irenaeus," Vols. I, II. Translated by Rev. A. Roberts and Rev. W. H. Rambaut. *Ante-Nicene Christian Library,* Vols. V, IX. Edited by Rev. A. Roberts and J. Donaldson. Edinburgh: T. and T. Clark, 1868, 1869.

Origen. "The Writings of Origen," Vols. I, II. Translated by Rev. F. Crombie. *Ante-Nicene Christian Library.* Vols. X, XXIII. Edited by Rev. A. Roberts and J. Donaldson. Edinburgh: T. and T. Clark, 1872, 1895.

Patrologiae Cursus Completus, Series Graeca, Vols. VI, VII, XI, 161 vols. Edited by J. P. Migne. Paris, 1857-1887.

Lexica, Encyclopedias, Apocalyptic and Apocrypha Literature

Andrews, E. A., ed. *A New Latin Dictionary.* New York, 1895.

Arndt, W. F., and Gingrich, F. W. *A Greek English Lexicon of the New Testament and Other Early Christian Literature.* 4th ed. A translation and adaptation of W. Bauer's *Griechisch-Deutsches Wörterbuch zu den Schriften des Neuen Testaments und der übrigen urchristlichen Literatur.* Chicago, 1957.

Bartelink, G. J. *Lexicologisch Semantische Studie over de Taal van de Apostolische Vaders.* Nijmegen, 1952.

Bromiley, G. W. *Theological Dictionary of the New Testament.* 5 vols. A translation of G. Kittel's *Theologisches Wörterbuch zum Neuen Testament.* Eerdman's, 1964-1968.

Buttrick, G. A., ed. *The Interpreter's Dictionary of the Bible.* 4 vols. New York, 1962.

Davidson, Gustav. *A Dictionary of Angels.* New York, 1967.

Hastings, J., ed. *A Dictionary of the Bible.* 5 vols. Edinburgh, 1898-1904.

——, ed. *Dictionary of Christ and the Gospels.* 2 vols. Edinburgh, 1906-1908.

——, ed. *Dictionary of the Apostolic Church.* 2 vols. Edinburgh, 1915-1918.

——, ed. *Encyclopaedia of Religion and Ethics.* 12 vols. New York, 1913-1922.

Lampe, G. W. H. *A Patristic Greek Lexicon.* 4 vols. Oxford, 1961-1965.

Liddell, H. G., and Scott, R., ed. *A Greek-English Lexicon.* Oxford, 1961.

Moulton, J. H., and Milligan, G. *The Vocabulary of the Greek Testament Illustrated from the Papyri and Other Non-Literary Sources.* London, 1914-1929.

The Apocrypha and Pseudepigrapha of the Old Testament, Vols. I, II. Edited by R. H. Charles. Oxford: Clarendon Press, 1913.

The Assumption of Moses. Translated by W. J. Ferrar. New York: Macmillan Co., 1918.

The Book of Enoch. Translated and edited by R. H. Charles. Oxford: Clarendon Press, 1893.

The Book of Jubilees. Translated by G. H. Schodde. Oberlin: E. J. Goodrich, 1888.

The Book of Wisdom. Translated with commentary by J. Reider. New York: Harper and Brothers, 1957.

The Manual of Discipline. Translated and annotated by P. Wernberg-Møller. Grand Rapids: Eerdmans, 1957.

Selected List of Secondary Sources

Aulen, Gustaf. *Christus Victor.* Translated by A. G. Hebert. New York: The Macmillan Co., 1956.

Barton, G. A. "The Origin of the Names of Angels and Demons in the Extra-Canonical Apocalyptic Literature to 100 A. D." *Journal of Biblical Literature,* XXXI, Part IV (1912), 156-157.

Berkouwer, G. C. "Satan and the demons." *Christianity Today,* V (June 5, 1961), 18-19.

Brunner, Emil. *The Christian Doctrine of Creation and Redemption.* London: Lutterworth Press, 1952.

Bultmann, Rudolf. *Jesus and the Word.* Translated by L. P. Smith and E. H. Lantero. New York: Charles Scribner's Sons, 1958.

——. *Primitive Christianity.* New York: Meridian Books, 1960.

——. *Theology of the New Testament.* 2 vols. New York: Charles Scribner's Sons, 1951-1955.

Buri, Fritz. *Theology of Existence.* Translated by H. H. Oliver and Onder. Greenwood, S. C.: The Attic Press, 1965.

Caird, G. B. *Principalities and Powers.* Oxford: Clarendon Press, 1956.

Campenhausen, Hans von. *The Fathers of the Greek Church.* London: Adam and Charles Black, 1963.

Campbell, James M. *The Greek Fathers.* New York: Cooper Square Publishers, 1963.

Carpenter, H. J. "Popular Christianity and the Theologians in the Early Centuries." *Journal of Theological Studies*, no. 14 (Oct., 1963), 294-310.
Chadwick, Henry. *Early Christian Thought and the Classical Tradition.* Oxford: Clarendon Press, 1966.
Conybeare, F. C. "The Demonology of the New Testament." *Jewish Quarterly Review.* VIII (1896-1897), 576-608.
——. "Christian Demonology." *Jewish Quarterly Review,* IX (1896-1897), 59-114, 444-470, 581-603.
Cross, F. L. *The Early Christian Fathers.* London: Gerald Duckworth and Co., Ltd., 1960.
Cullman, O. *Christ and Time. The Primitive Christian Conception of Time and History.* Translated by F. V. Filson. Philadelphia: Westminster Press, 1950.
Dibelius, M. *Die Geisterwelt im Glauben des Paulus.* Göttingen: Vandenhoeck and Ruprecht, 1909.
Duchesne-Guillemin, J. *The Western Response to Zoroaster.* Oxford: Clarendon Press, 1958.
Eitrem, S. *Some Notes on the Demonology of the New Testament.* Osloae: A. W. Brøgger, 1950.
Gokey, Francis X. *The Terminology for the Devil and Evil Spirits in the Apostolic Fathers.* Washington, D. C.: The Catholic University of America Press, 1961.
Goodenough, E. R. *The Theology of Justin Martyr.* Jena: Walter Biedermann, 1923.
Goodspeed, E. J. *A History of Early Christian Literature.* Chicago: University of Chicago Press, 1966.
Grant, Robert M. *After the New Testament.* Philadelphia: Fortress Press, 1967.
——. *Gnosticism and Early Christianity.* New York: Columbia University Press, 1959.
Hitchcock, F. R. M. *Irenaeus of Lugdunum: A Study of His Teaching.* Cambridge: University Press, 1914.
Jesus-Marie, Père Bruno de, ed. *Satan.* New York: Sheed and Ward, 1952.
Kallas, James. *The Satanward View: A Study in Pauline Theology.* Philadelphia: Westminster Press, 1966.
Kluger, R. S. *Satan in the Old Testament.* Translated by H. Nagel. Evanston: Northwestern University Press, 1967.
Langton, E. *Essentials of Demonology.* London: Epworth Press, 1949.
——. *Satan, A Portrait.* London: Skeffington & Son, Ltd., 1945.
Leaney, A. R. C. *The Rule of the Qumran and Its Meaning.* London: SCM Press, Ltd., 1966.
Leivestad, R. *Christ the Conqueror.* London: SPCK, 1954.
Leitzmann, Hans. *The Beginnings of the Christian Church.* Translated by B. L. Woolf. London: Lutterworth Press, 1958.
Ling, T. O. "Personality and the Devil." *Modern Churchman,* no. 5 (Jan., 1962), 141-148.
——. "Satan enthroned." *South East Asian Journal of Theology,* no. 3 (July, 1961), 41-53.
——. *The Significance of Satan.* London: SPCK, 1961.
Macgregor, G. H. C. "Principalities and Powers: The Cosmic Background of Paul's Thought." *New Testament Studies,* I (1954), 17-28.
Macquarrie, J. "Demonology and the Classic Idea of Atonement." *Expository Times,* no. 68 (Oct. - Nov., 1956), 3-6, 60-63.

Nock, A. D. *Conversion*. London: Oxford University Press, 1961.

Nygren, Anders. *Agape and Eros*. Translated by P. S. Watson. Philadelphia: Westminster Press, 1953.

——. *Christ and His Church*. Translated by A. Carlsten. Philadelphia: Westminster Press, 1956.

——. "Christ and the Forces of Destruction." *Scottish Journal of Theology*, IV (1951), 363-375.

——. *Essence of Christianity*. London: Epworth Press, 1960.

Papini, G. *The Devil*. New York: E. P. Dutton & Co., 1954.

Quasten, Johannes. *Patrology*. 3 vols. Utrecht: Spectrum, 1950-1960.

Rupp, Gordon. *Principalities and Powers*. New York: Abingdon-Cokesbury Press, 1952.

Schlier, Heinrich. *Principalities and Powers in the New Testament*. New York: Herder and Herder, 1962.

Stewart, J. S. "On a Neglected Emphasis in New Testament Theology." *Scottish Journal of Theology*, IV (1951), 292-301.

Taylor, V. *The Gospel According to St. Mark*. London: Macmillan Co., 1952.

Weatherhead, L. D. "The Problem of Demon-Possession." *London Quarterly and Holbron Review*, no. 174 (April, 1949), 118-119.

Weber, H. R. "Christ's Victory over the Satanic Powers." *Study Encounter*, II, No. 3 (1966), 160-165.

Ziegler, Matthäus. *Engel und Dämon im Lichte der Bibel*. Zürich: Origo, 1957.

PART TWO

Primary Sources

Pali:

Dīgha-Nikāya. 3 vols. Edited by T. W. Rhys Davids and J. E. Carpenter. Pali Text Society. London: Oxford University Press, 1890, 1947, 1960.

Dialogues of the Buddha. 3 vols. Translated by T. W. Rhys Davids and C. A. F. Rhys Davids. The Sacred Books of the Buddhists. Vols. II-IV. London: Luzac and Co., 1956, 1957, 1959.

Majjhima-Nikāya. 4 vols. Edited by V. Trenckner, R. Chalmers, Mrs. Rhys Davids. Pali Text Society. London: Luzac and Co., 1960, 1964.

The Middle Length Sayings. 3 vols. Translated by I. B. Horner. Pali Text Society. London: Luzac and Co., 1954, 1957, 1959.

Saṃyutta-Nikāya. 6 vols. Edited by M. Leon Feer. Pali Text Society. London: Luzac and Co., 1960.

The Book of the Kindred Sayings. 5 vols. Translated by Mrs. Rhys Davids and F. L. Woodward. Pali Text Society. London: Luzac and Co., 1950, 1952, 1954, 1956.

Aṅguttara-Nikāya. 6 vols. Edited by R. M. Morris, E. Hardy, and C. A. F. Rhys Davids. Pali Text Society. London: Oxford University Press, 1883, 1955, 1958, 1960.

The Book of the Gradual Sayings. 5 vols. Translated by F. L. Woodward and E. M. Hare. Pali Text Society. London: Luzac and Co., 1951, 1952, 1955.

The Dhammapada. Edited by S. Sumangala Thera. Pali Text Society. London: Oxford University Press, 1914.

The Dhammapada. Translated by F. Max Muller. The Sacred Books of the East. Vol. X (2nd ed.). London: Oxford University Press, 1924.

The Dhammapada. Translated by S. Radhakrishnan. London: Oxford University Press, 1954.

Udāna. Edited by Paul Steinthal. Pali Text Society. London: Oxford University Press, 1948.

Udāna: Verses of Uplift. Translated by F. L. Woodward. The Sacred Books of the Buddhists. Vol. VIII, titled *The Minor Anthologies of the Pali Canon: Part II*. London: Oxford University Press, 1948.

Iti-vuttaka. Edited by E. Windisch. Pali Text Society. London: Oxford University Press, 1948.

Itivuttaka: As It Was Said. Translated by F. L. Woodward. The Sacred Books of the Buddhists. Vol. III, titled *The Minor Anthologies of the Pali Canon: Part II*. London: Oxford University Press, 1948.

Sutta-Nipāta. Edited by D. Anderson and H. Smith. Pali Text Society. London: Luzac and Co., 1965.

Woven Cadences of Early Buddhists. Translated by E. M. Hare. The Sacred Books of the Buddhists, Vol. XV. London: Oxford University Press, 1947.

Sanskrit:

Ashṭasāhasrikā. Edited by R. Mitra. Calcutta: Asiatic Society, 1888.

Aṣṭasāhasrikā Prajñāpāramitā (*The Perfection of Wisdom in Eight Thousand Slokas*). Translated by E. Conze. Calcutta: Asiatic Society. Nu. 284, Issue 1578, 1958.

L'Abhidharmakośa de Vasubandhu. 6 vols. Translated by L. de la Vallée Poussin. Paris. Paul Geuthner, 1923, 1924, 1925, 1926.

Lalita Vistara. Edited by S. Lefmann. Halle: Waisenhauses, 1902.

Le Lalita Vistara. Translated by Ph. Ed. Foucaux. Annales du Musée Guimet, 1902-1908.

Lalita Vistara. Translated by R. Mitra (Chapters I-XV). Calcutta: Asiatic Society, 1886.

Le Traité de la grande vertu de sagesse de Nāgārjuna (*Mahāprajñāpāramitāśāstra*). 2 vols. Translated by É. Lamotte. Louvain: Bureaux du Muséon, 1944, 1949.

Le Mahāvastu (*Texte Sanscrit*). 3 vols. Edited by E. Senart. Paris: Société Asiatique, 1882, 1890, 1897.

The Buddha-Carita of Aśvaghosha. Edited by E.B. Cowell. Oxford: Clarendon Press, 1893.

The Buddha-Carita of Aśvaghosha. Translated by E. B. Cowell. Sacred Books of the East. Vol. XLIX. London: Oxford University Press, 1927.

The Mahāvastu. 3 vols. Translated by J. J. Jones. Sacred Books of the Buddhists. Vols. XVI, XVIII, XIX. London: Luzac and Co., 1949, 1952, 1956.

Saddharmapuṇḍarīka-Sūtram. Edited by U. Wogihara and C. Tsuchida. Tokyo: The Seigo-Kenkyukai, 1934-1935.

Saddharma-Puṇḍarīka (*The Lotus of the True Law*). Translated by H. Kern. Sacred Books of the East. Vol. XXI. London: Oxford University Press, 1909.

Śrāvakabhūmi of Asaṅga. Translated and edited text by Alex Wayman in: *Analysis of the Śrāvakabhūmi Manuscript*. Berkeley: University of California Press, 1961; and "Studies in Yama and Māra." *Indo-Iranian Journal*, III (1959), 112-131.

LEXICA AND ENCYCLOPEDIAS AND COMMENTARIES

Buddhaghosa. *Papañcasūdanī: Commentary to the Majjhima-Nikāya*. 4 vols. Edited by Dhammananda. Colombo: Tripitaka Publication Press, 1933.

Edgerton, F. *Buddhist Hybrid Sanskrit Dictionary*. 2 vols. New Haven, 1953.
Hastings, J., ed. *Encyclopaedia of Religion and Ethics*, IV (1912), VIII, (1916).
Malalasekera, G. P. *Dictionary of Pali Proper Names*. 2 vols. London: Luzac and Co., 1960.
——, ed. *Encyclopaedia of Buddhism*, II, 1. (1966), 1-14.
Mayrhofer, M. *A Concise Etymological Sanskrit Dictionary*. Heidelberg: Carl Winter Universitätsverlag, 1962.
Rhys Davids, T. W., and Stede, William, editors. *Pali-English Dictionary*. Pali Text Society. London: Luzac and Co., Ltd., 1959.
Williams, Monier. *A Sanskrit-English Dictionary*. Oxford: Clarendon Press, 1872.

SELECTED LIST OF SECONDARY SOURCES

Banerjee, A. C. *Sarvāstivāda Literature*. Calcutta: Calcutta Oriental Press, 1957.
Bareau, A. *Les sectes bouddhiques du petit vehicule*. Saigon: Ecole Française d'extrème Orient, 1955.
Conze, E. *Buddhism: Its Essence and Development*. New York: Harper and Brothers, 1951.
——. "Buddhist Philosophy and its European Parallels." *Philosophy East and West*, XIII, (1963), 9-23.
——. *Buddhist Thought in India*. London: George Allen and Unwin, Ltd., 1962.
——. ed. *Buddhist Texts Through the Ages*. New York: Harper and Row, 1964.
——. "Recent Progress in Buddhist Studies." *The Middle Way*, XXXIV, 1 (May, 1959), 6-14.
——. "Recent Progress in Mahayana Studies." *The Middle Way*, XXXIV, 4 (Feb., 1960), 144-150.
——. "Recent Work on Tantric and Zen Buddhism." *The Middle Way*, XXXV, 3 (Nov., 1960), 93-98.
——. "The Oldest Prajñāpāramitā." *The Middle Way*, XXXII, 4 (1958), 136-141.
——. *The Prajñāpāramitā Literature*. S-Gravenhage: Mouton and Co., 1960.
——. "Spurious Parallels to Buddhist Philosophy." *Philosophy East and West*, XIII, 2 (1963), 105-115.
Dutt, N. "The Buddhist Sects. A Survey." *B. C. Law Volume, Part I*. Calcutta: Indian Research Institute, 1945.
Dutt, S. *The Buddha and Five After Centuries*. London: Luzac and Company, Ltd., 1955.
Eliade, M. *Yoga: Immortality and Freedom*. Translated by W. R. Trask. New York: Pantheon Books, 1958.
Eliot, Sir Charles. *Hinduism and Buddhism*. 3 vols. New York: Barnes and Noble, 1954.
Foucher, A. *La vie du Bouddha*. Paris: Payot, 1949.
Frauwallner, E. *On the Date of the Buddhist Master of the Law Vasubandhu*. Rome: Serie Orientale, 1951.
Hardy, E. "Māra in the Guise of Buddha." *Journal of the Royal Asiatic Society*, 4 (1902), 951-955.
Hopkins, E. W. *Epic Mythology*. Translated by K. J. Trübner. Strassburg: K. J. Trübner, 1915.
Keith, A. B. *A History of Sanskrit Literature*. London: Oxford University Press, 1920.

——. *Religion and Philosophy of the Vedas*. Cambridge: Harvard University Press, 1925.
Lamotte, É. *Histoire du bouddhisme indien*. Louvain: Publications Universitaires, 1958.
Law, B. C. *Indological Studies Part IV*. Allahabad: Ganganath Jha Research Institute, 1962.
——. "The Buddhist Conception of Māra." *Buddhistic Studies*. Calcutta: Thacker, Spink and Co., Ltd., 1931, 257-283.
Levi, S. "Devaputra." *Journal Asiatique*. CCXXIV (Janvier-Mars, 1934), 1-21.
Ling, T. O. *Buddhism and the Mythology of Evil*. London: George Allen and Unwin, Ltd., 1962.
Masson, J. *Religion populaire dans le canon bouddhique pāli*. Louvain: Bureaux du Muséon, 1942.
Oldenberg, H. *Buddha: His Life, His Doctrine, His Order*. Translated by W. Hoey. London: Williams and Norgate, 1882.
Pande, G. V. *Studies in the Origins of Buddhism*. Allahabad: University of Allahabad, 1957.
Poussin, L. de la Vallée. "Cosmogony and Cosmology (Buddhist)," *Encyclopaedia of Religion and Ethics*, IV (1955), 129-138.
——. *Indo-Européens et Indo-Iraniens*. Paris: E. De Boccard, 1924.
——. "Māra." *Encyclopaedia of Religion and Ethics*, VIII (1958), 406-407.
Rahula, Walpola. *What the Buddha Taught*. Bedford: Gordon Frazer, 1959.
Rau, Wilhelm. *Staat und Gesellschaft im Alten Indien*. Wiesbaden: Otto Harrassowitz, 1957.
Senart, E. "Origins of Buddhism." Translated by M. Ray. *Indian Historical Quarterly*, VI (1930), 537-544, 665-678.
Streng, F. J. "The Problem of Symbolic Structures in Religious Apprehension." *History of Religions*, IV, 1 (1964), 126-153.
Thomas, E. J. *The History of Buddhist Thought*. London: Routledge, Kegan and Paul, 1949.
——. *The Life of the Buddha*. New York: Alfred A. Knopf, 1927.
Tucci, G. "The Demoniacal in the Far East." *East and West*, IV, 1 (April, '53), 3-11.
Wayman, Alex. "Studies in Yama and Māra." *Indo-Iranian Journal*, III (1959), 44ff., 112ff.
——. "The Meaning of Unwisdom (Avidya)." *Philosophy East and West*, VII, 1 and 2 (April, July, 1957), 21-25.
Windisch, E. *Māra und Buddha*. Leipzig: S. Hirzel, 1895.
Winternitz, M. *A History of Indian Literature*. Calcutta: University of Calcutta, 1933.

PART THREE

Selected Bibliography

Bartsch, H. W., ed., *Kerygma and Myth: A Theological Debate*. New York: Harper and Row, 1961.
Bishop, J. B. "Value of Myths, Images, Types and History for Apologetic." *Church Quarterly Review*, 164 (July-Sept., 1963), 269-280.
Bleeker, C. J. "The Future Task of the History of Religions." *Numen*, VII, 2-3 (Dec., 1960), 221-234.
Bouquet, A. C. "Christian Influences in Early Buddhism." *Modern Churchman*, 6 (Jan., 1963), 165-170.

Brandon, S. G. F., ed. *The Saviour God*. New York: Barnes and Noble, Inc., 1963.

Brown, James. *Subject and Object in Modern Theology*. London: SCM Press, Ltd., 1955.

Buber, Martin. *Images of Good and Evil*. London: Routledges, 1952.

Dewey, John. *Experience and Nature*. New York: Dover Publications, Inc., 1958.

Eliade, M. *Patterns in Comparative Religion*. New York: Sheed and Ward, 1958.

——. *Images and Symbols*. Translated by P. Mairet. New York: Sheed and Ward, 1961.

——, and Kitagawa, Joseph M., ed. *The History of Religions: Essays on the Problem of Understanding*. Chicago: University of Chicago Press, 1966.

Grabau, R. "The Necessity of Myth: An Answer to Rudolf Bultmann." *The Journal of Religion*, XLIV, 2 (April), 1964.

James, E. O. "The Influence of Folklore on the History of Religion." *Numen*, IX, 1 (1962), 1-16.

Jaspers, Karl, and Bultmann, Rudolph. *Myth and Christianity: An Inquiry into the Possibility of Religion without Myth*. New York: Noonday Press, 1964.

Jones, G. V. *Christology and Myth in the New Testament*. London: George Allen and Unwin, Ltd., 1956.

King, W. L. "Some Buddhist and Christian Concepts Compared." *South East Asia Journal of Theology*, 2 (April, 1961), 59-62.

——. "Myth in Buddhism: Essential or Peripheral?" *Journal of Bible and Religion*, 29 (July, 1961), 211-218.

Kramer, S. N., ed. *Mythologies of the Ancient World*. New York: Doubleday, 1961.

Langer, S. K. *Philosophy in a New Key: A Study in the Symbolism of Reason, Rite, and Art*. New York: New American Library, 1951.

Macquarrie, J. *The Scope of Demythologizing*. London: SCM Press, Ltd., 1960.

——. *An Existentialist Theology: A Comparison of Heidegger and Bultmann*. New York: Harper and Row, 1965.

Mascall, E. L. *Words and Images: A Study in Theological Discourse*. New York: Ronald Press Co., 1957.

Newbigin, L. "The Quest for Unity through Religion." *Journal of Religion*, XXXV, 1 (Jan., 1955), 17-33.

Otto, R. *The Idea of the Holy*. Translated by J. W. Harvey. New York: Oxford University Press, 1958.

Parrinder, G. *Comparative Religion*. London: George Allen and Unwin, Ltd., 1962.

Parsons, H. L. "Myth and Religious Knowledge." Unpublished Ph. D. dissertation, University of Chicago, 1946.

Reardon, B. M. G. "Myth, Metaphysics and Reality." *Hibbert Journal*, LV, 124-130.

Ricœur, Paul. *The Symbolism of Evil*. Translated by E. Buchanan. New York: Harper and Row, 1957.

Schlette, H. R. *Towards a Theology of Religions*. Translated by W. J. O'Hara. New York: Herder and Herder, 1966.

Sparks, I. A. "Buddha and Christ: A Functional Analysis." *Numen*, XIII, 3 (Oct., 1966), 190-204.

Smith, W. C. *The Meaning and End of Religion*. New York: Mentor, 1965.

Streeter, B. H. *The Buddha and the Christ*. London: Macmillan, 1932.

Tillich, Paul. *Christianity and the Encounter of the World Religions.* New York: Columbia University Press, 1963.
——. *The Interpretation of History.* New York: Charles Scribner's Sons, 1936.
Wach, Joachim. *The Comparative Study of Religions.* New York: Columbia University Press, 1961.
Wirz, Paul. *Exorcism and the Art of Healing in Ceylon.* Leiden: E. J. Brill, 1954.
Zaehner, R. C. *At Sundry Times: An Essay in the Comparison of Religions.* London: Faber and Faber, 1958.
Zuurdeeg, W. F. *An Analytical Philosophy of Religion.* New York: Abingdon Press, 1958.

INDEX